THE OREGON TRAIL

DEVIL'S TOWER, WYOMING

AMERICAN GUIDE SERIES

THE OREGON TRAIL

THE MISSOURI RIVER TO THE PACIFIC OCEAN

Compiled and written by the
FEDERAL WRITERS' PROJECT
of the
WORKS PROGRESS ADMINISTRATION

Sponsored by
OREGON TRAIL MEMORIAL ASSOCIATION, INC.
and published by
HASTINGS HOUSE   *Publishers*   NEW YORK

Republished 1972
SOMERSET PUBLISHERS — a Division of Scholarly Press, Inc.
22929 Industrial Drive East, St. Clair Shores, Michigan 48080

Library of Congress No. 70-145012
I. S. B. N. 0-403-01290-2

PRINTED IN THE UNITED STATES OF AMERICA
BY J. J. LITTLE AND IVES COMPANY, NEW YORK

FOREWORD

The Oregon Trail, third in the series of main-highway guidebooks prepared by the Federal Writers' Project, presents a story particularly pertinent to our times.

The great migration westward came largely as a result of the terrific depression of 1837; a depression brought on by speculation in railroads and canals and by overexpansion of industry. The great difference between then and now is to be found in the fact that today there are no longer western frontiers. Since we cannot migrate to undeveloped land as a solution for our troubles, we are now cultivating our neglected human and material resources. However, without a knowledge of the period between 1800 and 1870 it is impossible to understand the trends of our own times.

The American spirit of independence that carried thousands of emigrants from the East to the Pacific Coast is still alive, and though the problems to be solved require a new technique, the American people are competent to find a satisfactory solution.

HENRY G. ALSBERG
Director of Federal Writers' Project

WORKS PROGRESS ADMINISTRATION

F. C. HARRINGTON, *Administrator*
FLORENCE S. KERR, *Assistant Administrator*
HENRY G. ALSBERG, *Director of Federal Writers' Project*

CONTENTS

ALTERNATE ROUTE, NEBRASKA-WYOMING

SIDE ROUTES

APPENDICES

INDEX

ILLUSTRATIONS

NOTES ON THE BOOK

The Oregon Trail is primarily a guidebook, but it is also history, told, after the first chapter, in geographical rather than chronological or topical sequence. The explorers Lewis and Clark, the fur trader Manuel Lisa, the refugee Mormons, and the construction gang of the Union Pacific Railroad are tied together by campgrounds near the same place on the bank of the muddy Missouri. The first chapter gives the background and paints in the broad outlines of the story; it also introduces some of the leading characters whose activities and trials are related in their rich details, sometimes bizarre and occasionally tragic, in the following sections.

When possible the story has been told through extracts from the diaries and other writings of the actors and their contemporaries. Lewis, Clark, and the men who accompanied them, tell of the satisfactions of the explorer and also of the price paid for them in hunger, danger, and physical discomfort; the reactions of the Indians to the white expropriators appears in Clark's comments on little Sacajawea, the Shoshone guide and interpreter, and in conversations reported by other overland travelers. The nature of the wilderness, and of the traders who first dared to face it, is made clear through the story of the Astorians, as told by Irving, and the incredible, even though well-authenticated, epic of Hugh Glass's nine-month pursuit of revenge. The very human qualities and motives of the migrants who captured the West are presented through fragments from diaries, some of them never before published; these make clear, as no abstract discussion could, that the pioneering forefathers were not different from their descendants; they enjoyed the overland journeys in exactly the same way that modern Americans enjoy their holiday cruises and week-end ski trips. No motorist today is more interested in his speedometer records than were the pioneers in those of their ox-cart "roadometers."

No modern highway closely follows throughout any of the historic trails between the Missouri and the Pacific Northwest; but these trails were in many places merely broad courses and the routes changed from year to year. US 30, the modern trail to Oregon, with its feeders

xi

and its alternate route through Nebraska and Wyoming, most nearly follows the general course of the mass migration; almost every mile of its roadbed covers ruts made at one time or another by covered wagons.

Those reading the book as narrative are advised to turn to the Alternate Route description after finishing Section 3; the Alternate Route covers the section of the Mormon and Oregon Trails generally used before 1862, and Sections 4, 5, and 6 the short cut developed after that time.

Only adventurous travelers should attempt to follow the last quarter of the Alternate Route; though it will probably be improved soon, this section is now (1939) in very poor condition. The route can be followed, however, to Muddy Gap near South Pass in central Wyoming; this point is accessible from US 30 at Rawlins, Wyo., over paved US 287.

In order to give *The Oregon Trail* to the public at a low price, with a clarifying map and some illustrations, the wordage had to be limited. This has meant that editing was highly selective, that material not pertinent to the story of exploration and development was omitted.

Numerous advisers have given their time freely in checking the material. But it is impossible that any book covering such a range of history should be free from errors. If readers who find misstatements will report them to the Federal Writers' Project in Washington, corrections will be made in future editions.

The Oregon Trail contains no list of recommended accommodations; a Government-compiled publication cannot enter this field.

Population figures are from the last Federal census (1930).

KATHARINE A. KELLOCK
Tour Editor American Guide Series

WHY A TRAIL TO OREGON?

THE HISTORY of the Oregon Trail is the history of how two million square miles of land, some of the richest in the North Temperate Zone, came under the control of a weak new nation and made it one of the mighty powers of all time. The process took place in a period so brief that many men saw it all—saw a vast wilderness explored, acquired, settled, and united under one government. In 1800 half the territory now covered by the United States was either a blank on the maps or was decorated with imaginary topographical features and names of Indian "kingdoms"; it was claimed by European powers and inhabited by a few hundred thousand aborigines, most of whom still had a late Stone Age culture. In 1880 the region was occupied by more than 11 million citizens of the United States, and had been charted and divided into political subdivisions with stable governments; it had been spanned by two railroads, partly spanned by several others, and covered with a web of trails and telegraph lines; the aborigines had been either exterminated or penned up in reservations.

No other conquest in history has been accomplished with so little military force and leadership, and few with so little organized direction. Yet from the time, covering only a few weeks, when Napoleon, idol of dictators, and Thomas Jefferson, philosopher of democracy, had mutual interests and moved swiftly to realize them, the history of the West is filled with the names of those whose ideas and activities, at decisive moments, determined the course of events.

There were many trails to Oregon but their general direction was determined by Lewis and Clark when in 1804-5 they traveled up the Missouri to its headwaters, crossed the Continental Divide, and worked their way down the Columbia River to its mouth. The next transcontinental travelers, the Astorians, went only part way up the Missouri and swung southwest, crossing the Divide below what is now Yellowstone National Park in order to avoid the hostile Blackfeet Indians;

1

they followed the Snake River to reach the Columbia, where they retraced the route of Lewis and Clark. West of the Divide much of their
route was later part of the Oregon Trail. By the 1830's fur traders
had further shortened the distance to the Snake by leaving the Missouri
at the point where it turns north near Independence, Mo., which was
established in that period as a frontier supply post. Following the
Santa Fe Trail for a few miles they usually cut northwest to follow
the south bank of the Platte River and then the south bank of the
North Platte, swinging southwest through South Pass, which came
into use in 1824. From the pass they crossed to the Snake and more
or less followed the route of the Astorians to the Columbia. The fur
traders helped to blaze the way for the emigrant trains of the following decades.

ᵛThe Oregon Trail in time developed numerous cut-offs, feeders,
and outlets. As congestion increased around Independence, half a
dozen places to the north of it developed as outfitting points. Some
emigrants followed a route on the north side of the Platte, traversed
in 1847 by the first Mormon party, and reached the main trail at
Fort Laramie. The Overland route left the Oregon Trail near the
junction of the North and South Plattes, taking a short cut to Fort
Bridger in southwestern Wyoming. Two cut-offs, the Sublette and the
Lander, crossed north of Fort Bridger to reach the Snake. The route
to Salt Lake City—which was later extended to California—turned
southwest at Fort Bridger; two other trails to California left the
Oregon Trail along the Snake River.

ʾIn many places the trail was 10 to 20 miles wide, succeeding wagon
trains making detours to avoid the dust and ruts of those ahead of
them; in other places passing wheels wore a single pair of deep ruts
that are still visible. Fort Laramie, Fort Bridger, and Fort Hall—
established as trading posts rather than forts—were goals that determined the course of the trail in their neighborhoods.ʲ

The story of the Oregon Trail begins in the Middle Ages when men
were seeking a route to India. Newly discovered America was for a
time regarded as part of Asia, then as an annoying barrier on the
way to the Far East. The Spanish were the first to appreciate the fact
that the new land offered riches; within a few decades they had found
the culturally advanced native kingdoms in Mexico and in Central and
South America, had conquered and enslaved the inhabitants, and were
carrying fabulous fortunes back to Europe. The existence of America

had been known for more than a hundred years before the nations of northwestern Europe awoke to the fact that Spain and Portugal had already pre-empted the Western Hemisphere.

But the Spanish were primarily conquerors, not colonizers; hence they had made little attempt to establish themselves in the lands north of Mexico where the inhabitants were largely nomads—hard to tame— and still ignorant of the use and value of metals. Sir Humphrey Gilbert and his half-brother, Sir Walter Raleigh, were the first northern Europeans to attempt to take physical possession of land in the Americas. Gilbert was lost at sea before he had an opportunity to carry out his plans. Shortly afterward Raleigh succeeded in planting a colony on Roanoke Island in what is now North Carolina. Though his means were too limited to insure the success of the venture, which ended tragically, he did bring the potential wealth of the country to the attention of English merchants, with the result that 20 years later, in 1607, two more English colonies were started in America, one successful and the other unsuccessful.

Two years before this, however, the Sieur de Monts, a careful and far-sighted Frenchman, had made a successful settlement in eastern Canada, the first in the region north of Florida. The French, the English, the Dutch, and the Swedes then started colonization in earnest, the English more aggressively than the others. The English soon captured the Dutch and Swedish settlements, the inhabitants resigning themselves to English rule without prolonged struggle because of the English colonial policy that permitted a large measure of self-government and extended considerable religious and social toleration as long as the colonies returned profits to the proprietors and the Crown. This was the "wise and salutary neglect" that suffered "a generous nature . . . to take her own way to perfection," as Edmund Burke phrased it in defending the colonies before the Revolution.

Settlement was the decisive factor in establishing political ownership of the lands along the Atlantic seaboard, just as it was later to settle the question of ownership along the Pacific. The Spanish had made small military settlements in Florida and they continued to hold the region, except for a brief interval, until the end of the second decade of the nineteenth century; the French brought colonists to eastern Canada and held that region for 150 years; British supremacy between the French and Spanish possessions was established by the number of people who were persuaded to come over to live under British rule.

The settlements of the French grew slowly, in part because of the
severe climate of Canada and in part because of the monopolies granted
in the fur trade, the most important industry of the area.

The first attempts to penetrate the interior of the continent north
of the region held by the Spanish were made by the French, who worked
west chiefly along the shores of the Great Lakes. Between 1654 and
1660 two particularly enterprising Frenchmen, Medard Chouart, later
Sieur de Groseilliers (whose name was translated "Mr. Gooseberry"
in Hudson's Bay Company records), and his brother-in-law, Pierre
Radisson, crossed to the western end of Lake Superior and wintered
on the shores of Lake Nipigon. Upon returning to Quebec, they applied to the Governor for a license to trade for furs in the interior, but
he would grant it only on such exorbitant terms that they departed for
the West without it; when they came back to Quebec two years later
they were fined £10,000 for their illegal trading operations. After vainly
attempting to have their case reviewed in France, they approached Boston merchants with a plan for reaching the rich fur country of the
interior by way of Hudson Bay; the Americans sent a ship north to
test the practicality of the idea but because of the lateness of the season
the master turned back.

The Frenchmen then went to England where they quickly reached
the ear of Charles II; the royal family, always much interested in any
scheme that offered high profits, gave backing to the enterprise. In
May, 1670, after the ketch *Non Such* had visited the bay and confirmed
the reports of the Frenchmen, a charter was given to the King's dear
cousin, Prince Rupert, and his associates—"the Governor & Company
of Adventurers of England, trading into Hudson's Bay," a corporation that has come down in history as the Hudson's Bay Company.
The King, his brother (later James II), and his cousin were among the
first stockholders. The charter, covering trading rights in the vast region west of the country occupied by the French, gave to the company
complete feudal rights, including that of making war on infidels. The
company was also granted the territory, which was named Rupert's
Land, in which it was to operate; the payment to the Crown for this
enormous grant was to be two elks and two black beavers, paid annually whenever the sovereign should visit the land. The enterprise
was very profitable.

The French soon began to feel the effects of English competition
and attempted to end it, but with only temporary success; in 1713, when

the Treaty of Utrecht was signed, the west coast of the bay went to the British, and the French gave up all forts and posts near the bay. Not long after this, however, an obscure Irishman began attacking the company for its failure to find the Northwest Passage; its failure to explore and develop the interior from which it was receiving furs at its post on Hudson Bay; and for its failure to carry religion to the Indians. He finally succeeded in so arousing public opinion that in 1736 the company sent out a small exploring expedition; it accomplished little.

Meanwhile, French traders were slowly working westward along the shores of the Great Lakes, though the French Government, embroiled in European affairs, gave little encouragement to the missionaries and adventurers who had dreams of extending French domain and of finding a route to the Pacific Ocean. In 1673 Marquette and Joliet explored the country south of Lake Superior, reaching the Mississippi River; La Salle crossed from Lake Michigan to the Mississippi, resting "upon the majestic bosom" in February, 1682, and descended it to the Great Gulf. On April 9 he took possession for "Louis Le Grand, Roy de France et de Navarre Régne." As Parkman said, "by virtue of a feeble human voice, inaudible at half a mile," he claimed for France "the vast basin of the Mississippi from its frozen northern springs to the sultry borders of the Gulf; from the woody ridges of the Alleghenies to the bare peaks of the Rocky Mountains—a region of savannas and forests, suncracked deserts and grassy prairies."

'Between 1731 and 1743 Pierre Verendrye and his sons also worked their way westward and southward from Lake Superior into the Dakotas; some contend they reached the foothills of the Rockies, then known as the Stonies. By the Treaty of Paris (1763), France lost Canada and her possessions east of the Mississippi, except the port of New Orleans, to Great Britain; all of Louisiana west of the Mississippi went to Spain by cousinly arrangement, Spain supposedly holding Louisiana for France in order to keep it out of British hands.

Among the British troops brought to Canada were many young Scots who, facing the prospect of return to a poverty-stricken homeland, determined to remain in America. They were later joined by some Scottish Jacobeans. The Scots rapidly took over the fur trade along the St. Lawrence River; one of them, Alexander Henry, spent the years 1760-66 in the Middle West, exploring for some distance north of Lake Superior toward the Hudson's Bay Company domain. By 1770 the aggressive newcomers were beginning to divert trade from this powerful rival and a conflict had begun that did not end until 1821. In 1783-4 some of the Scots, led by Benjamin and Joseph Frobisher and Simon Mc-Tavish, organized the North West Company, and established a post at Grand Portage, on the northern shore of Lake Superior, as the center of their trading activities. Other Scots, among them Alexander Mackenzie, formed a rival company, but because competition was expensive, the differences between the groups were ironed out in 1787, the second group joining the North West Company. An extensive organization was developed, with an army of partners, sub-partners, clerks, interpreters, and boatmen, that met at a grand annual rendezvous on the Great Lakes, later celebrated in song and legend.

In addition to being a trader, Alexander Mackenzie was an explorer. In 1789, while his penny-pinching partners objected to his expense accounts, he traveled with two canoeloads of Indians and French Canadians down the river that now bears his name to its mouth on the Arctic Ocean. In 1792, still against the will of his partners, and therefore without notifying them, he left his post in central Canada, accompanied by one Scot, two French Canadians, and two Indians, went up the Peace River, crossed the Divide on July 17, 1793, and shortly afterward reached the Pacific Coast. Mindful of the grumbling partners, he immediately returned to his post in central Canada.

In 1798 several members who disliked the dominating McTavish left the North West Company to form the New North West Company, known as the XY, which in turn became so aggressive that order in the fur country was disrupted, the traders of the Hudson's Bay, the North West, and the XY Companies demoralizing the Indians with liquor to gain their trade and instigating Indian attacks on one another. Mackenzie joined the XY in 1801.

In 1796 David Thompson, a young English surveyor, had been sent out by the North West Company to survey the 49th parallel west of the Great Lakes in order to determine whether the company posts were in Canada or the United States. During the winter he visited the Mandan village on the great bend of the Missouri near which Lewis and Clark were to spend the winter of 1804-5. Later, in 1806, he was sent out again and went through the Rockies to the head of the Columbia, where he wintered in 1808-9.

Since the sixteenth century the Spanish had been sending expeditions north to explore what is now Texas, New Mexico, and Arizona.

After the cession of Louisiana to Spain in 1763, Spanish traders began to work their way up the Mississippi, and in 1793 a Spanish trading company was granted a license to explore and trade along the Missouri River; the company's activities lasted only four years but they extended to the Dakotas.

The English were slow to penetrate inland, making little attempt to look beyond the Appalachians, though a few, such as Maj. Robert Rogers, whose story was told by Kenneth Roberts in *Northwest Passage*, could not forget the dream of a northern route to the Orient. After the Treaty of Paris of 1783, which gave the United States the country east of the Mississippi between Canada and Florida, settlers began to move across the mountains in large numbers.

Thomas Jefferson, who was notable for the diversity of his interests even in an age when many believed that it was possible for one man to cover the full range of knowledge, was early fascinated by the vast, little-charted area beyond the Mississippi River. In 1783 Jefferson suggested to George Rogers Clark that he lead an exploring expedition through it; and he expressed the belief that England had colonization designs for the region, even though it belonged to Spain. Nothing came of the plan, so three years later Jefferson, while Minister to France, encouraged John Ledyard, a Yankee who had traveled around the world with Capt. James Cook, to attempt to explore the western country by traveling across Siberia, proceeding to the west coast of North America, and penetrating inland toward the Missouri. But Ledyard was arrested by the Russian authorities when near the Pacific shores, and sent back to Europe.

In 1793 Jefferson, as a vice-president of the American Philosophical Society, made arrangements for a French botanist, Michaux, to attempt an overland journey to the Pacific by way of the Missouri River, and persuaded members of the society to subscribe to a small fund for the expedition; the botanist, however, became embroiled in French politics and the plan was abandoned. The report of Capt. Robert Gray of Boston, who had visited the mouth of the Columbia River in 1792, convinced Jefferson of the existence of the legendary River of the West with headwaters close to those of the Missouri, which would provide a nearly complete water route between the Mississippi River and the Pacific Ocean. He constantly studied maps and reports. In 1801, the year in which the account of Alexander Mackenzie's successful trip across

Canada to the Pacific was published, Jefferson became President of the United States.✓

Just when Jefferson determined to use his official position to further the realization of his long dream of finding a route to the Pacific Ocean is unknown. But he knew that the idea was also cherished by Meriwether Lewis, because in 1793, when Jefferson was trying to send the French botanist west, Jefferson's neighbor, Lewis, then only 19, had begged to be permitted to go with the party. Doubtless they had often discussed the problems and joined in conjectures before Jefferson, about to assume the Presidency, asked Lewis to leave the Army and become his secretary.

Between 1800 and 1802 Napoleon, in a series of secret negotiations, had coerced the stupid Charles IV of Spain into retroceding Louisiana to France in return for a small Tuscan kingdom for Charles' son-in-law and the promise that the territory should not be alienated to any other power. The public transfer of New Orleans, planned to take place in October, 1802, was deferred because of an uprising in Santo Domingo. Though news of the agreement was not made public, the diplomatic grapevine brought it quickly to Jefferson.

In the summer of 1802 Jefferson quietly sent Lewis to Philadelphia, scientific headquarters of the country, to learn the "technical language of the natural sciences, and readiness in the astronomical observations."

The ruthless energy of Napoleon and the colonial ambitions of his minister Talleyrand were well known to Jefferson and his advisers. The transfer of Louisiana from Spain to France filled them with consternation, particularly because of the increasing swarms of settlers that poured over the mountains into the Northwest Territory, Kentucky, and Tennessee; the Mississippi River provided the main marketing outlet for their products. To add to the tenseness of the situation, word arrived in 1802 that the Spanish Intendant at New Orleans, still in command as the French had not yet taken possession, had arbitrarily closed the port of New Orleans to products from the United States. Jefferson endeavored to keep his followers under control but could do nothing to quiet the rule-or-ruin Federalists, who screamed for war and demanded the seizure of New Orleans. He conferred with the Spanish Ambassador, who knew of no orders from Spain on the matter, and sent official representations to Madrid. Jefferson also wrote to Robert Livingston, his Minister to France, on the need of negotiations with the French to safeguard the interests of the United States in New Orleans.

On January 18, 1803, a month after Congress met, Jefferson sent a secret message to Congress, asking for funds for exploration west of the Mississippi; as a pretext for the message he used the expiration of an act establishing governmental trading posts among the Indians and the need of extending it. This message was exceedingly tactful; it pointed out the necessity for acquiring more land for white settlers—east of the Mississippi—by domesticating the Indians and proving to them that they needed less land to live on, and it pointed out the advantages of raising the standard of living of the aborigines to increase their consumption of manufactured goods. It went on to remark that it might be worth while for Congress to find customers for the private traders deprived of incomes by the extension of the act and the establishment of more governmental trading posts among the Indians in the United States, and that there were numerous tribes along the Missouri who should be able to pay for goods with valuable furs. It added that if a few men, 10 or 14 with an officer, were sent up the Missouri they could report on these trade prospects and might also find a short portage to the Columbia, which would provide a commercial route for the Pacific trade free from competition with the French and Spanish traders who were along the Mississippi and lower Missouri. The men needed for the enterprise could easily be spared from the military posts, and their army pay, continuing while they were away, would lessen the amount of money that would have to be appropriated for the expedition; $2,500 was the sum suggested. Congress made the appropriation and by midsummer plans were well under way for the start. (Jefferson had expected the expedition to leave in the spring, having underestimated the time it would take to collect supplies and select men.)

At the time Jefferson made his proposal for this expedition, the Federalists were carrying on a campaign against him that has seldom, if ever, been equalled in America for virulence; word from Spain that the Intendant had acted without authority in closing New Orleans did not stop their attempts to instigate war and to discredit the President. When, shortly afterward, Congress, at the President's request, authorized negotiations to buy an outlet at the mouth of the Mississippi, their rage went beyond all bounds. Why buy what could be seized? The President appointed James Monroe as special envoy to assist Robert Livingston in conducting negotiations, in part because there were instructions for Livingston that were too delicate to be trusted to paper, and in part because Monroe was trusted by the westerners, whom the Federalists were trying to alienate from the Jeffersonian leadership.

Monroe sailed on March 8, 1803. Jefferson and Madison in last minute conferences had formulated the lines of negotiation. The envoys were to attempt to buy the Floridas and New Orleans; if acquisition of the Floridas were impossible, the acquisition of New Orleans and some territory near it on the east bank of the river should be attempted; if the second offer failed also, the envoys should attempt to purchase some land on which the United States could build its own port of deposit at the mouth of the Mississippi; and if Napoleon rejected all offers to buy, the envoys were to attempt to negotiate a treaty permitting goods to pass freely through New Orleans.

There was dramatic neatness in the series of events that determined the future of the United States—Charles IV's move to provide for a son-in-law; the Negro Toussaint's successful resistance of Napoleon's attempt to suppress the Santo Domingan revolt, which diverted Napoleon from his plans for immediate extension of the colonial empire; and the virulent attacks of the Federalists, which forced Jefferson to act swiftly in clearing up the question of a trade outlet on the Mississippi. Acting on hurried instructions from Jefferson, Livingston had approached Talleyrand on the subject of obtaining New Orleans, pointing out that in case of war with England a bit of extra money might be useful to France and that the sale of New Orleans would free France from the need of defending her American possessions. Talleyrand, scornfully dismissing the proposal, said that his master was planning to send a minister to Washington to negotiate a treaty covering American relations in Louisiana. Shortly after this, at a diplomatic reception, Livingston heard Napoleon address the British Minister in terms that indicated he had suddenly determined to fight, whether England wanted to or not.

In making his plans for war, Napoleon remembered Livingston's proposal, which Talleyrand had apparently not feared to communicate to his master. On April 11, knowing that he could not trust Talleyrand, Napoleon abruptly summoned Barbé-Marbois, his young Minister of Finance, who was friendly to the Americans and also faithful to the First Consul, telling him, "I renounce Louisiana. . . . Have an interview this very day with Mr. Livingston." That day Talleyrand asked Livingston, who believed he was joking, whether the United States would like to have all Louisiana and what it would pay for it. Monroe arrived in Paris that night. Late the following evening Livingston was asked to visit Barbé-Marbois' home. After various preliminaries Barbé-Marbois quoted Napoleon's statement: ". . . let him give you one hundred million of francs . . . and take the whole country." The price and the proposal staggered Livingston; Barbé-Marbois added quickly that he thought the sum suggested was too high but that sixty million francs ($15,000,000) seemed fair and he would like an immediate decision. Livingston protested that the whole thing was impossible; that neither he nor Monroe had authority to negotiate such a purchase or to pledge such a sum. Barbé-Marbois was friendly but firm, reminding him that Napoleon was mercurial in temperament and it was quite possible the offer might be withdrawn if it were not speedily accepted; the terms were all or nothing. Both Livingston and Monroe, to whom he reported the conversation, were impressed by the warning, but neither knew how tenuous was the string offered to them.

Word of the offer reached the Consul's brother, Joseph; he took it immediately to Lucien Bonaparte, who had negotiated the transfer of Louisiana from Spain to France and shared Talleyrand's imperialistic dreams. Lucien and Joseph dashed post-haste to their brother, who was in his bath when they arrived; they ranted without effect, the Consul splashing them with bath water to show his contempt. But he realized the danger of the Chambers' finding out about the offer and pressed Barbé-Marbois to obtain a decision. Still the Americans hesitated, the magnitude of the deal and their lack of authority to handle it terrifying them. They knew Jefferson's desires, however, and on May 2 with great trepidation completed the purchase; the price to be paid was 80,000,000 francs, 20,000,000 of it going to satisfy claims of American citizens against the French. Later they exulted a bit at their own daring, appreciating the fact that they had more than doubled the size of the United States.

The news reached Jefferson late in June but was not made public until July 14. The President, though delighted, was troubled by the unconstitutionality of the affair, while the Federalists raged, fearing the result of acquiring more land to be peopled by agrarians. But the national pride was touched and the treaty was ratified. The size of the area bought was uncertain; though the United States later asserted that the purchase included the Oregon country, it was unable to establish any claim to land west of the Rockies by the deal with Napoleon.

Thus the Lewis and Clark expedition, secretly authorized to extend the "external commerce of the United States" but announced to the

Spanish and French authorities as an "innocent literary journey," became in part a legitimate enterprise needing little camouflage.

Jefferson, who had studied every available map and report on the country west of the Mississippi, himself drew up the plans for the exploring expedition. It was to proceed up the Missouri, find the headwaters of the Columbia, and travel down that stream to the Pacific Ocean; it was to confirm Indian tales reported by early travelers about the Shining Mountains at the head of the Missouri, report on climate, topography, and inhabitants of the country; and it was to find out what men of other nations were entering Louisiana and Oregon to trade. (*See Jefferson's Instructions in APPENDIX.*) In addition to Jefferson's lists of points on which he wanted information, Lewis carried others prepared by eminent scientists of the American Philosophical Society, including printed English vocabularies with spaces for the Indian equivalents.

The equipment was carefully planned; besides the usual supplies of food—including soup cubes—clothing, ammunition, scientific instruments, and medical supplies (the list of which is surprisingly modern and comprehensive when examined today), the explorers carried large quantities of goods to be presented to the Indians—medals, plumed hats, gaudy military coats, garters, and even odds and ends for "women of Consideration."

Jefferson had desired that at least the co-leader of the party should be a scientist well trained in many fields. He came to the conclusion, however, that the primary qualification for both leaders should be experience in handling Indians and in meeting wilderness conditions. Lewis chose his long-time friend, William Clark, a younger brother of George Rogers Clark; no choice could have been more fortunate, the two men complementing each other and working in perfect harmony.

Lewis left Pittsburgh in August, 1803, and, meeting Clark at Louisville, proceeded to St. Louis, where they recruited a staff to accompany them on their journey, had boats built, and added to the supplies. The party started up the Missouri on May 14, 1804, "in the presence of many of the neighboring inhabitants and proceeded on under a jentle brease," according to Captain Clark, whose orthography is convincing argument against the preciosity of spelling rules. That the explorers had no false modesty about the importance of their expedition is shown by Captain Lewis' notes as the party was starting into the unknown territory after the winter spent among the Mandans: "The little fleet altho' not quite so rispictable as those of Columbus or Capt. Cook, were still viewed by us with as much pleasure as those deservedly famed adventurers ever beheld theirs. . . . We are now about to penetrate a country at least two thousand miles in width, on which the foot of civilized man has never trodden. . . . I could not but esteem this moment of my departure as among the most happy of my life."

The long journey up the Missouri to the Mandan village was a course of training in which the party of what Clark called "robust healthy hardy young men" was disciplined, tested for loyalty and endurance, and forged into a working unit. At the end of the winter the misfits and malcontents were weeded out and sent back to civilization with some of the boatmen, the most trustworthy carrying "Sundery articles to be sent to the President of the U.S."—horns of mountain rams, animal skins and skeletons, plants, Indian clothing and utensils, a parcel of roots "highly prized by the natives as an efficatious remidy in cases of the bite of a rattle Snake or Mad Dog," a tin box containing insects and mice, a "liveing burrowing Squirel of the praries," four live magpies, and a living prairie hen; the list is a commentary on the range of Jefferson's interests.

Throughout the journey the explorers worked hard to satisfy the President's mighty curiosity, the petty officers as well as the leaders sitting down each night, in rain, snow, or fair weather, to bring their journals up to date. Apparently the only question that they dared not risk attempting to satisfy was the one asking "What is the State of the pulse in both (Indian) Sexes, Children, grown persons, and in old age, by feeling the Pulse Morning, Noon & Night &c.?"

While at winter quarters on the Missouri the leaders faithfully carried out Jefferson's instructions to make friends among the Indians; sent firm but tactful warnings to British trappers that the country now belonged to the United States and that the Indians must not be made hostile to American traders; spent hours collecting countless scraps of gossip based on hearsay and experience concerning the country they were to face; and hired the half-breed Charbonneau, chiefly for the sake of Sacajawea, one of his wives, who was a stolen Shoshone "Squar" (squaw), and could act as an "interpeter" beyond the mountains. The "Squar," starting out with a newborn child on her back, became one of the most esteemed members of the party, bearing difficulties uncomplainingly, nursing the sick, interceding for the party when among her kin, advising on routes, and saving lives by teaching the white men how to dig for roots and utilize other resources of the harsh mountain country. The deep affection Clark developed for her appears in the official *Journals*, in which he sometimes called her "Janey."

The charming *Original Journals of Lewis and Clark* exhibit the fine judgment of the two commanders that enabled them to carry out their mission with the loss of only one man—and he of a "Billiose Chorlick" early in the journey. They met handicaps and barriers— precipitous passes in very high mountains, volcanic deserts where game and water were lacking, and rivers choked with rocks and rendered dangerous by falls—much of which the reports of Mackenzie and others had not led them to anticipate; yet they managed to reach the Pacific Coast in safety in the dismal mid-November rains of 1805, too tired and starved for much rejoicing, eager only to make some kind of shelter and find food.

After leaving the coast in March, 1806, the party was divided near what is now Missoula, Mont. Clark swung south to come down the Yellowstone, and Lewis went north with a very small party to explore the Marias River. At the northern limits of his side trip Lewis killed one of a band of Blackfeet who were making off with his horses and supplies; the tribesmen never forgot this act, and carried on relentless warfare against the whites until after many decades the whites had almost exterminated them. The two parties united at the mouth of the Yellowstone and made the return trip to St. Louis with speed, arriving there September 23, 1806. The men wept with joy when they again saw a cow, symbol of civilization. The people of St. Louis, Sgt. John Ordway reported, "gathred on the Shore and Hizzared three cheers."

Patrick Gass, a sergeant, was the first to publish his *Journal*, because both Lewis and Clark were immediately given responsible administrative positions and had little time or skill to prepare the polished accounts they thought the material deserved. The condensed Lewis and Clark *Journals*, edited by Nicholas Biddle and Paul Allen, appeared in 1814; the publisher made only $154.10 net profit. In spite of the meager circulation of these books, they did in time stir many restless minds and stimulate interest in the Far West.

When Jefferson told Congress that the Missouri country would provide new customers for the traders, he spoke better than he knew. In the winter of 1808 Manuel Lisa, an experienced trader born of Spanish parents in New Orleans, organized the St. Louis Missouri Fur Company, and turned over to it a post he had established in 1807 at the mouth of the Bighorn River, in what is now Montana. In 1810 Andrew Henry, a member of the firm, crossed the Divide and built a small post, known as Fort Henry, on the North Fork of the Snake River. Before Lisa's death in 1820 the company had aroused the envy of other businessmen by its profits.

The second important fur-trading venture was made by John Jacob Astor, who had come to the United States from Germany in 1784. He had early entered the fur business, beginning with beating and dressing, progressed to the collection of pelts from hunters in rural New York State, and eventually dealt with the traders of Montreal. Astor had long been annoyed by the fact that many of the furs he bought in Canada, and paid duty on, had been collected by North Westers south of the International Line; he had been planning ways and means of invading this part of the field when, first, the Louisiana Purchase and then the Lewis and Clark reports stirred him to action. He planned to establish posts in the Middle West and at the mouth of the Columbia River, from which he could carry furs direct to the Orient, the principal fur market, with an advantage over the Canadian traders who, because of the monopoly held by the East India Company, had to send their furs to the Far East by way of London.

The American Fur Company was incorporated in April, 1808, and the Pacific Fur Company in June, 1810. Washington Irving told the story of the enterprise, from Astor's viewpoint, in *Astoria* (1836). Utilizing his wide acquaintance among the Canadian traders, Astor persuaded three veteran Nor' Westers, including Alexander McKay, who had accompanied Mackenzie to the Pacific Coast, to join him as partners in the Oregon enterprise. He also brought in Wilson Price Hunt, who had had some experience in fur operations around St. Louis. The partners and clerks were divided into two parties, one to go around the Horn in the *Tonquin* with supplies for the post, and the other, under the leadership of Hunt, to go overland to the Columbia, establishing friendly relations with the Indians on the way and selecting sites for trading posts.

Both parties set out in 1810 but were dogged by calamity and misfortune. The members of the group that went by sea quarreled with the martinet who was the ship's captain, and with one another. The boat finally reached the mouth of the Columbia late in March, 1811, where the calamities of the voyage were crowned by the loss of eight men as a result of the captain's error in judgment in attempting to enter

the river. The land crew, including clerks and partners, left the ship
to establish Astoria and on June 1 the captain took the ship up the
coast for trade. Lacking any understanding of the Indians, he created
enmity that resulted in the complete destruction of the ship and everyone
aboard.

Astoria had been left in charge of Duncan McDougall, one of the
Nor' Westers. The fort had been built and trading had begun when the
land party, led by Hunt, straggled in by small groups after a series of
misadventures, chiefly resulting from Hunt's lack of experience in the
wilderness. There were now approximately a hundred men at the post,
a number that lessened the danger of Indian attack but did not add to
the harmony. On July 15 David Thompson, surveyor for the North
West Company, completed his methodical progress down the Columbia
to find to his chagrin that the Americans had reached the river ahead
of him. In London the representatives of the North West Company, unaware that Astor had stolen a march on them, were petitioning for
exclusive trading rights along the Pacific Coast between Alaska, occupied by the Russians, and California, held by the Spanish.

In the meantime, on June 18, 1812, the United States had declared
war against Great Britain. Astor, who had heard of the London activities of the North West Company, was working frantically but in vain
to obtain naval protection for his Pacific post. Word of the war arrived
in Astoria on January 15, 1813, one of the Astor party having picked
it up from members of a North West expedition along the Columbia.
The Astorians became discouraged; they were certain that Astor would
be unable to send a supply ship that would take away the considerable
number of pelts they had collected. The Nor' Westers who visited them
encouraged the feeling and made McDougall regret that he had em-
barked on such an amateurish enterprise. Astor had managed to send
a ship, but his plans were again dogged by bad luck; the ship did not
arrive until after the partners had sold the collected furs to the North
West Company, rather than risk sending them overland. The Nor'
Westers returned in the fall, triumphantly exhibiting the message dated
May 9, 1813, saying that a British frigate was on its way to "destroy
everything that is American on the N.W. coast." McDougall then took
it upon himself to sell all the property of the Pacific Fur Company to
the North West Company; the terms were not as illiberal as some of
McDougall's critics have contended. While the Astorians were winding
up their affairs the British frigate arrived and on December 12 took

possession of the country and the post for Britain. While the sale was a lucky stroke for the Astor company; it was later an embarrassment to the United States in claiming the territory by priority of settlement.

The War of 1812 did not last long, being unpopular in the United States to such an extent that some of the New England States threatened to secede from the Union; England was also willing to end hostilities because her attention was deeply occupied with European affairs—Napoleon was insecurely held on Elba. Negotiations following the war resulted in the settlement of the boundary between Lake Superior and the Oregon region, but the Oregon question was evaded by an agreement made in 1818, on "joint occupation" for a period of 10 years. In the following decade the Russians accepted a southern boundary at 54° 40′ (the Alaskan Line) on the coast and the Mexicans a northern boundary at 42° (the present Oregon-California Line). The joint occupation agreement on Oregon was later renewed but from 1818 on, nationals and officials of both Great Britain and the United States, as well as those of other countries—notably Spain and Russia—kept wary eyes on the country, watching one another's activities and waiting for situations that could be turned to their advantage. In the two decades before migration of settlers to Oregon began, the country was visited by a stream of spies, some of whom were naval and army officers ingenuously pretending to be sportsmen, health seekers, or journalists.

Astor's plans for capturing the fur trade of the Great Lakes and the upper Mississippi had been hampered by the War of 1812, but some of the terms of the peace negotiations were to his advantage. In 1816 Congress passed an act, largely through Astor's efforts, excluding foreigners from participation in the American fur trade except in subordinate capacities. While this nominally ended the activities of the British south of the International Line, considerable poaching was carried on. British agents did not scruple to carry to the Indians the liquor forbidden by law in the trade, and made continuous efforts to prejudice the aborigines against United States traders and stir up attacks on them; these were the same tactics used by the British companies against one another.

The cutthroat competition between the North West and the Hudson's Bay Companies reached a crisis in 1818. Early in the century the Earl of Selkirk, moved by the suffering of the landless Scots, had bought a controlling interest in the Hudson's Bay Company in order

to obtain land for settlement along the Red River of the North. The
Nor' Westers, very much opposed to settlement in the area they depended on to provide buffalo meat for their inland staffs, carried on a
warfare against the settlers and the Hudson's Bay Company officials
that resulted in several deaths in 1818. At this point, with Parliamentary
interference imminent, officials of the two companies, exhibiting the
British ability to compromise in the face of a crisis involving profits,
began to work for the amalgamation of the two groups.

The North West leader in the movement was Dr. John McLoughlin,
a nephew of the veteran Nor' Wester, Alexander Fraser; he had married the capable half-breed widow of Alexander McKay, who was killed
in the explosion on the Astor ship. The companies were united in 1821
under the name of the older company. In the summer of 1824, in recognition of his ability, McLoughlin was made Chief Factor of the Department of the Columbia, which embraced the country west of the
Rockies between Russian Alaska and Mexican California.

The North West Company had done little to develop trade in this
area, though it held Astoria (Fort George) and maintained several
posts. McLoughlin set out almost immediately for his new post, closely
followed by the energetic George Simpson, field Governor of the new
Hudson's Bay Company. The Governor made the journey from York
Factory on Hudson Bay to Fort George on the Columbia in 84 days,
proof not only of his energy but also of the efficient organization of
the Hudson's Bay Company and the control it had over the Indians
of Canada.

The new Chief Factor and the Governor soon decided that Astoria
was in a poor position; the Governor wanted to move the headquarters
north to the mouth of the Fraser River, but McLoughlin preferred to
keep it on the Columbia and his desire prevailed. He selected the new
site, naming it for the British commander Vancouver whose expedition
had gone up the river in 1792 just after the Bostonian, Captain Gray,
had entered the mouth. Fort Vancouver became the capital of the country between Alaska and Oregon. Under George Simpson the Hudson's
Bay Company developed a policy of withholding liquor from the Indians (within British territory) and of conserving the fur-bearing animals by limiting operations whenever signs of depletion appeared.
McLoughlin quickly established respect for the company among the
Indians, thus making trading operations orderly and reasonably safe.

When Fort Vancouver was established in 1824 it was placed on the north bank of the Columbia because the realistic Hudson's Bay Company Council had come to the conclusion that when the Oregon question was settled there would be a compromise; the company, and Great Britain, hoped to hold the land north and west of the Columbia River, which embraced more than half of the present State of Washington. McLoughlin was told that he must, as far as possible, make the Department of the Columbia independent of outside supplies by raising foodstuffs around his post. This he undertook to do at once.

In 1816 Astor's American Fur Company began to be active in the Great Lakes and the upper Mississippi fur trade, making its headquarters at Mackinac Island. By 1822 its business had expanded to the point that a Western Department was established with headquarters at St. Louis and activities covering the Illinois, the middle Mississippi, and the Missouri areas.

In the same year the *Missouri Republican* carried this advertisement: "To enterprising young men. The subscriber wishes to engage one hundred young men to ascend the Missouri river to its source, there to be employed one, two, or three years. For particulars enquire of Major Henry . . . who will ascend with, and command, the party. . . ." It was signed by William H. Ashley. Many of the men assembled by Ashley in this enterprise appear sooner or later in every history, no matter how brief, of the American fur trade. Among them were Jedediah S. Smith, the trailmaker who was the only praying Methodist among the wild and reckless fur-trading crew; Andrew Henry, who had built the post on the Snake in 1810 and had survived a sanguinary struggle with the Blackfeet; William Sublette, who in 1826 with Smith and David Jackson bought out Ashley's interests in the fur company, that later provided the only serious opposition to the Astor operations and gave trouble even to the Hudson's Bay Department of the Columbia; Jim Bridger, canniest of all western scouts, explorer of the Great Salt Lake and a creator of folklore; Thomas Fitzpatrick, who was a leader of the party that early in 1824 discovered, or rediscovered, South Pass, through which went most of the early travelers; Étienne Provot, another trailmaker; Hugh Glass, whose duel with a grizzly bear is a classic of the early West; James Beckwourth, the gaudy liar whose autobiography long filled small boys with envy; Mike Fink, the tough keelboatman whose exploits passed rapidly into legend; Carpenter, who was killed by Mike; and Talbot, who in turn killed Mike.

In 1821-22 the Astor interests had had the governmental trading posts abolished; this gave the trade completely to private concerns, resulting eventually in a virtual monopoly for the Astor interests east of Oregon. Long before that had been achieved, however, private competition had thrown the Indian tribes into turmoil similar to that which had forced the Hudson's Bay-North West Company merger. Rival groups plied the Indians with banned liquor, and stirred them up against other tribes, against the traders of other companies, and even against factions within their own companies, by bewildering them with contradictory statements—all inculcating contempt for white men and white government. Though the monopoly of the Hudson's Bay Company in Canada and in the Oregon country had a quieting effect, making the country fairly safe for the passage of small groups of white persons, the Astor monopoly increased the tension because of the intracompany competition. Another result of the rivalries was the early exhaustion of the fur field, since conservation was impossible under the circumstances.

Rufus Sage, who traveled through the West before the great migration began, came to the conclusion that vice was all the white men had given to the Indians. One early traveler reported that an Indian chief, noting the conduct of the white men with the Indian women, asked innocently whether there were any white women; another reported that an Indian had asked him seriously whether the whites were not deliberately debauching them with intent to weaken them. An emigrant wrote that the only English words some tribes knew were "Whoa," "Gee," and "God damn," which they used as polite greetings; he added that one company that asked Indians where there was good camping ground was told that there was plenty of grass nearby for the "Whoa-haws" but no water for the "God-damns."

Almost from the beginning the relations between the whites and the Indians were strained, the people of the two races having different ethical values and material standards. Joseph Whitehouse of the Lewis and Clark expedition summed up the friendliest white attitude toward the Indians: "they are or appear as yet to be the most friendly people I ever Saw but they will Steal and plunder if they can git an oppertunity. . . . Some of them & indeed most of them have Strange & uncommon Ideas, but verry Ignorant of our forms & customs. but quick & Sensible in their own way & in their own conceit &c &c."

The first white men in a region were greeted with curiosity and were often welcomed because of the gadgets they brought. Nonetheless, even when the welcome was warm and friendly, the white men were ex-

Catlin

CHINOOK WOMAN
The Chinooks called their neighbors Flatheads

NEBRASKA SETTLERS (1886)

asperated by the aborigines, chiefly because of the Indian attitude towards private property. Among all tribes there was a limited amount of personal property, and title to it was respected within the tribe. Nontribal property was legitimate loot in the complicated game of skill that played a large part in Indian warrior life. Scoring rules for the game were intricate; so many points went to the man who could steal such property, the number dependent on the value of what was taken. War was a sporting event. Many points went to the man who took a prisoner; if the attempted capture resulted in death, it was still counted provided the scalp was obtained, because the Indians believed that body and spirit were one. Killing with a tomahawk was more meritorious than killing with an arrow because it involved greater physical risk. A great hero was a man who could touch an enemy before he killed and scalped him. Enemies were those who had scored unfairly against the tribe or who had humiliated its members.

Training in theft was given from the earliest years, property within the tribe being used for this vocational guidance. The small boy caught stealing was thoroughly shamed by his parents as a bungler. The Indian who could slip into the Lewis and Clark camp and make off with a knife or a kettle was merely a clever fellow, in the eyes of his tribesmen; and the Indians did not understand why the visitors should particularly resent this if they had been lax about guarding their property. Had the whites stolen in return, the Indians would have regarded it as wholly natural. Friendly chiefs were quite willing to force the return of stolen odds and ends if the visitors could point out the unskilled person who had taken them.

The whites, misunderstanding this attitude, frequently beat Indians for theft, not realizing that the Indians considered death less humiliating. Once a tribal member had been beaten, his tribe felt that it could save face by nothing short of capturing—dead, if necessary—as many of the beater's fellows as possible; and since all white men looked alike to them, they avenged themselves on the first party to appear after the humiliation.

On the other hand, the Indians had a deep sense of justice and of gratitude. McLoughlin controlled those in his area by punishing offenders whose guilt could be clearly demonstrated, rewarding those shown worthy of trust, caring for the sick among the Indians as faithfully as he cared for ailing whites, and by observing Indian taboos and demanding that the Indians observe his; the Indians called him the White-Headed Eagle. Fort Vancouver was never attacked.

McLoughlin, however, could not entirely prevent the Indians from selling to his rivals, because of the agreement on joint occupancy of the Oregon country, renewed in 1827. In 1826 American traders, probably belonging to the aggressive Ashley company, had been so successful in underselling the second Hudson's Bay expedition into the Snake River country that Peter Skene Ogden, its leader, reported he was happy to return to Fort Vancouver without serious loss. When American traders came to the area by sea or land the Chief Factor received them cordially but used all his influence to make their quests for furs fruitless. The competition of one ingenious Yankee, Capt. William McNeill, who arrived in 1832 with a shipload of such gay novelties as jumping-jacks, wooden soldiers, and whistles—which seemed far more desirable to the Indians than the Hudson's Bay staples—was suppressed only by the purchase of the ship, its cargo, and the captain's services for the Hudson's Bay Company.

Occasionally Dr. McLoughlin smothered competition with courtesy; in 1828 Jedediah Smith limped into Fort Vancouver after having lost part of his men and all his furs among the Umpquas of southern Oregon. The Chief Factor had personal sympathy for Smith, a brave man, but he acted largely as an overlord for the Hudson's Bay Company when he sent an expedition to punish the Umpquas and recover the furs; no molestation of whites would be tolerated in his domain. Governor Simpson, who was visiting the post, approved the purchase of the furs at market price to save Smith from the dangers of transportation overland with a small escort, at the same time making it clear that in doing so the company was trusting Smith to keep out of the Oregon area in the future. The praying Methodist did not violate the obligation.

In the meantime, however, more serious attacks on McLoughlin's territory were developing. The English colonies had been settled by protestants against authority in church and state, protestants against unfavorable economic conditions, and protestants against the dullness and monotony of life in settled communities. The great majority of the settlers were people who had different values from those who stayed at home, counting physical risk and hardship a small price to pay for adventure, fortune, or freedom to do as they pleased. Some found what they had sought; others did not, and they moved restlessly on from place to place. People dissatisfied with Massachusetts had settled Connecticut and New Hampshire; people dissatisfied with Connecticut and New Hampshire had settled Vermont and upper New York; people dissatisfied with New England and nearby States had settled Ohio. People who had left the seaboard for Kentucky, Tennessee, and the Northwest Territory had moved across the Mississippi River soon after Louisiana was acquired, many abandoning fertile farms they had cleared, because of some undefined dissatisfaction and the vague belief that Utopia must exist somewhere west.

All explorers, nearly all pioneers, and certainly all the fur traders belonged to this restless breed, though many who write of their adventures do not understand their heroes; they judge them by their own stay-at-home values and waste "heroic," "intrepid," "hardy," "valiant," and like words on them until the adjectives are meaningless. When, after a hard winter in a hut along the Missouri, Lewis wrote that the moment of departure for the untrodden wilderness was among the happiest of his life, he was voicing the feeling of all who followed him westward. Time and again the traders and mountain men vowed that they were through with hardships and were going back to the security of the settled East; but the first person who asked them to return to the mountains was sure to start them west again. Those who returned to the East, even briefly, spread unrest and stirred up the adventurous blood dormant in most of the descendants of the first pioneers.

In the early decades of the nineteenth century a large part of the population of the United States was in a particularly disturbed state of mind. The more perfect union envisioned by the Constitution had not abolished taxes or created idyllic communities; the new factories, belching forth smoke and cinders, provided many new comforts but did not pay wages that enabled the hands to buy them in quantities; farmers were receiving lower prices for their products because of competition from the newly settled lands; the blow dealt to the spiritual authority of the churches by the Revolution had robbed many of their feeling of spiritual security; and the ideas let loose by the French Revolution, widely aired by those who had fled to America to escape the reactionary regimes of the post-Revolutionary period, added to the mental ferment. Messiahs appeared daily, offering mesmerism, socialism, vegetarianism, love-communism, Millerism, dress reform, transcendentalism, and countless other panaceas for social, economic, and religious ills. Almost every prophet gained at least a few followers, some a great many.

The *Journals* of Lewis and Clark and of other explorers, the diaries and letters of travelers and journalists, turned public attention to the Far West. European philosophers, poets, and novelists had long been romanticizing the American wilderness and, to some extent, the pioneers. James Fenimore Cooper, however, was the first American to idealize the frontiersmen. Washington Irving began the literary exploitation of the Far West. The romantic attitude gradually spread downward from the literate to the illiterate, and restless migrants who had never read a book in their lives began to see themselves as participants in heroic drama—and to act and pose accordingly.

One of the first to advocate emigration to the Oregon region was Hall J. Kelley, a teacher in a school near Boston, who began writing letters and memoranda to the newspapers on the subject in 1818, basing his statements largely on his own interpretations of what Lewis and Clark had reported. In time he organized emigrant meetings, addressed memorials to Congress for aid, and eventually founded an Oregon Emigration Association to travel west in 1832. His first appeals were commercial and agrarian; but as the clergy, fearful of losing more parishioners, and factory owners, determined not to have their cheap-labor market diminished, began to attack him and his propaganda, his writings became somewhat socialistic.

Kelley interested the well-to-do Nathaniel Wyeth in the scheme. Wyeth clearly indicated the state of mind of the average emigrant when he wrote: "I cannot divest myself of the opinion that I shall compete better with my fellow men in new and untried paths than in *those which require only patience and attention.*" But Wyeth early discovered Kelley's impracticality and determined to lead his own expedition, but as a fur trader, not a settler. His plans were like those John Jacob Astor had made earlier; a ship would carry supplies for the Indian trade to the Columbia and Wyeth would travel overland to meet it. In late October, 1832, Wyeth reached Fort Vancouver after many difficulties resulting from his lack of experience; his ship had not arrived. Dr. McLoughlin, liking the young man, took him into the Hudson's Bay mess with his usual hospitality, but at the same time warned him frankly that he would do all he could to oppose his business venture. Wyeth did not learn for many months that his ship had been wrecked and that it was useless for him to remain in Oregon.

In 1832 Capt. Benjamin de Bonneville also arrived in Oregon, ostensibly as a fur trader but, judged by the maps and reports he made and by recently discovered pay-roll records, actually as a United States secret intelligence officer. The *Adventures of Captain Bonneville*, written by Washington Irving from Bonneville's notes, was read by many people, who in 1837, the year the book was published, were sharing the results of the disastrous financial crash that had been caused by mad speculation in public utilities and unsound public and private financing. To them the West began to seem a place of refuge, offering unlimited land without mortgages.

It was a rule of the Hudson's Bay Company that an employee reaching the end of his term of service must return to the point of enlistment for discharge. A number of French Canadians employed in the Department of the Columbia asked McLoughlin's permission to settle near Fort Vancouver when their time was up; they liked the country and had taken wives from local tribes. Ignoring the company regulation, the doctor sent them down the Willamette and aided them with tools and supplies; he did this partly from kind-heartedness and partly, perhaps, because he had an idea that settlement south of the river by loyal Canadians might enable him to hold the country. As the settlement expanded and the number of half-breed children increased, he became anxious to provide education and religious training. He several times asked headquarters to obtain a clergyman for the post, but none was sent in spite of promises.

In 1831 four members of the Flathead tribe had journeyed to St. Louis to ask for instruction in the white man's religion, having heard from a wandering band of Canadian Iroquois of the superior efficiency of the "medicine" of the "black robes" (priests). Their action aroused such interest in religious circles that in 1833 the General Conference of the Methodist Episcopal Church appointed the efficient Jason Lee "Missionary to the Flatheads." Lee rapidly organized a small party of assistants and, learning that Nathaniel Wyeth was returning to Oregon to make another attempt to compete with the Hudson's Bay Company, obtained permission to travel overland with the Boston merchant. In July, 1834, the party reached the Snake River, where Wyeth established a small post, which he named Fort Hall; the party reached Fort Vancouver on September 16. McLoughlin greeted them cordially, in spite of his knowledge of Wyeth's intentions, and was soon advising Lee that it was dangerous to establish a mission among the Flatheads and that he had a congregation ready for his ministrations along the Willamette. In giving this advice the Chief Factor spoke as a Hudson's Bay man,

eager to keep the Americans well south of the Columbia. Lee accepted
the advice and almost at once set out to build his mission.

Despite Dr. McLoughlin's disapproval, Wyeth built a post close to
Fort Vancouver, but he was no match for his entrenched rival and after
a very discouraging struggle he left the field.

Another arrival at Fort Vancouver in 1834 was Hall Kelley, who
had traveled from Boston by way of California. During his first visit
Wyeth had told Dr. McLoughlin of Kelley's activities and the doctor,
ordinarily kind and courteous, had worked up an intense hatred of the
man who was trying to stimulate what was, in the Factor's opinion, an
invasion of a country he had developed. When Kelley arrived, penni-
less, almost alone, and preceded by a report that he had stolen horses
in California, the doctor permitted him to live at the post but treated
him as a pariah. Kelley lingered miserably until 1836, his hatred of
McLoughlin increasing daily. When Kelley returned to Boston his
stored-up venom found outlet in a bitter pamphlet in which he accused
the doctor of tyranny and of activities inimical to the American cause.
This pamphlet was called to the attention of the Secretary of State, who
at once arranged to have a Captain Slacum investigate the situation on
the Columbia. Slacum's report, which was not free from bias, aroused
considerable feeling in the United States.

In the meantime, more missionaries had arrived along the Columbia.
Other religious people besides the Methodists had been moved by the
Flathead plea; in 1834 an interdenominational board appointed the
Rev. Samuel Parker and Dr. Marcus Whitman to study the needs. In
1835 the two men traveled with fur traders to the annual rendezvous
in the Green River Valley of western Wyoming. When they reached the
valley Dr. Whitman had seen enough Indians to be convinced that he
need go no farther before reporting to the board that the aborigines
needed religious attention. Parker traveled on with only a few Indians,
arriving at Fort Vancouver on October 16 immaculately dressed and
wearing a plug hat, as was his wont. The Chief Factor, though somewhat worried by the advent, was courteous as usual; but this missionary
was not to be diverted to the Willamette Valley. After looking over
sites for missions he left Vancouver for Boston by way of the Pacific.

Not long after Parker's departure for reinforcements, the Hudson's
Bay Company answered the doctor's six-year-old prayer for a clergyman; the Rev. Herbert Beaver arrived from London with his wife and
within a short time managed to set the post by its heels. Neither the

clergyman nor his wife had anything but scorn for the Indians and they disapproved of the Hudson's Bay contract marriages, going so far in their dislike of inter-racial marriage as to snub the doctor's wife, who was a half-breed and married by contract. The situation was made increasingly tense by the severely critical letters the clergyman wrote to London; it culminated in 1838, when the doctor lost his temper and caned Mr. Beaver. The act was unfortunate for Dr. McLoughlin because the Beavers, after their return to England, helped to work up opposition to the Chief Factor's activities. Up to this time the doctor had been accorded great respect from headquarters. He had extended his posts to the north and east, was raising enough foodstuffs to enable him to have a surplus for exportation, and was also trading in the Sandwich Islands.

About the time Mr. Beaver put in his delayed appearance, Dr. Whitman and the Rev. Henry Spalding arrived at Fort Vancouver with their wives—the first white women to make the overland trip. Dr. McLoughlin treated the party hospitably and, when they insisted on going at once to found missions near Walla Walla and on the Clearwater River, gave them what assistance he could, by permitting them to replenish their exhausted supplies from his stores; he warned them, however, of the danger of isolating themselves inland near the treacherous Cayuses.

In the meantime Jason Lee had called for reinforcements, and in the summer of 1837 two ships arrived with supplies and more missionaries, bringing the total in the Willamette Valley to 60.

The Chief Factor watched their arrival with mixed feelings; the Protestant missionaries had made slight progress, their type of religion having little appeal for the natives. Indian converts had been few and the French Canadians, who were Roman Catholics, had held aloof. The doctor began to hear rumors that the Americans were turning their attention to real estate and politics and were considering the setting up of a provisional government. As the failure to win the Indians became more apparent, the missionary group became concerned to show some other results to their financial backers. In 1838 Jason Lee determined to visit the East and place a memorial before Congress asking that Oregon be made a part of the Union.

In the same year the Chief Factor took his first vacation away from the Columbia since he had arrived there in 1824; he went straight to London to lay before his chiefs his plans for the extension of Hudson's Bay activities. In addition to obtaining permission to trade into

Russian Alaska, with Russian consent, he was also authorized to make settlements south of Puget Sound, as a means of reinforcing Britain's claim to the territory that is now the State of Washington.

In May, 1840, not long after McLoughlin's return to his post, Jason Lee reappeared, by way of the sea, at the head of a party of 52 persons. When the doctor asked why they had come, Lee assured him that they were to work in the mission. Not long after this, however, it became quite apparent that many were interested in settlement rather than in missionary work. Long afterward the Chief Factor was to learn that Lee on his trip east had traveled widely on lecture tours, mixing his discussion of Indian needs with large doses of propaganda on the desirability of Oregon as a place of settlement. No professional imperialist could have been more enthusiastic than Lee about the justness of seizing Oregon for the United States. Lee's speeches and the *Journal* of his travels, published in 1838, did much to spread the Oregon fever. The question of the ethical propriety of Lee's imperialistic activities has provided meat for a hundred years of argument; he had accepted much help from the doctor in establishing his mission, with full knowledge that McLoughlin would have opposed him if his announced purpose had been commercial or imperialistic. It is probable that Lee was less sensitive than Jedediah Smith and that to him McLoughlin was merely a symbol representing Britain, which the average American believed should be outwitted by fair means or foul.

Less easily condoned was the act of the Reverend Mr. Waller, who deliberately pre-empted land by the Falls of the Willamette that McLoughlin had taken possession of in 1830 and where he had blasted out a millrace. McLoughlin gave notice of the claim when Waller started to build, but permitted the Methodist as a tenant to erect a small building, even giving him some lumber. Later Waller and others ignored the doctor's claim entirely and did all in their power to take from him the spot to which he had planned to retire.

In 1841 Governor Simpson, then Sir George, arrived at Fort Vancouver on an inspection trip. McLoughlin had been permitted far more freedom than were most Chief Factors, but he knew that in allowing the missionaries to establish themselves so strongly he had betrayed company policy. Though Sir George was noncommittal, it was clear that he was not satisfied.

The Hudson's Bay Company was well aware that there was a growing sentiment in the United States for the seizure of Oregon; in fact,

American claims disputed title to all the West Coast country up to the Russian boundary. The American claim rested in part on the fact that Robert Gray had visited the mouth of the Columbia in 1792, though it was Vancouver's lieutenant who, in the same year, had explored the river for a hundred miles and verified its course; it also rested on the explorations by the Americans, Lewis and Clark. The British, however, could show that they had been developing the country, had made some settlements, and had established civil rule for British subjects in the territory. The weakness of the American claim was apparent and the missionary-imperialists in the critical years were frank, in the States if not in Oregon, in stressing the need of rushing settlers in to attain predominant numbers for the United States. Conservative members of the Government had resisted the shouts of jingoes for military penetration of the Oregon country, as they had resisted pleas for forts near the Rockies to protect the fur traders. Settlements, however, were rapidly increasing between the Mississippi and Indian territory, particularly since the depression of 1837 had added to the popular unrest.

In May, 1841, a group of people assembled at Independence, Mo., for migration to California; they had been collected largely by John Bidwell who had heard stories of the country from a traveling Frenchman. Most of the would-be emigrants became discouraged and withdrew from the party, which became so small that the remainder joined some trappers, including Thomas Fitzpatrick, on their way to Green River, and a party of Roman Catholic priests, including Father Pierre DeSmet, who were journeying to the Flathead country at last to answer the call for "black robes." When the priests left them at Soda Springs, the party, now consisting of 64 people, was split; half of them, fearing to attempt the uncertain California route, followed the better-known trail to Whitman's mission at Walla Walla and then went down the Columbia.

In 1842 the real march on Oregon began. In this year the imperialists, led by Sen. Thomas H. Benton of Missouri, had succeeded in having an official trail-exploration expedition sent as far west as the Wind River Valley; this was led by Benton's new son-in-law, J. C. Frémont. Frémont's report, issued early in 1843, roused wide enthusiasm; in 1843 he again went out and he spent most of the two following years exploring foreign land—Oregon and the Mexican possessions in what is now the United States. His reports of these expeditions became the chief guidebook of later emigrants. At the time Frémont was making his first trip, a party of about a hundred started for Oregon under the leadership of Dr. Elijah White, a member of the Willamette mission who had quarreled with Jason Lee but was returning with the peculiar Federal title of "Indian subagent for Oregon." McLoughlin's agent at Fort Hall sent a guide to lead them to the Willamette. This party did not pass Fort Vancouver, but McLoughlin later helped many of its members by extending credit at the company commissary to them. In the following year nearly half the members of the White party moved on to California; their arrival had, however, stimulated the Americans in the Willamette Valley to form a loose civil government for themselves. The British subjects in the valley first joined the movement, but withdrew when they discovered the nationalistic character of the activities.

At the time the organization meeting was held nearly a thousand persons were assembling at Independence, Mo., and preparing to start west. White in 1842 had brought news of this assembly and also orders to Dr. Whitman that part of his missions were to be closed because the board was tired of the dissension among the workers and disappointed in the number of conversions. Whitman and his colleagues determined to disregard the instructions. In the fall of this year Whitman suddenly decided to rush east, regardless of the weather. After a quick trip across the mountains, he went straight to Washington to urge his ideas on Government officials, asking for forts to protect emigrants along the Oregon Trail; he then visited New York, where he met Horace Greeley and filled him with enthusiasm for the disputed territory; and finally he went to Boston to consult with his board. Almost immediately he started west again, lecturing as he went, to join the travelers at Independence and turn them toward Oregon.

About 875 persons straggled into Oregon in November and December of 1843; like those who preceded them, they were assisted in various ways by the Hudson's Bay Chief Factor of the Columbia. In the following year the settlers reorganized and strengthened their provisional government, and welcomed 1,400 more arrivals. Still Dr. McLoughlin extended credit to the straitened newcomers, who promised repayment in wheat and other commodities to be produced on the new lands; it is possible that he yet hoped to redeem himself in the eyes of his superiors by making Fort Vancouver the export center for the territory.

In 1845, which saw the arrival of more than three thousand immigrants, the provisional government was fully established. In the same year the Hudson's Bay Company forced the resignation of its Chief Factor on the Columbia; after winding up his affairs he moved south in an attempt to regain the land he had laid claim to 15 years before and in the expectation of some repayment from the many newcomers he had helped. Many of the settlers had not paid their debts to the Hudson's Bay Company and McLoughlin's later years were embittered because he had to use his lifetime savings to reimburse the company. Though he soon became a citizen of the United States, his land claim was not recognized until five years after his death.

A leader of one 1845 section was Joel Palmer, whose *Journal,* published in 1847, gave sound advice to future emigrants (*see AP-PENDIX*).

By 1846 the boundary controversy had become acute; Polk's campaign slogan—"Fifty-four forty or fight"—and the Mexican War had whipped the United States into a state of imperialistic belligerency. War between the United States and Great Britain seemed so inevitable that the representatives of the two countries hastily brought the 30-year negotiations to an end with a compromise extending the international boundary westward along the 49th parallel to the Strait of Georgia.

The same force—settlement—that had brought Oregon territory into the Union was already bringing in the Southwest; by 1853 war and purchase had rounded out the present boundaries of the United States.

The acquisition of vast western lands swelled the stream of migration to all parts of the West. By 1848 the Oregon Trail was deeply rutted. The discovery of gold in California in that year drove it deeper into the prairies, for it carried the great bulk of the gold seekers—at least to a point west of South Pass.

Much maudlin sympathy has been wasted on the pioneers; few of them asked for it. They were taking part in one of the great mass movements of history—and they knew it, as is shown by the diaries they kept under difficult conditions, by the letters they wrote to the home-town newspapers and to friends, and by the efforts they made to leave their names on various rocks along the way. To many the journey was an exhilarating picnic, with gossip, chatter, love-making, sightseeing, and adventure providing them with something to boast about for the rest of their lives. If the hardships were greater than they anticipated, the majority was undismayed. Cholera epidemics along the trail in

1849, 1850, and 1852 took heavy toll, as such epidemics did in cities. On the whole the emigrants had such good health on the trail that hordes of sick and anemic persons journeyed to the Missouri to travel at least for a time with the parties. Had the emigrants stayed at home, the average annual death rate would have been 500 in every 20,000; probably the death rate on the trail from natural causes was lower than at home. Most deaths not resulting from epidemics were the result of rashness or carelessness. Loaded guns in the hands of amateur frontiersmen were a leading cause of accidents.

Every party had some members who were sure that they could find shorter and better routes than could experienced guides; the tragic experience of the Donner party (*see SECTION 7*) took place because the members acted on advice given in a letter written by a man of whom they had never heard.

As Army posts were opened along the way, the officers became increasingly annoyed by the foolhardiness of the travelers; finally, to save themselves the labor of rushing about rescuing the foolish, they forcibly though without authority organized the trains under military rules and passed them along under escort.

While many of the emigrants feared the Indians and were always alert, others could not be made to take reasonable precautions against surprise. The Indians stole when they could and caused occasional deaths during raids, but they were not serious menaces until the sixties, when they began to realize that the invaders were driving away and killing off the buffalo and other animals on which the natives depended for their food and clothing. By this time, moreover, the Indians had become thoroughly disillusioned of any hopes that the whites would keep the land treaties. By these agreements the whites took the best lands and gave the Indians the worst; in addition comparatively little of the promised compensations in money and goods ever reached the aborigines. Even the Army officers sent to quell uprisings when the Indians became desperate, reported, with a stern sense of justice, that the natives had just cause for their frantic last stands. For many years the forces sent against the Indians were inadequate, but when at length the Government undertook to finish the job of expropriation, the results were swift and final.

` Great hardship was caused by the settlers' determination to carry their prized possessions with them. Many a cherished chest and spinet on the West Coast was carried overland at the price of semistarvation.

By 1850 the immigrants were beginning to clamor for quick mail service and better transportation, but it was 1859 before an overland stage went as far west as Colorado. The Pony Express, which gave the first fast mail service to California, was inaugurated in 1860; though it lasted only 16 months and ruined its promoters, it provided the country with one of the most exciting series of relay races in history. In 1861 a telegraph line connected the Pacific Coast with the East. After much talk about building a railroad to the Far West, the Federal government accepted the responsibility. A Congressional act permitted the Central Pacific to built eastward from Sacramento and the Union Pacific to build westward from Council Bluffs until their lines should meet, with a bait of princely land grants to stimulate rivalry between the two companies for distance covered. The most formidable engineering difficulties were encountered at the western end, but the building of the Union Pacific was a far more dramatic enterprise; it was carried through at a time when many of the Indian tribes of the plains were actively and fiercely hostile. On May 10, 1869, at Promontory, Utah, a golden spike was driven into a cross-tie of California laurel, celebrating the junction of the rails pushed from the East and the West, and the completion of an iron span across the continent.

Wagons continued to follow the Oregon Trail until late in the eighties, but the days of pioneer travel were over and the physical frontier was almost gone. Many who went west remained only a short time, then turned back to settle in the Middle West, or to resettle in their native States east of the Mississippi. Relatively few of the immigrants found the quick wealth and happiness they had sought. Through the years the migrations grew steadily smaller; they have not yet stopped, though there is no free land today.

The biological genes transmitting the characteristics that drained Europe of much of its vitality and made the United States an empire extending from coast to coast have not been bred out.

THE OREGON TRAIL

US 30

The Missouri River to the Pacific
2,110 miles

Alternate Route
Nebraska–Wyoming
570.4 miles

CAVALRY ESCORTING THE MAIL

THE MAIL

INDEPENDENCE COURTHOUSE, MISSOURI (1855)

Missouri-Iowa

Independence, Mo.—Kansas City—St. Joseph—Council Bluffs, Iowa (Missouri River); 218.1 m. US 24, US 71, and US 275.

Burlington Route and Missouri Pacific R.R. roughly parallel route between Kansas City and Council Bluffs.

Paved roadbed.

Accommodations chiefly in towns.

> *". . . from this river is time reconed & it matters not how far you you have come, this is the point to which they all refer, for the question is never, when did you leave home? but, when did you leave the Mississouri river?"*
> —Mrs. Frizzell, *Across the Plains to California in 1852.*

"Last spring, 1846," wrote Francis Parkman in *The California and Oregon Trail,* "was a busy season in the city of St. Louis. Not only were emigrants from every part of the country preparing for the journey to Oregon and California, but an unusual number of traders were making ready their wagons and outfits for Santa Fe. The hotels were crowded, and the gunsmiths and saddlers were kept constantly at work in providing arms and equipment for the different parties of travellers. Almost every day steamboats were leaving the levee and passing up the Missouri, crowded with passengers on the way to the frontier.

"In one of these, the *Radnor,* . . . . my friend and relative, Quincy A. Shaw, and myself left St. Louis on the twenty-fifth of April on a tour of curiosity and amusement to the Rocky Mountains. The boat was loaded until the water broke alternately over her guards. Her upper deck was covered with large wagons of a peculiar form, for the Santa Fe trade, and the hold was crammed with goods for the same destination. There were also the equipments and provisions of a party of Oregon emigrants, a band of mules and horses, piles of saddles, and a multitude of nondescript articles, indispensable on the prairies.

". . . . In five or six days we began to see signs of the great western movement that was taking place. Parties of emigrants, with their tents, and wagons, were encamped on open spots near the bank, on their way to the common rendezvous at Independence."

Section 1. Independence to Council Bluffs (Missouri River), 218.1 m. US 24, US 71, and US 275.

INDEPENDENCE, **0 m.** (949 alt., 15,296 pop.), is a pleasant residential and manufacturing suburb of Kansas City, Mo., lying about five miles south of the Missouri River and a dozen miles west of the mouth of the Kansas. There is little in its appearance today to suggest

37

that it was at one time the busiest town in the United States west of
St. Louis.

A few settlers appeared in the area after 1808, when little Fort
Osage was established some miles to the east; it was chiefly a Government trading post. Missouri became a State in 1821 but Independence
was not organized until 1827, after the Indians occupying the territory
had been sent (1825) west of the State Line, and Fort Leavenworth,
some miles up the Missouri, had been garrisoned.

Traders and trappers from the United States were roaming toward
the Rockies soon after the Louisiana Purchase was made. A few pene-
trated to Santa Fe, then under Spanish rule, though the Mexicans were
attempting to obtain independence. These early traders in the Southwest
were treated with suspicion and hostility by the Spanish. In the fall of
1821 a party of 20 traders and trappers went up the Arkansas, crossed
to and explored the headwaters of the Rio Grande, and in the following
summer returned to Missouri by a route to some extent approximating
the later Santa Fe Trail; this was called the Fowler expedition for
Jacob Fowler, second in command, who reported the results of the
explorations. Not long after this expedition started out William Beck-
nell, a trader, returned from Santa Fe with the report that the Mexicans
were free from Spanish domination and eager for trade with the United
States. In 1825-27, through the effort of Thomas Hart Benton, an
expansionist and Missouri's first Senator, three United States commis-
sioners were sent out to survey a trail to the Southwest; since the
area that is now New Mexico was then Mexican territory, they did not
work beyond the United States boundary, but as far as they went they
laid out the Santa Fe Trail. Though the route nominally started at
Fort Osage, Independence soon became the headquarters of the Southwest traders. It maintained its importance in this capacity until after
1868, when construction of the Atchison, Topeka & Santa Fe Ry. began.

This area, rather than St. Louis, became the jumping-off-place for
the West and the Southwest because traders could avoid 250 miles of
travel over mire and rough roads by traveling up the Missouri River to
the point where it made a sharp bend at the beginning of its long swing
north. By 1830 the town had a busy blacksmith shop and other facilities
needed by those setting off on long journeys overland through unsettled
territory.

The earliest traders along the Santa Fe Trail used pack horses, but
they soon acquired mules, which were abundant in Mexico and had a
reputation for sturdiness, sure-footedness, and ability to carry heavy
loads. Later traders found oxen even better for the purpose. The first
wagons used on the Santa Fe Trail were made in Pittsburgh, Pa., but
"Murphy wagons," originally made by a man of that name in St. Louis,
soon became popular. Later Samuel Weston and other local men manufactured trail wagons, and in the last years of the prairie-schooner traffic there were wagonmakers in a number of nearby towns.

A loaded wagon weighed from three to seven thousand pounds. Ten or twelve mules, or six yoke of oxen, were needed to pull each wagon; reserve animals were driven with the train to take the places of those that gave out.

In the thirties and forties a trip or two to Santa Fe was the popular means of occupying the "Wanderjahr" before young men settled down to business and family life; those who could afford it went as traders and the rest took employment with the trains. The skilled employees were the packers and drivers, who received each month between $25 and $50 and "found." Wealthy young men often accompanied the trains as tourists, paying for their own equipment and sometimes paying also for protection on the route. Yet others accompanied the trains for only a hundred miles or so.

Josiah Gregg, the trader who made his first trip on the trail, as a health seeker, in his *Commerce of the Prairies* (1844) related that "among the concourse of travellers at this 'starting point,' besides traders and tourists, a number of pale-faced invalids are generally to be met with. The Prairies have, in fact, become very celebrated for their sanative effects—more justly so, no doubt, than the most fashionable watering-places of the North. Most chronic diseases, particularly liver complaints, dyspepsias, and similar affections, are often radically cured; owing, no doubt to the peculiarities of diet, and the regular exercise incident to prairie life, as well as to the purity of the atmosphere of those elevated unembarrassed regions. An invalid myself, I can answer for the efficacy of the remedy, at least in my own case. Though, like other valetudinarians, I was disposed to provide an ample supply of such commodities as I deemed necessary for my comfort and health, I was not long upon the prairies before I discovered that most of such extra preparations were unnecessary, or at least quite dispensable. A few knick-knacks, as a little tea, rice, fruits, crackers, etc., suffice very well for the first fortnight, after which the invalid is generally able to take the fare of the hunter and teamster. Though I set out myself in a carriage, before the close of the first week I saddled my pony; and when we reached the buffalo range, I was not only as eager for the chase as the sturdiest of my companions, but I enjoyed far more exquisitely my share of the buffalo, than all the delicacies which were ever devised to provoke the most fastidious appetite."

At the time Gregg wrote his book, the transient population of Independence had been augmented by emigrants, missionaries, tourists, journalists, and traders bound for Oregon and, in some cases, for California. After 1838, when Washington Irving's books on the West were becoming popular and Jason Lee made his lecture tour through the States bordering on the Mississippi, the Oregon fever burned higher annually. One of Lee's converts, Thomas J. Farnham, a lawyer who a few years earlier had migrated from Vermont to Illinois, became very enthusiastic; he was going to trade in the Oregon country and

take possession of it for the United States. He reached Independence
early in 1839 with others who wanted to join him in the venture, and
was elected leader of the company, which called itself the Oregon Dragoons and carried a flag embroidered by Mrs. Farnham with the slogan
"Oregon or the Grave." The group was poorly equipped, each member
having contributed only $160 to the enterprise. Despite the fact that
there were no experienced hunters in the party, the supplies were sufficient for only 400 miles of travel; Farnham had believed they could
live on game. (The naive belief that the trip overland could be made
with limited facilities and equipment was not singular to this group;
many of the tragedies of the trail resulted from ignorance of the fact
that a man had to be reasonably well-to-do to make the journey.)
Farnham's experiences are described in his *Travels in the Great Western
Prairies* (1841).

Each year thereafter emigrants straggled into Independence and
the towns farther north, alone or in small groups; some reached the
town early in April, and joined those who in the previous year had
arrived too late to start. May was considered the best month for departure. Because of the danger of Indian attacks and lootings, emigrants and other travelers usually endeavored to find or organize a
party in the Missouri outfitting towns with which they could travel.
Despite the seriousness of the business of making the last arrangements, of buying equipment and foodstuffs, of having wagons repaired
and horses shod, and of finding suitable fellow travelers, there was
generally a festive air along the Missouri in the spring. The newcomers
collected information and misinformation, made friends and enemies,
changed proposed destinations, and behaved in general as though they
were on a picnic. The children frolicked and the women cooked, sewed,
gossiped, and did the family washings.

When a wagon train had been assembled, a quasi-military organization was formed. Instructions were given by Capt. R. B. Marcy in
the *Prairie Traveler:* "After a particular route has been selected to
make the journey across the plains, and the requisite number have arrived . . . their first business should be to organize themselves into a
company and elect a commander. The company should be of sufficient
magnitude to herd and guard animals, and for protection against Indians. . . . In the selection of a captain, good judgment, integrity of
purpose and practical experience are the essential requisites. . . . His
duty should be to direct the order of march, the time of starting and
halting, to select the camps, detail and give orders to guards, and,
indeed, to control and superintend all the movements of the company.
An obligation should be drawn up and signed by all the members of
the association, wherein each one should bind himself to abide in all
cases by the orders and decisions of the captain and to aid him by
every means in his power . . . . and they should also obligate them-

selves to aid each other, so as to make the individual interest of each member the common concern of the whole company."

A typical pact made by emigrants is found in Silas Newcomb's *Journal* (1850-1):

"At a meeting of a Company of Californians on the Banks of the Missouri, May 6th, 1850, the following Preamble and Resolutions were unanimously adopted:

"Whereas we are about to leave the frontier, and travel over Indian Territory, exposed to their treachery, and knowing their long and abiding hatred of the whites; also many other privations to meet with. We consider it necessary to form ourselves into a Company for the purpose of protecting each other and our property, during our journey to California.

"*Therefore Resolved,* That there shall be one selected from the Company, suitable and capable to act as Captain or Leader.

"*Resolved,* That we, as men, pledge ourselves to assist each other through all the misfortunes that may befall us on our long and dangerous journey.

"*Resolved,* That the Christian Sabbath shall be observed, except when absolutely necessary to travel.

"*Resolved,* That there shall be a sufficient guard appointed each night regularly, by the Captain.

"*Resolved,* That in case of a member's dying, the Company shall give him a decent burial."

The reason for this last pledge is easily found. In 1830 Asiatic cholera had, with the aid of a Mecca pilgrimage, spread into Europe, and by 1832 had appeared to a serious extent in American port cities, particularly New Orleans. By 1833 it had moved up the Mississippi and some of its tributaries. The bacteria causing the disease live in human discharges and are transmitted chiefly through infected water and foodstuffs. Europe was experiencing a second serious cholera epidemic in 1847-8, when a wave of emigration to the United States brought thousands eager to settle in the lands newly acquired in the Far West. Many of these European immigrants brought cholera with them, and infected those who followed them up the Mississippi and down the Ohio. By the middle of June, 1848, Dearborn County, Ind., with a population of two thousand, was burying 14 people a day. In January, 1849, more than a hundred victims of cholera were landed at St. Louis; in that year 4,500 to 6,000 died of the disease in that city alone. Fleeing westward from the plague-stricken city, the emigrants carried the disease with them. In 1849 nearly sixty thousand people passed through Independence and other outfitting towns north of it along the river, most of them with California as their goal. They carried death across the country.

The early symptoms of cholera often pass unrecognized and many who thought they were escaping from the disease had already contracted it; they polluted the campgrounds along the Platte, and those who came behind them picked up the bacteria far from the stricken centers. The onset of the acute stage of the infection is sudden and terrifying; some who started the day's journey on the trail, apparently in good health, were writhing with pain by noon, and were in graves by sundown. Lacking any knowledge of the cause of this horror, fellow travelers, pressing handkerchiefs to their noses, fled from those who became ill, often leaving people to die alone. Some who fled were likewise deserted in a day or two. "It is sometimes just a case of Death snapping his finger at you and you are gone," wrote one forty-niner. The disease spread to the Indians, who, believing that the whites were poisoning them, retaliated by senseless attacks. In 1849 cholera was carried as far west as the Mormon Ferry on the North Platte. The epidemic was not so acute in 1850-1, but there was a resurgence in 1852.

Mercifully, the period of suffering with cholera was brief; though the death toll on the trail can never accurately be estimated, it was probably lower there than in some of the worst-infected cities and the death rate did not raise a barrier of fear against further migrations; even in the epidemic years many thousands made rollicking starts from the frontier.

Those who left it in the neighborhood of Independence followed the Santa Fe Trail for about 40 miles, passing through Westport and crossing into the Indian lands. They then turned northwestward and crossed the Kansas somewhere in the neighborhood of the present Topeka. There the caravans usually stopped to consider plans and reorganize their companies. Some would-be emigrants had had enough of frontier life when they reached this point, and turned back. From Kansas the trail—early called the Oregon and later the California—continued northwestward in the general direction of Grand Island in the Platte River, at intervals meeting feeders from other towns along the Missouri.

The inhabitants of Independence early attempted to divert the flow of business from other settlements that were growing up near the river. By 1846 they had laid a rock road to the bank of the Missouri and established stores near the wharf.

The year 1850 saw the first overland mail and stagecoaches leave this town for Salt Lake City, by Government contract with Samuel H. Woodson; in the following year a summer service was extended to California. The coaches first ran on a monthly schedule; in the early sixties the overland stage left each day. The *Missouri Commonwealth* for July 1860, described the new mail and passenger coaches as "in elegant style, each arranged to convey eight passengers. The bodies are beautifully painted and made water-tight, with a view of using them as boats in ferrying streams." There were six mules to each coach. The mail was guarded by eight armed men.

Until after the railroads had been built there was a steady stream of private vehicles on the trail in summer; a few emigrants of the gold-rush period rode horseback, traveling without wagons, and others pushed or pulled their belongings in carts.

The rush in the 'fifties was so great that supplies often ran low and prices advanced. Repeated orders were sent to St. Louis but river boats bringing provisions also brought additional people eager to begin the westward trek. Cargoes arrived here for points along the trails as well as for local consumption and for the caravans. On the riverbanks were unloaded boxes, barrels, hogsheads, and crates filled with sugar, dry goods, bacon, rice, dishes, and glassware; there were also barrels of liquor from Kentucky and occasional casks of brandy from France. Local freighting finally became so heavy that Independence men formed a company to build a railroad from the landing to the town. The train used on this road consisted of Independence-built flatcars drawn by mules, and it ran along three or four miles of hand-hewn hardwood rails. In the late fifties river commerce turned to the new City of Kansas, which offered a better landing place; and Independence gradually lost its commercial importance.

Mormonism was introduced into Independence in 1830, when five elders of that faith arrived to spread their gospel among the Indians. Discouraged in their attempt, they sent one of their number back to report defeat. But Joseph Smith had a vision in which he saw Independence as the City of Zion, and sent other elders into the Ohio and Mississippi Valleys to seek converts and bring them here. Smith himself with other officials of the church arrived in the summer of 1831 and bought 40 acres of land. Two years later the Mormon *Evening and Morning Star* reported that Mormons and their families living here numbered more than 1,200, about a third of the total population of the county. Many gentiles resented the influx, and their bitterness increased as the Mormon influence grew. There were minor persecutions; the Mormon newspaper editor was tarred and feathered; then came mob violence, and in 1834 the Mormons agreed to move to Clay County. But they found themselves equally unwelcome in other parts of Missouri; in 1838 Gov. Lilburn Boggs asked Gen. John B. Clark to take command and subdue the Mormons. After further imprisonments and disturbances, the Saints left the State and in time built up Nauvoo, Ill., as their headquarters.

In COURTHOUSE SQUARE is the brick JACKSON COUNTY COURTHOUSE, part of which was erected in 1836. While Independence is the seat of Jackson County, the courthouse here serves only the eastern part of the county; that in Kansas City serves the western part.

The FIRST JACKSON COUNTY COURTHOUSE (*open weekdays 8 a.m.-6 p.m.*), 107 W. Kansas Ave., was built in 1827 at the southeast corner of Lynn St. and Lexington Ave. The building cost $150, and is of white-oak and walnut logs cut by a slave. Weatherboarding, put on the west end to preserve the structure, and a porch have been added.

Construction on the AUDITORIUM, south side of W. Walnut St. be-

tween S. River Blvd. and Grand Ave., was begun in 1926; it belongs
to the Reorganized Church of Jesus Christ of Latter-Day Saints. When
the building is completed its cost is expected to exceed $1,500,000. The
structure, of massive proportions, was designed by Henry C. Smith
of Independence. The circular main arena, with a seating capacity of
seven thousand, is topped with a large elliptical, unsupported dome.

West from Independence on US 24.

KANSAS CITY, **9 m.** (963 alt., 399,746 pop.) (*see MISSOURI
GUIDE*).

Railroad Station. Union Station, 24th and Main Sts., for Chicago & Alton
R.R.; Chicago, Milwaukee, St. Paul & Pacific R.R.; Atchison, Topeka & Santa Fe
Ry.; Chicago, Burlington & Quincy R.R.; Kansas City Southern Ry.; Missouri,
Kansas & Texas R.R.; Missouri Pacific R.R.; St. Louis-San Francisco Ry.; Union
Pacific R.R.; Wabash Ry.; Chicago, Rock Island & Pacific Ry.; Chicago Great
Western R.R.; and Kansas City, Kaw Valley & Western R.R.

Accommodations. Numerous first-class hotels with standard rates.

Points of Interest. Municipal Auditorium, Liberty Memorial, Nelson Gallery of
Art and Atkins Museum of Fine Arts, and Livestock Exchange.

Kansas City embraces the early town of Westport, which was built
just east of the Missouri Line, four miles south of the Missouri River.
Westport is now bounded by Main, Thirty-fifth, and Forty-seventh Sts.
Westport Avenue, once part of the Santa Fe Trail, is a short distance
south.

Before settlers arrived at this place it was a camping ground of
traders. In 1831 the Rev. Isaac McCoy entered a claim for a tract of
land here and in the following year John C. McCoy, his son, opened a
store and platted the townsite.

John McCoy was canny in opening a store at this point, since the
Santa Fe Trail ran by his door and he could cater to the most urgent
needs of those returning from Santa Fe and the wilderness and catch
some of the outfitting overflow from Independence. The first consign-
ments of goods came to McCoy through Independence; but he soon
found a rocky ledge along fairly deep water in the Missouri within a
few miles of his land, and in the fall of 1832 the *John Hancock* chugged
up to land goods there.

Four years later Missouri was increased by two million acres by
"extinguishing the Indian title" to the triangle formed by the Missouri
River, the western extension of the State's northern boundary, and the
extension of the western boundary. This addition to slave territory was
immediately thrown open to settlement and both Westport and Independence, at the inverted apex, benefited by the rush of immigrants.
Before many years local workshops were turning out wagons, harnesses,
saddles, tents, covers for prairie schooners, yokes and bows for oxen,
candles, and other commodities.

The gold rush brought on a further boom; here, as elsewhere along the river, stores of foodstuffs and equipment were quickly exhausted. Orders rushed to St. Louis and other wholesale markets could not be filled rapidly enough to meet the demand. The goods available sold at fantastic prices as the fortune hunters sought to hurry their departures in order to overtake and pass those who had already left for California.

In the fall of 1849 cholera broke out among Mormon immigrants camped on the edge of the town; soon afterward many Westport inhabitants became victims of the disease and others left the town, never to return. For a time the normal activity of the area was paralyzed.

In spite of the competition being offered by the City of Kansas, Westport continued to thrive and was particularly prosperous between 1855-60. It was incorporated in 1857.

The HARRIS HOME (*open on request*), 4000 Baltimore Ave., Westport's social center in the early 1850's, was removed in 1922 from its original site at the corner of Main St. and Westport Ave. This building was used as a nursing home for wounded Civil War soldiers on both sides after the Battle of Westport.

The REARDON HOME (*private*), 4260 Clark Ave., is one of the oldest structures in the former Westport. It was built of logs by an early-day blacksmith for his Irish bride. The logs have been covered with weatherboards.

The JOSEPH STEGMILLER HOME (*private*), 708 Westport Rd., was built in the early 1850's by one of the pioneer wagonmakers.

The SITE OF THE DEATHPLACE (1881) OF JIM BRIDGER, the trapper and scout, at the northwest corner of Westport and Pennsylvania Aves., is now occupied by a red-brick liquor store. Bridger settled late in life on a farm that was here.

The SITE OF THE HARRIS HOUSE, a widely known hostelry run by Col. and Mrs. John Harris, is at Fortieth and Main Sts. Among its famous guests was John C. Frémont, who in 1843 started on his second western exploring expedition from nearby Kansas Landing on the Kansas River.

Frémont, who was born in 1813, had as a lad gained many friends by his alert mind and personal charm; one of these friends obtained an appointment for him in the U.S. Topographical Corps, where he became a protégé of the distinguished Frenchman, Jean Nicholas Nicollet, whom he accompanied in 1838 on an exploring expedition to the western tributaries of the Mississippi. This expedition gave him social entree in Washington during his work on the Nicollet report. He soon met Jessie, the delightful and intelligent daughter of the Missouri warhorse, Sen. Thomas Hart Benton, and the young people before long evaded Benton's opposition to what seemed an undistinguished match by eloping. Benton swallowed his resentment and immediately began to further his expansionist dreams by promoting his son-in-law's exploration ambitions. In 1842 the young man was sent on a preliminary reconnaissance along the Platte River to the Rockies; the object of his activities, as conceived by the powerful Benton, was to provide a guidebook for settlers who would take possession of Oregon for the United States, and maps for the use of military expeditions that might be needed to complete the work if the settlers failed.

When Frémont returned from this journey he found to his dismay that it was beyond his powers to write the kind of report that he and Senator Benton wanted—one that would stir the imagination as had Irving's *Adventures of Captain Bonneville* (1837). His 18-year-old wife, an unusually gifted person, supplied the skill he lacked; Frémont dictated to her daily and his report was published by Congress early in 1843, about the time he left on his second expedition, which was to carry him to Oregon and California. The report added to his prestige in the Capital. His wife and her parents traveled west to St. Louis with him, and before continuing his journey he asked her to open all mail addressed to him. He was still completing his preparations here in Westport when he received a letter from his wife, sent by special messenger; without explanation it told him to leave immediately. Frémont's faith in Jessie was such that he did not question the command; writing "Good-bye. I trust and GO," he hastily set out the next morning on the two-year expedition that was to determine his future career and help to fulfill his father-in-law's schemes. Not until after his return did he learn that Jessie had sent her peremptory letter because she had opened an order from the War Department instructing him to return immediately to Washington to explain why he was taking a howitzer with him into Oregon and into Mexican territory. Jessie attributed the order to jealousy on the part of Frémont's chief, who, she believed, wanted to send his son as leader of the glory-giving western expedition.

Francis Parkman also lived at the Harris House while preparing to go west in 1846. Parkman wrote: "Westport was full of Indians, whose little, shaggy ponies were tied by the dozen along the houses and fences. Sacs and Foxes, with shaved heads and painted faces; Shawnees and Delawares fluttering in calico frocks and turbans; Wyandottes dressed like white men, and a few wretched Kanzas wrapped in old blankets, were strolling about the streets or lounging in and out of the shops and houses." He then added this observation: "Whiskey, by the way, circulates more freely in Westport than is altogether safe in a place where every man carries a loaded pistol in his pocket."

On US 24 (Independence Ave.) in downtown Kansas City is the junction with US 71-69; R. here on US 71-69, which leads north, crossing a free bridge over the Missouri River. US 71 (L) leaves US 69 (R) in North Kansas City, swinging northwest toward the Missouri River.

At TRACY, **41.2 m.** (777 alt., 169 pop.), is a junction with Mo. 92.

Left on this paved road and across the Missouri River, in the center of which is the Kansas Line, **6.8 m.** At **7 m.** is the FORT LEAVENWORTH MILITARY RESERVATION.

Soon after the establishment of Fort Atkinson (*see SECTION 2*), the first military post of importance along the Missouri River, the War Department came to the conclusion that the post should have been placed nearer Independence, then the outfitting point for those setting out for the West. Fort Leavenworth was established on March 7, 1827, and the older fort to the north was abandoned three months later. In the early decades of the post's existence, the chief function of its commander was to police the nearby Indian reservations. Later he occasionally provided military protection for trading expeditions. Fort Leavenworth, now the seat of the Command and General Staff School of the U.S. Army, is garrisoned by demonstration troops of several branches of the Army.

Grant Avenue is the main thoroughfare of the reservation. Behind the old, widespreading trees that line the streets are well-kept lawns and clusters of trim buildings.

Frontier garrisons were often lax in discipline. The situation became so critical here that on April 28, 1832, Gen. Winfield Scott ordered: "Every soldier or ranger who shall be found drunk or insensibly intoxicated after the publication of this order will be compelled, as soon as his strength will permit, to dig his grave at a suitable burying place large enough for his own reception, as such grave cannot fail to be wanted for the drunken man himself or for some drunken companion."

In 1834 the efficiency of the fort was increased by the arrival of the First Dragoons, which had been organized the preceding year at Jefferson Barracks in Missouri. This was the first cavalry regiment of the Army and was formed as an experiment; Congress had been reluctant to establish many military posts in the West, and the infantry could not be moved with the speed requisite for the pursuit of well-mounted nomads. Military advisers had come to the conclusion that demonstration parades of a well-equipped cavalry regiment might impress the Indians living in remote places with the might of the Federal Government and frighten them into keeping the peace. The Dragoons left Fort Leavenworth on May 29, 1835, and followed the Platte to the Rockies. The commander held councils with the Otoe, the Omaha, and the Pawnee, admonishing them that they must behave; their leaders were placated with presents. Other conferences were held in Colorado. The troopers returned to this post in the fall in good condition after a 1,600-mile journey on horseback.

Later the fort became the principal point of departure for troops and supplies being sent to posts farther west, and was stocked with large numbers of horses, mules, oxen, and wagons. It was an outfitting point for troops during the Mexican War. A host of officers later well known acquired their training during service at this post.

Although Congress originally designated Fort Leavenworth as the temporary capital of the Territory of Kansas, it heeded objections of the Secretary of War that suitable quarters were not available. Andrew H. Reeder, first Territorial Governor, arrived here October 7, 1854, on a river steamer, *Polar Star*, accompanied by his secretary and the U.S. Attorney for the Territory.

At the south end of Scott Ave. is the COMMAND AND GENERAL STAFF SCHOOL, housed in Sheridan, Grant, Sherman, and Wagner Halls.

The STONE WALL, part of the defenses erected by Col. Henry H. Leavenworth, is near the junction of Scott and Grant Aves.

On the northwest corner of McPherson and Riverside Aves. is the U.S. PRISON ANNEX, formerly the U.S. Military Prison and Disciplinary Barracks, opened in 1875 for military prisoners, who had previously been confined with civilian convicts. The walls and buildings are of gray stone quarried on the reservation. During the World War this prison confined a large number of prisoners who had been convicted of publicly opposing the Government's participation in the war and refusing on non-religious grounds to obey the Selective Service Act; it also contained a number of people convicted of espionage.

In 1929 the prison was placed under the jurisdiction of the Department of Justice, which had once previously (1895-1906) used the building as a Federal prison. The old prison, now an annex of the LEAVENWORTH FEDERAL PENITENTIARY, is used principally for the confinement of narcotic addicts.

The NATIONAL CEMETERY (*open 9 a.m.-4 p.m.*), Biddle Ave., contains hundreds of neatly aligned small stone markers over the graves of soldiers who served in various American wars. Here is the GRAVE OF GEN. HENRY H. LEAVENWORTH, the fort's founder, who died July 21, 1834, while leading an expedition against the Pawnee. His body was first buried at Delhi, N. Y.

South from the military reservation on US 73E.

LEAVENWORTH, **9.7 m.** (760 alt., 17,466 pop.) (*see KANSAS GUIDE*).

After the passage of the Kansas-Nebraska Bill in 1854, large numbers of squatters moved across the river to settle on this spot; the land, which had been part of the Delaware Indian territory, was to have been platted and sold to the highest bidders, a fact that the newcomers did not realize until after they had organized a company and platted the town. Leavenworth was not legally organized until 1857. In the meantime William H. Russell, Alexander Majors, and W. B. Waddell had organized a freighting company with headquarters here, close to Fort Leavenworth. This soon became the leading firm of its kind operating in the West, owing its prosperity in large part to contracts for freighting military supplies. Business boomed in 1857 when the firm obtained the contract to transport supplies for the troops sent to Utah Territory. The freighting operations alone would have brought local prosperity. The streets were constantly filled with dust raised by the moving freight trains, and with shouting, free-spending teamsters.

The members of the freighting firm were ambitious; in April, 1859, when the banks of the river were again filled with frantic hordes of gold seekers, this time with wagons labeled "Pike's Peak or Bust," they enlarged their services to include stage transportation to the mining area. In May, Russell, of the freighting firm, united with John S. Jones and others to establish the Leavenworth and Pike's Peak Stage and Express, with weekly service over a route running almost directly west. At first the coaches traveled in pairs for protection; the first ones westbound reached Denver in 19 days. Soon the firm obtained the Missouri River-Salt Lake City mail contract and transferred its stages to the Oregon Trail; coaches bound for Denver left the route at Julesburg (*see SECTION 4*).

Early in 1860 the Central Overland California and Pike's Peak Express Company, an outgrowth of the Russell, Majors, and Waddell firm, was chartered by the Kansas Territorial Legislature.

Horace Greeley in his *Overland Journey* thus describes the establishment at Leavenworth: "Russell, Majors & Waddell's transportation establishment, between the fort and the city, is the great feature of Leavenworth. Such acres of wagons! such pyramids of extra axletrees! such herds of oxen! such regiments of drivers and other employees! No one who does not see can realize how vast a business this is, nor how immense are its outlays as well as its income. I presume that great firm has at this hour two millions of dollars invested in stock, mainly oxen, mules and wagons. (They last year employed six thousand teamsters, and worked 45,000 oxen.)"

The new stage company gradually bought up competing lines. Having a practical monopoly on all overland transport and freighting, Russell was anxious to obtain an overland mail contract from the Government for daily service. To do this, he felt that it was necessary first to demonstrate the practicality of the central route he proposed to use. The idea of the Pony Express (*see below*) was therefore hit upon. Sen. W. M. Gwin of California, whose constituents were in favor of a central rather than a southern mail route, was the most important backer of the plan. The Central Overland California and Pike's Peak Express Company was operated successfully for two years, but the costly Pony Express demonstration and the company's failure to obtain the overland mail contract sent it into bankruptcy. In March, 1862, Ben Holladay bought the line at public sale. He reorganized the firm and named it the Overland Stage Line.

North from Tracy on US 71.

ST. JOSEPH, **76.1 m.** (814 alt., 80,935 pop.) (*see also MISSOURI GUIDE*), generally known as "St. Joe," is built on the bluffs above the Missouri River. Joseph Robidoux, later an employee of Astor's American Fur Company, opened a trading post here in 1803. Prior to the Platte Purchase in 1836, "Uncle Joe," as Robidoux was called, had practically no competition and few neighbors; after the Indians had been expelled he had both. In 1842 he platted the town and named it for his patron saint.

St. Joseph soon became the leading freight depot in the district despite the fact that the trails between the town and the junction with the Oregon Trail lay through rugged country with few watering places. The town increased rapidly in size, being one of the chain that shared prosperity as outfitting points for westbound travelers.

Eleaser Ingalls' *Journal* (1850-1), in describing the community he found here, voiced a complaint made of all the river towns: "St. Joseph is quite a village, and doing quite a great deal of business at this time; but the way they fleece the California emigrants is worth noticing. I should advise all going to California by the Overland Route to take everything along with them that they can, as every little thing costs three or four times as much here as at home. The markets are filled with broken down horses jockeyed up for the occasion, and unbroken mules which they assure you are handy as sheep. It is the greatest place for gambling and all other rascality that I was ever in. We had to stand guard on our horses as much as if we were in the Indian Country. It is said that one or two men have been shot by the Emigrants, while in the act of stealing."

In the same year Silas Newcomb wrote: "This place contains some two thousand five hundred inhabitants and at present is a very busy place on account of the California emigration which seems to centre here; hills and dales are white with their camps. Many have crossed the river and encamped on the west side in the Indian Territory. Find all classes well represented here and to find a drunken Indian at every square is nothing uncommon. Place contains four good sized Hotels, about twenty Stores and the residue is made up of groceries, bakeries, &C."

By 1851, when the gold fever was abating, the community's businessmen began shipping supplies overland to the thousands who had recently passed through on their way to the Pacific coast. Many herds of cattle were driven from this town across the country to California, where they were rested and fattened before being placed on sale. From the early freighting business developed the present wholesale activities of the city.

On February 13, 1859, Joseph Robidoux drove the last spike, a golden one, according to the fashion of the day, to complete the Hannibal & St. Joseph R.R. line whose advent gave impetus to the town's development.

In St. Joseph on the evening of April 3, 1860, a rider, generally believed to have been Johnny Frey, mounted a pony in the Pike's Peak stable and started westward, thereby inaugurating the Pony Express. At about the same time Harry Hoff took off from Sacramento, Calif. (*see above*). This first relay race to the West required 10 days. The St. Joseph *Gazette* of April 4, 1860, described the event: "Yesterday evening at 7:00 and fifteen minutes, the first carrier of the Pony Express left the office of the company in this city. . . . At the hour of starting, an immense crowd had gathered around the Express office to witness the inaugurating of the novel and important enterprise—Mayor Thompson, in a few remarks to the spectators, briefly alluded to the significance of the Express from our city over the Central Route. Mr. Majors, being loudly called for, responded in a speech characterized by his usual practical manner of thought, in which he reviewed the rapid changes which have taken place in the condition and prospects of the West, predicting that the day is not far distant when other and powerful communities will spring up in the shadow of the mountains, a region lately regarded as wild and sterile beyond the power or desire of reclamation . . . But a dozen years ago the entire season was thought scarcely time enough to make the trip from Missouri to California, and companies of a less number than fifty, armed and organized, were deemed too weak to venture on the perilous route. Now a single man, aye, a defenseless woman, so far as Indians were concerned, need fear no evil." (Mr. Majors could not foresee the uprisings of the following decade.)

Another St. Joseph newspaper of the same date, the *Weekly West*, contained the following: "The rider is a Mr. Richardson, formerly a sailor, and a man accustomed to every degree of hardship, having sailed for years amid the snow and icebergs of the Northern ocean. He was to ride last night the first stage of forty miles, changing horses once in five hours; and before this paragraph meets the eyes of our readers, the various dispatches will have reached the town of Marysville on the Big Blue, one hundred and twelve miles distant, an enterprise never before accomplished, even in this proverbially fast portion of a fast country."

Most old-timers, however, agreed that the *Weekly West* reporter was in error as to the identity of the rider.

During the 16 months of the Pony Express service, such men as Bob Haslem and Jack Keetley carried the mail. There were about 180 riders; relay stations were usually about 9 to 15 miles apart. Some of the riders were attacked by Indians and had narrow escapes; several keepers of relay stations were killed, but only once was a mail pouch lost and not recovered. Letters had to be written on thin paper, and transcontinental delivery for the thinnest cost $5. In 1861 the service came to an end upon the completion of the first transcontinental telegraph line.

One of the most picturesque tourists who ever traveled west through St. Joseph was Richard Burton, English scholar, adventurer, diplomat, and later the translator of the *Arabian Nights*. During his travels in the Near East, Burton had developed a lively curiosity about polygamy and came to America in 1860 chiefly for the purpose of visiting the "City of the Saints," which became the title of his report of the journey. As a traveler of wide experience in primitive lands he was equipped for every emergency; in addition to the usual supplies he carried a rifle, a brace of revolvers, a Bowie knife, a whistle for stopping railway trains as was the custom in rural England of the day, reference books, an air gun to entertain the aborigines, opium to relieve the tedium of the plains journey, and patent notebooks; he also carried a top hat, a morning coat, and a silk umbrella to enable him to call on Brigham Young in formal attire.

The EUGENE FIELD HOME (*private*), 425 N. 11th St., is a two-story gray-brick house, where the poet and his bride lived when he was editor of the St. Joseph *Gazette* (1876-80).

The JOSEPH ROBIDOUX HOUSE (*private*), 219-25 Poulin St., is part of Robidoux Row; here the founder of St. Joseph lived at the time of his death in 1868. It is a long story-and-a-half brick structure with a stone foundation.

The JESSE JAMES HOUSE (*open daily 9 a.m.-5 p.m.; adm. 10¢*), 1318 Lafayette St., is a small shabby one-story frame cottage. Here, on April 3, 1882, the outlaw was killed by Bob Ford. James had been living here under the name of Howard.

North of St. Joseph US 71 is united with US 275-59. At **90 m.** L. from US 71 on US 59-275.

At **164.1 m.** US 275 crosses the Iowa Line and runs through an area of large vineyards. About September acres of blue Concord grapes are seen from the highway.

COUNCIL BLUFFS, **218.1 m.** (984 alt., 42,048 pop.) (*see IOWA GUIDE*).

Railroad Stations. 1115 W. Broadway for Chicago & North Western Ry., Union Pacific R.R., and Wabash Ry.; 1216 W. Broadway for Illinois Central R.R.; 1201 S. Main St. for Chicago, Rock Island & Pacific Ry., and Chicago, Milwaukee, St. Paul & Pacific R.R.; 900 S. Main St. for Chicago Great Western R.R.; and 407 Eleventh Ave. for Chicago, Burlington & Quincy R.R.

Accommodations. First-class hotels with standard year-round rates.

Points of Interest. Mormon Trail Memorial, Father DeSmet Memorial, and Lewis and Clark Monument.

Council Bluffs is one of the most important railroad transfer points in the United States. Manufacturing plants here produce a wide range of articles, including playground equipment, apiarists' supplies, artificial limbs, batteries, candy, and wheels.

In 1804 Lewis and Clark held council with the Indians on a bluff some distance up the river and called the area Council Bluff. In 1827 Francis Guittar was appointed agent of the American Fur Company to establish a post here that was called Hart's Bluff.

Father Pierre DeSmet in 1838 wrote of the place: "We arrived among the Pottawattamies on the afternoon of May 31. Nearly 2,000 savages, in their finest rigs and carefully painted in all sorts of patterns, were awaiting the boat at the landing. I had not seen so imposing a sight nor such fine-looking Indians in America." The Jesuit missionary and his companions went at once to talk with the half-breed chief, Billy Caldwell, who was happy to have the white teachers come among his people. For three years a mission was operated here.

A military post, Fort Croghan, was established on the site in 1842 to keep the Indians in order while they were being removed to lands farther west. Few were left when the vanguard of the Mormons arrived in the early summer of 1846. After an Illinois mob had killed Joseph Smith, the Mormons at Nauvoo lived under constant threat of violence. Brigham Young, who soon became their leader because of his executive ability, was convinced that it was useless for the Latter-Day Saints to attempt to establish themselves permanently in the East or the Middle West; so he made plans to evacuate the settlement on the Mississippi and salvage what he could of the local property by sale. He sent scouting groups ahead to examine routes through Iowa, and at the end of February, 1846, started off with the first of the emigrants—men, women, and children. The weather was bitterly cold and the people suffered greatly; but, comforting each other and sure that they were acting under divine guidance, they managed to maintain an amazing cheerfulness. As they plowed through the snow and mud, a brass band led by the English Captain Pitts provided lively music. Their provisions were limited, but the inhabitants of the scattered settlements showed tolerance toward them and paid willingly for evening entertainment by the band. Young established several relay stations along the route in Iowa, leaving small groups to plant crops for the provisioning of later Mormon migrants.

When the vanguard reached this place it was too late in the season to start the overland trip to an undetermined goal. Young therefore decided to spend the winter in this area and prepare for the arrival of other refugees. A second factor entering into his decision was the formation of the Mormon Battalion; soon after the group had arrived here a U.S. Army captain visited them to recruit for the Mexican War. Young made an agreement that the Mormons should enlist but merely perform guard service in California and not be sent to the front. He was forced to this decision by the dire need of his followers, who had limited opportunities for employment that would add to the community funds.

WAGON TRAINS (c. 1871)

BLOCK HOUSE NEAR OMAHA

The headquarters of the Mormon colony here was near the old fort at a place called Miller's Hollow; this later became a semipermanent Mormon relay station and was called Kanesville for Thomas L. Kane, a U.S. Army officer who was long helpful to the Saints. The community was also known as Winter Quarters, as was the camp on the west side of the river at this point (*see SECTION 2*). Ruling over the community was Orson Hyde, priest, editor, lawyer, and one of the leaders among the Twelve Apostles of the Church.

During the California gold rush of 1849, westward travel over the trail on the north side of the Platte increased greatly, and Kanesville became one of the jumping-off-places. The Mormon population in this district reached its peak in 1848, but there were still several thousand here in 1852, when word came that all the faithful should go on to Utah. Farms, cabins, and stores were immediately sold to the incoming settlers, often at a great sacrifice. A few Mormons remained to provide assistance to the Saints who had been recruited abroad to fill up the Promised Land.

After the Mormon departure, Kanesville was for a time without government, for the Mormons had ruled not only the church but also the town. The remaining inhabitants adopted the name of Council Bluffs.

In 1863 the town was chosen as the eastern terminus of the Union Pacific R.R. Actual construction of the railroad to the West was begun in 1866. By 1870 five railroads had made connections with the Union Pacific here.

Thomas Beer (1889-   ), best known for his *Mauve Decade* (1926) and a biography of Stephen Crane (1923), was born here. Amelia Jenks Bloomer (1818-1894), active in the women's rights movement, lived in the town from 1855 until her death. Mrs. Bloomer, an advocate of dress reform, while serving as editor (1848-54) of *The Lily* advertised a costume designed by Elizabeth Smith Miller. The public has since associated her name with the baggy lower part of the costume, dubbed "bloomers."

In Council Bluffs is the junction with US 30-Alt. Left on it, crossing the Missouri River on the Douglas St. toll bridge (*car and driver 15¢, passengers 5¢ each*); in the middle of the river is the Nebraska Line.

Nebraska

Omaha (Missouri River)—Fremont—Grand Island—Kearney—North Platte—Sidney—Kimball—Wyo. Line; 460.8 m. US 30-Alt. and US 30.

Union Pacific R.R. and United Air Lines parallel route throughout.

Union Pacific, Chicago & North Western, Interstate Transit, and Burlington Trailways buses follow route.

Accommodations available at short intervals in eastern section, less frequently in western section; hotels chiefly in cities.

Road hard-surfaced throughout.

Change between Central Standard and Rocky Mountain time at western limit of North Platte.

US 30 is the chief east-west road traversing Nebraska. The eastern two-thirds of it follows the long curves of the Platte River on the north bank; at the confluence of the North and South Platte Rivers US 30 crosses to the north bank of the South Platte, follows it for a time, and then runs almost directly west. The Platte, which one writer described as "a thousand miles long and six inches deep" and Washington Irving called "the most magnificent and most worthless" of streams, was important in western history because it formed a natural guide for the emigrant routes.

The east-bound Astorians (1812-13) were the first known white men to follow the north banks of the North Platte and Platte Rivers to a point below Grand Island; there they obtained a canoe from the Indians to complete the wearisome journey they had been pursuing on foot with a single pack horse. Ashley's men (1824-25) traveled along the north bank of the Platte, and switched to the north bank of the South Platte, as US 30 now does, instead of following what later became the major emigrant trail.

The Long party (1819-20) approached the Platte River from the south near the center of the State and followed the south banks of the Platte and South Platte Rivers. Wyeth's party (1832-33), on its way west, also reached the Platte near the center of the State.

The first large group of emigrants to travel west along the north bank of the Platte and of the North Platte were the Mormon Pioneers of 1847. Thousands of Mormons and non-Mormons followed the route in the next decade. The Oregon Trail was south of the Platte, and most of its feeders from the Missouri reached the river near Grand Island; it followed the south bank of the North Platte to Fort Laramie in Wyoming, where the Mormon Trail joined it.

In only a few places—where natural conditions forced traffic into a single track—were the emigrant trails anything but broad general courses. Succeeding parties drove to the right or left of tracks left by

54

earlier trains, in order to avoid dust, to find grass and fuel, or to find drinking water and camp sites unpolluted by their predecessors. Every train had a few companies that attempted short cuts, hoping to reach the day's camp first and occupy the best places. After the big migration had begun, those who started late constantly attempted short cuts, fearing that the hordes ahead of them would pre-empt all the desirable land before they arrived; some of the worst tragedies of the trail were the result of these breaks from the beaten path.

US 30 runs through one general type of country—prairie; and there is little if any contrast between the undulating hills of eastern Nebraska and the flat land of the central and western sections. The highway touches the edge of the sand hills west of Gothenburg.

Section 2. Omaha (Missouri River) to Kearney, 191.1 m. US 30-Alt. and US 30.

US 30-Alt. leads west from the Nebraska Line, **0 m.** Below the bridge rolls the "Big Muddy," useless from the standpoint of modern navigation, though the channel is now being deepened in the hope of making the stream again navigable. Between its banks at this point passed the white traders and explorers who gradually toiled farther and farther upstream until they arrived at the western end of what is now North Dakota. Up this river went Meriwether Lewis and William Clark with the party that was to make the first and second transcontinental journeys across the broadest part of North America. Up and down the river went Manuel Lisa and Andrew Henry on the earliest trading expeditions carried on west of the Mississippi by citizens of the United States; and up this river went the Astorians. The stream has also borne most of the other men famous in the western fur trade, from Ashley, Smith, and Fitzpatrick to Hugh Glass and Mike Fink.

The Missouri, like the Mississippi, changes its course with a frequency that is exasperating to those who hopefully built on its banks. The lower part of Council Bluffs, Iowa, was swampy river bottom less than a century ago; a third of the blunt peninsula that is the northeastern part of Omaha is still under the jurisdiction of Iowa, though cut off completely from that State by the river and surrounded on the other sides by Omaha.

OMAHA, **0 m.** (1,040 alt., 214,006 pop.) (*see NEBRASKA GUIDE*).

Railroad Stations. Union Station, 10th & March Sts., for Union Pacific R.R.; Burlington Route; Chicago & North Western Ry.; Chicago Great Western R.R.; Chicago, Milwaukee, St. Paul, & Pacific R.R.; Rock Island Ry.

Points of Interest. Creighton University, Omaha Municipal University, Joslyn Memorial Art Gallery, Douglas County Courthouse, South Omaha Stockyards, and others.

The early journalist, J. Hanson Beadle, wrote in the *Undeveloped West:* "Omaha was laid out in 1854, soon after the organization of Nebraska Territory, and for several years gave little promise of future greatness; in fact, it was quite outrun by the little settlement of Florence, six miles north, of which the Omahas now speak patronizingly as a 'very pretty suburb', destined in their sanguine view to be the Spring Grove or Brooklyn to their future Gotham. . . . Omaha contained, in 1860, two thousand people; in 1864, four thousand; then the Union Pacific got fairly under way, and in three years the population doubled. A census taken by the city authorities a few days before my arrival (June, 1868) returned the population at 17,600, and the next year they made it 25,000. One year thereafter came a fearful epidemic and swept away 12,000 of these—at least, that strikes me as the easiest explanation, for the National Census of 1870 only credited Omaha with some 13,000 people. . . .

"The growth of Omaha was encouragingly rapid; but the Western mind is queerly constructed, and great on anticipation. The air is light, dry and healthy, and the world looks big west of the Missouri; every man feels that the range of all outdoors is his pasture, and is hopeful as a millionaire if we have a few corner lots, and ten dollars in his pocket. Hence magnified reports, and glowing promises of more rapid growth in the next two years; and thousands of young men in the Northern and Eastern States imagined that all they had to do was to come to Omaha, and fortune would shower her favors on them. There was an immense immigration in 1868, of just such material as a new State does not want, and for every clerk's or bookkeeper's position there were a hundred applicants. . . . But each of the disappointed wrote to his friends or to the press, and for the rest of that year Omaha was the best abused city in the West. . . ." (*For Omaha's fulfillment of the early hopes, see NEBRASKA GUIDE.*)

Right from Omaha **5 m.** on US 73 to the SITE OF WINTER QUARTERS, in the Florence section of Omaha. When the first section of the Camp of Israel, as the Mormons called their emigrant train, reached the Missouri in midsummer of 1846, it camped on the Council Bluffs side of the river to make preparations for the long trip west (*see SECTION 1*). Brigham Young, one of the most farsighted leaders in the history of mass migrations, was planting a colony at Kanesville to provide shelter and foodstuffs for the later emigrants. As other Saints arrived he sent them across the Missouri to form a camp here; one of the chief advantages of establishing a camp on the western bank was that the crossing of the broad river with wagons, cattle, and people—always a problem—would be over when the first spring day favorable for travel should arrive.

The winter of 1846-7 was unusually severe, and a lack of proper food caused scurvy and other diseases. Some Saints were smothered to death by snow that crushed the roofs of their dwellings.

Early in 1847 the Pioneers, as the first party was called, had completed their preparations. On April 7 a small band set out for a rendezvous on the Elk Horn, 25 or more miles west. In the following week there was a busy rushing back and forth between this camp and Winter Quarters; the personnel of the advance party changed daily.

Appleton Harmon wrote on April 13: "Brother Kimball said to me last night that he wanted that I should git readey and go with the Pioneers & drive an ox team for him. I consulted my Father, left my wife and child in as good circumstances as I could which was but poor as best got my clothes readey and started about 4 A.M. in company with Br Everett Jacobs & traveled 4 miles camped in hollow for night."

On April 14 William Clayton, Clerk of the Camp of Israel, wrote in his *Journal:*

"This morning severely pained with rheumatism in my face. . . . At 11:00 a.m. Brigham and Dr. Richards came. Brigham told me to rise up and start with the pioneers in half an hour's notice. I delivered to him the records of the K. of G. and set my folks to work to get my clothes together to start with the pioneers. At two o'clock I left my family and started in Heber's carriage. . . . We went about 19 miles and camped on the prairie."

The spring of 1863 saw the last Mormon wagon train leave Florence. The place was also used by the forty-niners as an outfitting station and camping place.

US 73 continues north to FORT CALHOUN, **15.8 m.** (100 alt., 309 pop.), a sedate, tree-shaded community on a bluff above the Missouri. It is near this spot that in 1804 Capt. Meriwether Lewis and Lt. William Clark held a conference with Indians and named the place Council Bluff. John C. Calhoun, Secretary of War, in 1818 planned to send a military expedition up the Missouri to advance the interest of the fur traders by enforcing the law forbidding foreigners—that is, British subjects—to trade for furs in the United States (*see WHY A TRAIL TO OREGON?*), and to push trade to the Pacific. The expedition, under Col. Henry Atkinson, reached this place in September, 1819, and established what was called Camp Missouri. A grandiose plan for military penetration to the Columbia was eventually dropped and in 1820 the camp was moved a mile south and became a permanent army post, Fort Atkinson. After the fort had been abandoned in 1827, the settlement disappeared for nearly 25 years; when a new one appeared it was named in honor of Calhoun.

Right from Fort Calhoun on Court St. **0.5 m.** to the SITE OF FORT ATKIN-SON, now a farm. There are no traces of the fort, which during its brief life had barracks for a thousand men, a brickyard, a limekiln, a sawmill, a gristmill, and other facilities.

US 30-Alt. follows Dodge St. in Omaha.

As the highway moves westward the tracks of the Union Pacific R.R., which curves southward to leave the city, again near it. The building of this railroad was one of the dramatic flourishes in the history of the United States. Though there had been agitation from the late 1830's on for the construction of a railroad to connect the East with the Pacific Coast, and though there was general agreement that the Federal Government should help to finance it, action was long delayed by sectional jealousies and political logrolling. A survey of possible routes was authorized in 1853. It was not until 1862, however, when southern opponents of northern routes had been removed from Congress by the secession of the southern States, that a route was finally decided on and the Pacific Railway Act was passed. Two years later a second act increased the munificent subsidies to the builders and gave the Government merely a second mortgage on the road.

The Union Pacific Railroad Company was to build westward to the borders of Nevada and the Central Pacific Railroad Company was to build eastward from the Pacific Coast to meet the Union Pacific. The

Union Pacific was granted a two-hundred-foot right-of-way, land for all necessary buildings, and the right to take earth, stone, timber, and "other materials" from the public lands for construction purposes. In addition, "for the purpose of aiding construction . . . and to secure the safe and speedy transportation of mails, troops, munitions of war, and public stores thereon," the company was granted "every alternate section of public land . . . to the amount of five alternate sections per mile on each side of said railroad, on the line thereof and within the limit of ten miles on each side of said road." The Government also issued bonds of $1,000 each at the ratio of 16 bonds to a mile. Because of the higher cost of construction in the mountains, the number of bonds issued per mile to the Central Pacific Company for some sections of the route was doubled or trebled. The Union Pacific obtained 4,846,108 acres of land in Nebraska alone.

The building of the Union Pacific began in earnest on July 10, 1865, at the time the Indians were becoming frantic in the face of white invasion (*see WHY A TRAIL TO OREGON?*); the road builders were special targets of attack. According to the chief engineer of the road, "every mile had to be surveyed and built within range of the rifle and under military protection."

The thousands of railroad workers were housed in tents and portable shacks; every few weeks the shelters and facilities were packed upon freight cars and moved westward to the end of the completed section. And in their wake followed gamblers, whiskey vendors, sneak thieves, and unattached women, who earned for the camp the nickname of Hell-on-Wheels. Occasionally the portable community left behind it the germ of a settlement, such as Cheyenne or Laramie; but for the most part only a series of rubbish dumps and trampled ground remained to mark its progress across the plains.

Rivalry soon developed between the workers of the two companies; the westward line advanced 250 miles in 1866, 240 miles in 1867, and 425 miles in 1868. When the two sets of rails met at Promontory, Utah, on May 10, 1869, the whole country had been whipped into a state of frantic excitement by the race.

The railroad companies were in excellent position to profit by the settlement of the area, because the acres nearest the long thin strip of rails were, inevitably, the ones most desired by pioneers; those nearest railroad stations brought top prices. The companies were little discommoded by the proviso designating alternate sections as public lands open to settlement under the Homestead Act of 1862; dummy homesteaders and obliging local officials usually remedied the Congressional obtuseness on this point. The boom literature of the homesteading period of the West makes the more recent Florida boom literature seem sedate.

Many settlers who had cherished visions of fine landed estates engendered in the days when "Vote yourself a farm" was a political campaign slogan, rushed west without carefully investigating the fertility and advantages of the advertised areas; their disillusionment was proportionate to the magnitude of their dreams.

WATERLOO, **21.2 m.** (1,122 alt., 432 pop.), is on the west bank of the Elkhorn River. The place was laid out in 1871 and named by the Union Pacific R.R. for the Belgian battlefield.

VALLEY, **24.8 m.** (1,140 alt., 1,039 pop.), was first named in 1867 by John Sanders for himself. The town was later called Platte Valley by the citizens, but when it was incorporated the first part of the name was accidentally omitted, and the name became simply Valley, though the precinct is still called Platte Valley. Railroad officials called the place Valley Station because it was the first station established on the Union Pacific in the valley of the Platte River. At Valley are stock and feed yards; here cattle in transit to Omaha are fed and watered.

At **38.4 m.** is FREMONT (1,195 alt., 11,407 pop.), a college town and agricultural trading center on the north bank of the wide, muddy Platte River just opposite Fremont Island. The city is a distributing center for the rich Elkhorn Valley farm land. It once gave promise of becoming an industrial town, but the hopes of the citizens on this point early disappeared; nonetheless the town has poultry-packing plants, creameries, and incubator factories.

On August 23, 1856, the first claim stake was driven for "Pinney, Barnard, & Co.'s Town Site." Since no surveyor's chain was handy when the town was laid out, a rope, which may have stretched, was used. That, at least, has been offered as the explanation of some for the irregularities in the first plat. The town was named Fremont in honor of John C. Frémont, who was then Republican candidate for the Presidency; it is said that this was the company's answer to some Democrats 25 miles to the west, who had named a town Buchanan. Frémont had many admirers among the settlers because of his valuable maps and reports. A resolution passed in 1856 by the Fremont Town Association, which developed from the earlier company, provided that two lots be given anyone erecting a hewn-log house 16 by 20 feet and a story and a half high within the following six months. The association agreed to furnish timber for the cabins, as well as firewood for a year.

The town prospered even before the railroad arrived. It was on the military road between Omaha and Fort Kearney—a fact commemorated in the name of the town's main street—Military Avenue—and provided a convenient supply point for soldiers and emigrants. During the Pikes Peak gold rush of 1858-9 there was a steady stream of through travelers. Merchants were able to make extra profits as disappointed miners sold their outfits cheaply on their way home; these could be resold at high prices to the next westbound group.

Encouraged by the prospect opening before their city when the Union Pacific R.R. routed its line through Fremont in 1866, the citizens established the Fremont *Tribune*. In 1869 the rails of the Sioux City & Pacific R.R. joined those of the Union Pacific at this point. This was an occasion for bell ringing, parades, and speeches on the future of Fremont and the Elkhorn Valley. Of even more importance was the building of the Elkhorn Valley R.R. branch, which was begun in 1870. The town was incorporated a year later.

Here is MIDLAND COLLEGE, coeducational, so named because it is near the center of the country. The institution, established at Atchison, Kan., in 1887, was the only college founded directly by the Board of Education of the General Synod of the Lutheran Church, now the United Lutheran Church in America. In 1919 the campus and buildings of the Fremont Normal School and Business College were purchased by the college, with the help of liberal subscriptions from Nebraska Lutherans and Fremont citizens. The present 10-acre campus holds six buildings.

It was not far from Fremont that the Mormon Pioneers made their final arrangements for the overland trip. The company included 143 men, 3 women, and 2 children. They had 72 wagons, 93 horses, 52 mules, 66 oxen, 19 cows, 17 dogs, and a number of chickens, in addition to supplies of food, clothing, agricultural and craft implements, books, musical instruments, and furniture. For real as well as psychological security the party carried one cannon. The men were organized into companies with "Captains of 100's," "Captains of 50's," and "Captains of 10's," following good biblical precedent, as they started west "to find a home where the Saints can live in peace and enjoy the fruits of their labors," and where they would "not be under the dominion of gentile governments, subject to the wrath of mobs," as Clayton wrote. Clayton carried on the duties assigned to him, though suffering acutely from the "rheumatism" in his face.

BARNARD PARK, formerly called Dead Man's Park, was the cemetery of the settlers.

FREMONT CITY PARK was planned when the town was laid out. In it are two monuments, one honoring Abraham Lincoln and the other commemorating Fremont soldiers killed in the World War.

At Fremont US 30-Alt. joins US 30, which crosses the Missouri some miles north of Omaha.

At **42.4 m.** (L) are the wooded FREMONT STATE RECREA-TION GROUNDS (*adm. free; camping facilities; fishing permitted 4 a.m.-10p.m.*). Here are 15 sand-pit lakes stocked with bass, crappies, sunfish, catfish, and bullheads. Signs indicate the varieties of fishes found in each lake and the legal limits of each catch.

At **43 m.** (L) is the NEAPOLIS MARKER, a white stone monument almost obscured by bushes; it is a reminder of the establishment of the capital of Nebraska Territory at Neapolis, two miles south of this point, in January, 1858.

In spite of the slow steady rise of the land from east to west the country through which US 30 runs in Nebraska has a monotonous flatness that is depressing to people born among the hills and mountains of the East and West. But overland travelers of early days were grateful for the easy passage it offered. They even spoke of these plains with affection because on westbound journeys they usually crossed them at the time of the year when the grass was fresh and green and meadow larks were crying their triumphant "Spring is here." The people who chose to settle along the Platte and force livings from the land had to face extremes of heat and cold, floods, prairie fires, blizzards, hailstorms, drought, lack of wood, and great loneliness. Only the hardiest remained. The little towns along the route, the solid farm buildings, and the occasional schools and public institutions are the results of unremitting toil. The groves about farmhouses and the trees in public parks and along streets are not gifts of nature; every single one has been coaxed and coddled into growth.

AMES, **45 m.** (1,231 alt., 500 pop.), was named for an official of the Union Pacific R.R., probably Oakes Ames. About 1880 the Standard Cattle Company had a cattle-feeding station here.

For about a mile between Ames and North Bend the highway runs past tall trees.

NORTH BEND, **53.2 m.** (1,275 alt., 1,108 pop.), was settled on July 4, 1856, by several Scottish families from Illinois. Not far from this place Clayton decided that his facial "rheumatism" came from a decayed tooth. He asked Brother Luke Johnson to pull it, but before this could be done the amateur dentist was told to take the Revenue Cutter fo a nearby lake for the use of Pioneer fishermen. (The Revenue Cutter was a bullboat, a tub-shaped craft made of leather. "Brother Johnson drives the team which draws the boat," Clayton explained, "and rides in the boat as in a wagon.") Clayton decided to go with the fishermen and on the trip discussed the possibility of constructing an instrument to measure mileages. The Pioneers were eager to leave signboards for the benefit of the Saints behind them; the guesses on distances traversed had been so divergent that Clayton, to obtain exact mileages, had resorted to the tedious device of counting the revolutions of a wagon wheel. There was no time to draw the tooth when the fishermen returned, and the clerk spent another sleepless night and day before he could again ask Brother Luke's services. Unfortunately the nippers extracted only half the tooth and Clayton had to endure many more days of pain.

SCHUYLER, **68.2 m.** (1,350 alt., 2,588 pop.), seat of Colfax County, was named, as was the county, for Schuyler Colfax, Vice President of the United States in 1869 when the town was platted. Schuyler was the first shipping point on the Union Pacific for cattle driven north from Texas.

At **81.8 m.** is a junction with a country road.

Right on this road is the COLUMBUS POWER HOUSE of the Loup River Project (*see below*), **1.8 m.**, where three turbines under a 112-foot head of water develop 39,900 kilowatts.

COLUMBUS, **86 m.** (1,447 alt., 6,898 pop.), seat of Platte County, was founded in 1856 by a group from Columbus, Ohio. It was settled 10 years before the Union Pacific R.R. reached this point and was a stopping point for emigrants traveling on the north bank of the Platte. The population is in part of German, Swiss, and Polish descent.

Most of the town's 26 industrial plants are typical of those found in midwestern towns of this size. A SHOE FACTORY makes wooden-soled shoes for use in packing houses, foundries, steel mills, and other places where leather and composition soles disintegrate rapidly. At the LIVE-STOCK SALES PAVILION a sale is conducted every Saturday, beginning at 1 p.m. and often lasting until midnight.

The town, which is on the Loup River near its confluence with the Platte, is the headquarters of the LOUP RIVER PUBLIC POWER DIS-TRICT PROJECT, first called the Columbus-Genoa Project. In 1936 the State's three major power and irrigation projects were co-ordinated into what has been called a little TVA, extending 200 miles across central Nebraska. The main purpose of the Loup River Project is power development; it is intended to augment a system supplying Columbus, Fremont, Norfolk, Lincoln, Omaha, Sioux City, and other points. A 35-mile canal, supplied by a diversion dam at Genoa, is tapped at the Columbus Power House (*see above*) and at the Monroe Power House.

At Columbus the Mormon Pioneers left the bank of the Platte to follow for a time the north bank of the Loup, which runs directly west, not far from the Platte, and is hard to ford near its mouth. The crossing of streams was always a major and time-consuming chore in the ox-cart days. In some places wagons could be taken through the waters without danger to the contents, but in others the goods had to be removed and ferried over on rafts. On the plains it was often difficult to find wood to make the rafts, so in time the beds of some emigrant wagons were made with calked seams, in order that they might be turned into clumsy barges.

The country for hundreds of miles north and northwest of the Platte, and the Platte itself—though farther upstream—provided the stage for the saga of Hugh Glass. Glass was a member of the party with which Andrew Henry started for the Yellowstone Valley in the fall of 1823, traveling up the Missouri and then the Grand, which is in the northeastern section of what is now South Dakota. One day Glass, who was a hunter and often traveled somewhat in advance of the main party, found himself suddenly confronted by a grizzly bear and her cubs. (The grizzly is one of the most ferocious and dangerous animals in the world—as some San Francisco gamblers proved long ago when they staged a fight between a grizzly and a tiger; the tiger was dead in a few seconds.) Before Glass could shoot or retreat, the animal had seized him and bitten out a large chunk of his flesh, which she dropped to her younglings. Glass screamed for his fellows but before they could kill the bear he had been mangled from head to foot.

Though he was not yet dead, his injuries were so frightful that Henry and his followers did not believe it possible for him to survive; they could not carry him with them, and because of the approach of winter they did not dare stay with him till he died. With the aid of a purse of $80, two men were persuaded to stay with Glass to bury him decently. But Glass lingered, and on the fifth day his volunteer nurses, fearful lest they be left too far behind their companions, determined to leave him; slipping away, they took with them all his belongings—his gun, knife, flint, and other essentials of wilderness life. These they gave to Henry, and asserted that Glass had died.

When Glass awoke and realized that he had been deserted, he was filled with a rage that provided the vitalizing will to live. For a short period he lay in the thicket, subsisting on fruits and berries; then, still unable to stand, he started to drag himself to the nearest post, Fort Kiowa, on the Missouri a hundred miles away. At a time when it seemed that he could not reach the river because of lack of food, he had a bit of luck; he came upon wolves attacking a buffalo calf and, as the wind was toward him, the wolves did not scent his approach. As soon as the cowardly animals had killed the calf, he frightened them away and, lacking a knife and flint, ate the flesh raw. Resuming his dogged journey he took part of the calf with him

The day he arrived at the post he met another trapping party on its way up to the Yellowstone and, in spite of his condition, set off posthaste with it. Some distance north of the present Bismarck, N.D., the trappers were attacked by Aricaras; all were killed but Glass, who was rescued by Mandans and taken to nearby Fort Tilton.

The same day he started again on his interrupted journey, this time traveling alone, though with a kit. He arrived at the Big Horn post, in the present Montana, 38 days later, only to find that those on whom he planned to take revenge had left for Fort Atkinson (Council Bluff). Off went Glass, joining a party of four carrying a report to that place. The couriers followed the Powder River south, crossed to the North Platte, where they built bullboats of buffalo hide, and started down stream. Somewhere along the river they met a band of Aricaras whose chief had been killed a year before in a brush with trappers; the Indians seemed friendly, however, and invited them into the current chief's tepee. Too late the whites realized that they had walked into a trap. Two of them were killed and the others escaped independently.

Glass was once more alone. Though he had lost the rest of his outfit, including his gun, he still had his flint and knife. As he said later, "These little fixin's make a man feel right pert when he is three or four hundred miles from anybody or anywhere." He started again for Fort

Kiowa, to the northeast. By this time spring had arrived; weak-legged young buffalo calves were numerous in the region, so he had no difficulty in finding food. Reaching Fort Kiowa he immediately started off down river. In June he walked into the fort at last to face those who had deserted him. Reports of his superhuman journey and vengeful desire had already reached the fort; he was received with awe and expectation, but his rage had been completely exhausted by the nine-month trek. Nothing happened.

DUNCAN, **94.1 m.** (1,495 alt., 241 pop.), laid out in October, 1871, was first named Jackson.

Left from Duncan on a marked graveled road to the KUENZLI MUSEUM, **2.5 m.** (*open 7 a.m.-6 p.m.; adm. 15¢, children 10¢*), owned by Dr. Frank Kuenzli and his son, Lindo. Dr. Kuenzli, a Swiss, came to America with his father in 1879 and studied to become a veterinarian. His interest in animal and plant life early led him to preserve specimens. In the museum are hundreds of curious articles from all parts of the world: reptiles, octopi, Australian birds and butterflies, pioneer and Indian relics, and military equipment. Free lectures on the collections are given daily. On Sundays and holidays the lectures are often continuous.

CLARKS, **115.8 m.** (1,623 alt., 540 pop.), was named for Silas Clark, a Union Pacific R.R. official. The town's first white settler came in 1867, and found the Pawnee quite friendly.

At **118.5 m.** is a junction with State 16.

Left on this graveled road and across the river to the Dexter farm, **2 m.**, on which is the SITE OF THE GRAND PAWNEE HUNTING AND BURIAL GROUNDS, as well as the SITE OF A PAWNEE VILLAGE. A second village site lies southwest of the farm. A hundred years ago the course of the Platte River was a mile farther south than it now is, and the two villages stood on the former riverbank. Neither village site has been excavated or investigated to any great extent, as the land is now under cultivation. Traces of the houses can be found by examining the banks of the ditches where the charred remains of the house poles and posts are imbedded in the soil. Burnt clay and charcoal from the fireplaces are also present. Such relics as arrowheads, hoes, axes, pipes, tomahawks, and flintlock muskets have been unearthed.

At **127.1 m.** is CENTRAL CITY (1,699 alt., 2,474 pop.). Years ago this section was a wide tract of rolling prairie with little vegetation and few trees; some miles away from this spot stood a lone giant cottonwood that served as a landmark for travelers on the trail. This tree, 10 or 12 feet in circumference at its base, stood tall and straight and was easily discernible for miles. In 1858 a ranch, known as the Lone Tree, was established here; it later became one of the "20-mile stopping places" of the stage on its weekly trips. Later, when the Union Pacific R.R. station was built three miles from the ranch, a station was established here and called Lone Tree.

A settlement grew up around the Lone Tree station—a town of three stores, six houses, and a tavern owned by a man named Parker, who claimed the land around the lone tree. Later the town of Central City was laid out around the railroad station and the Lone Tree settlers moved to it.

Right on Avenue C and its graveled continuation to NEBRASKA CENTRAL COL-LEGE, 2.5 m., a small coeducational school established in 1899 by members of the Society of Friends.

At **127.7 m.** is a junction with River Road.

Left on this dirt road to the LONE TREE MONUMENT, **3 m.** (L). This stone monument, about 10 feet tall, resembles the trunk of a tree. The pioneer passion for carving names on everything in sight caused the death of the original giant cottonwood tree, which was blown down in 1865. The region along the Platte River is now well wooded.

CHAPMAN, **135.2 m.** (283 pop.), was named by the local section boss, who was also the first postmaster, for his superior officer, the road-master of this section of the Union Pacific.

LOCKWOOD, **143 m.**, only a point on the railroad, is distinguished by a marker alongside the right-of-way.

Left from Lockwood on a graveled road to a junction at **0.7 m.**; L. here to the GOTTSCH-TRAMM GRAVES, **1.2 m.**, on the farm of William Johnson (*visitors welcome*). Early in January, 1868, when the Loup River was frozen solid and snow covered the ice, two men went off to hunt deer, accompanied by two boys, Christian Gottsch and Christian Tramm. On the second day the men left camp alone, leaving the boys in charge of the supplies. When the men returned, they found that the boys had been killed, presumably by Indians; the team, blankets, robes, and other supplies were missing. The boys were buried on the Gottsch homestead.

GRAND ISLAND, **149 m.** (1,861 alt., 18,041 pop.), was named for the narrow, 42-mile-long strip of land lying nearby between two channels of the Platte. French trappers first called this strip La Grande Isle. In 1856 a detachment of cavalry killed 10 Cheyenne on the island in reprisal for an attack the Cheyenne had made on a carrier of the U.S. mail.

In 1857 a group of Germans from Davenport, Iowa, started a west-ward trek in the general direction of the present Grand Island, believ-ing that the national capital would be moved to the center of the country and wanting to be early settlers in such a region. The three leaders of the band traveled with a four-mule team, while the others followed in five covered wagons drawn by oxen. They settled here.

During the sixties the Union Pacific reached the settlement, a post office and flour mills were established, and a General Land Office opened. It was not until 1872, however, that the town was incorporated.

The town is a distribution and shipping point for a large agricul-

tural area. Old buildings, showing the German predilection for elaborate architecture, contrast with more recent structures; the economy
and thrift of the early German inhabitants are exemplified in the neat,
narrow, downtown streets. The town is flanked by railroads and dotted
with manufacturing plants.

The agriculture of the territory surrounding Grand Island is of a
diversified nature. Although this region has been counted as part of the
Wheat Belt, large crops of sugar beets, rye, oats, barley, and corn are
also grown.

One of the outstanding commercial activities of the town is its horse
market. There are two good-sized livestock markets.

The AMERICAN CRYSTAL SUGAR COMPANY PLANT (*open to the public*) was one of the first beet-sugar factories in the Plains States.
Though in February, 1873, the Grand Island *Independent*, in an article
on the beet-sugar industry in Europe, made the suggestion that beets
could be grown in Nebraska, it was not until 1887 that any practical
action was taken. In that year Nebraska soil was tested and found adapt-
able to the culture of sugar beets; seed was imported from France and
Germany, and $100,000 raised by subscription for the new factory.

PIONEER PARK was the site of the first Hall County Courthouse.

Twenty-five miles or so northeast of Grand Island the Mormon Pioneers, on April 24, 1847, began to raft their belongings across the
Loup. Not far away they saw the remains of a large Indian village.
Indians were several times found lurking in the vicinity of the Mormon
camp in this area, but thanks to the vigilance of Brigham Young's well-
organized guard the emigrants were not molested. Once or twice men
on guard were caught asleep; but though Young severely reprimanded
them for endangering their fellows by such laxness, Clayton made ex-
cuses, commenting that it was hard for men who had been driving and
walking all day in the open air to keep from nodding.

While by this time of the year travel by ox-cart was fairly comfortable on the prairie, it was never entirely so for long. Many pioneers
felt at times as Clayton's mother had in crossing Iowa on the flight
from Nauvoo; Clayton had noted in his *Journal* that she felt too sick
to ride in the wagon and had walked all day in the rain.

It was perhaps in part a memory of the extreme discomfort sometimes experienced when riding in the jolting, lurching wagons and of
the number of emigrants who preferred to walk that caused Brigham
Young in 1855 to plan the handcart expeditions across the plains to
Salt Lake City. Between 50,000 and 60,000 people had reached Utah
by 1855, many of them Mormons who had followed the route laid out
by the Pioneers. Perhaps the majority were converts recruited in northwestern Europe, chiefly in the British Isles. While Young made great
effort to have the emigrants finance their own journeys to Utah, the
Saints in the West had made heavy contributions to the Immigration
Fund. Utah crops were very bad, however, in 1855, and early in 1856

a large company of new Saints left Liverpool. Since the Utah Saints could give little toward outfitting the many hundreds of converts with ox-carts and supplies for the trip west, it was determined that two-wheeled carts should be built to carry the smallest children and rigidly limited amounts of food and clothing; the men and women were to pull them from the Missouri to Salt Lake City.

The Handcart Expedition left in five brigades for the thousand-mile walk; those in charge of arrangements along the Missouri lacked Young's foresightedness and were not prepared to send off the final groups until very late in the travel season. The brigades that started early reached Salt Lake City without serious hardship, though many went through a painful period while their muscles and feet were hardening. Those leaving late underwent severe trials, walking over the prairies during the hottest part of the year and reaching the mountains after the weather had become bitterly cold. In one division of 401 people, 67 froze or starved to death. When word of the situation reached Utah, ox-carts were commandeered and sent to meet the last division. Young repeated the handcart experiment in the following year to prove that the plan was sound, but after 1857 the Saints went west with teams.

ALDA, **156.7 m.** (1,916 alt., 153 pop.), was named for an emigrant's child born here in 1860. On the site of the town was once a Pawnee Indian village.

At **164 m.** is the junction with a graveled road.

Right on this road to the Howe Farm, **1 m.**; R. on a private dirt road leading across the field to a decaying elm tree, **2 m.**, on the banks of Wood River, that marks the Site of a Pioneer Tragedy. The Smith and the Anderson families came to the Platte River Valley in January, 1862. One morning Smith, his sons, and an Anderson boy started to the Platte to fell trees for the construction of cabins. At noon Anderson arrived and saw Smith's wagon standing in the willows. The men and horses were gone. In the sand of the river bed lay Anderson's son, face downward, his body filled with arrows, while a few feet away was Smith, grasping the hands of his sons. All had been killed, presumably by the Sioux. The surviving members of the families returned to their former home.

When WOOD RIVER, **164.6 m.** (1,967 alt., 751 pop.), was laid out in 1874 by the Union Pacific R.R., it had already been settled for two or three years. The moving of the railroad station resulted in the moving of the town.

SHELTON, **172 m.** (927 pop.), grew from a settlement known as Wood River Center that stood several miles east of the present town. A Mormon party from England, led by Edward Oliver, was traveling to Salt Lake City when a broken axle forced them to camp and attempt to repair the break. The wagon was irreparably damaged, and Mrs. Oliver persuaded her husband to turn back. The family spent the winter in a log hut on the banks of Wood River and decided to remain; Oliver built the first store. The community that grew up near them was later named Shelton in honor of Nathaniel Shelton, another settler.

In Shelton is the SITE OF A LOG STOCKADE, once used as a shelter against Indians and as a depot for the Great Western Stage, which ran through the town. The town had a newspaper, the *Huntsman's Echo*, in 1858.

GIBBON, **178.2 m.** (2,000 alt., 825 pop.), came into existence as a soldiers' colony. The cheap land offered by the Homestead Act of 1862 and the advance of the Union Pacific R.R. caused Col. John Thorp of West Farmington, Ohio, to advertise and promote a colonization plan with the co-operation of the Union Pacific and the War Department. Offers included free home sites along the Union Pacific R.R. and reduced railroad fares to these points. Soldier colonists were recruited, largely from New York, Pennsylvania, Ohio, and Massachusetts. The men arrived here on April 7, 1871. Each soldier was entitled to file claim on a quarter section of land, and 61 such claims were drawn up. At the time of the drawing for lands, numbers from 1 to 61 were placed in a hat which was shaken. The drawings were made for choice rather than for prescribed lands—that is, number 1 had first choice, number 2 had second, and so on. Until they established their homesteads, the colonists lived in freight cars.

When the colony reached its twentieth birthday the settlers held a celebration; though the last member of the original group has died, a "reunion" has since been held every year on April 7.

At **180 m.** US 30 traverses the FORMER JAMES E. BOYD RANCH, which was earlier called Nebraska Center. The ranch became a caravan stop and supply station; Boyd, who later served as Governor of Nebraska (1891-1892), acquired the ranch about 1858. Doubtless the earliest settler felt that this site—about 3 miles from the Platte and 12 or 13 miles northeast of Fort Kearney—would have some measure of protection from Indian attacks, and offer opportunities for trade with emigrants.

The ranch had the first brewery in this region. The small plant, on the banks of the Wood River, made about 10 kegs of beer at a time, which were sold near the fort and at Dobytown for $6 to $8 each. There was also an icehouse here; the storage hole can be seen from the highway.

KEARNEY, **191.1 m.** (2,146 alt., 8,575 pop.), seat of Buffalo County, lies on a flat plain on the north side of the Platte River. The town was named for Fort Kearney, known originally as Fort Childs; the misspelled name of the fort honored Gen. Stephen Watts Kearny. The first settlement on the present townsite was called Kearney Junction. The Union Pacific R.R. and the Burlington & Missouri River R.R. (now the Chicago, Burlington & Quincy) had received grants of land from the Government, and the charter of the Burlington required that

THE PLATTE FERRY

PONY EXPRESS STATION, GOTHENBURG, NEB.

it make connection with the Union Pacific somewhere east of the 100th meridian. They met at this point and the plat of the town was filed on October 27, 1871.

At one time it was hoped that because of its central geographical position Kearney might become the capital of Nebraska. Local boosters once held a convention in St. Louis to launch a drive for making Kearney the capital of the United States. The population was larger during the eighties and nineties than it is today.

Surrounded by a fertile, irrigated region, Kearney is an important shipping point for grains and livestock. Industrial plants include a cigar factory, a candy factory, and flour mills.

Here are a STATE HOSPITAL with accommodations for 160 tubercular patients, and a STATE TEACHERS COLLEGE, which has an enrollment of more than two thousand. Both institutions are at the western end of the town (R).

Kearney is near the western end of the long low strip of land, called Grand Island, that divides the Platte for many miles.

The several eastern feeders of the emigrant route best known as the Oregon Trail united—insofar as any trails united on the prairies—on the south shore of the Platte near the head of Grand Island. Endless confusion has resulted from the fact that the names of the emigrant roads were popular, rather than official; that the same general section of an overland route might bear different names at different periods, as the goals of the major migrations changed; and that the routes themselves might move a hundred miles to the right or to the left within a year's time. One foresighted forty-niner predicted this, saying that future generations would not realize how slight the things were that brought major switches in the directions taken by succeeding wagon trains, even in the same year. The establishment of a new trading post or a ranch, the drying up of a spring or the finding of a new one, the outbreak of an epidemic at a camp site, a prairie fire, the pollution of a watering spot, the creation of a slough around a ford—any one of these was sufficient to turn the course of thousands of wagons. As a result, hundreds of towns in a very wide band have erected markers indicating that they were on the Oregon Trail, and old-timers, upholding their towns' right to the honor, tell of ruts they saw in the early days. Many emigrants bound for Oregon and California used the trail on the north side of the Platte, known as the Mormon Trail because the first large groups to use it were Saints; but some Mormons also used the route on the south bank. Emigrants bound for the West traveled on the north or south bank of the Platte according to where they crossed the Missouri.

Left from Kearney on State 10, a paved road, crossing the Platte to FORT KEARNEY STATE PARK, 7 m. (*camping free; picnicking and other recreational facilities*). The park includes 80 acres of grass and giant cottonwoods, on the site of the famous frontier military post. Still visible on the grounds are rifle pits and other earthworks, one of the corner blockhouses, and a grass-covered mound that was the magazine in which munitions were stored for use along the trail between this point and Fort Laramie.

The first Fort Kearney was a blockhouse on the Missouri River at what is now Nebraska City; it was built and occupied in 1846-1847. The post was transferred to this place in order to give emigrants protection against Indian attacks.

Lt. Daniel P. Woodbury, who chose the site, returned here from the first Fort Kearney in June, 1848, with 175 men, who began the construction of the post, first making adobe blocks; they also set up a sawmill and erected sod stables. Plans drawn in 1852 show that the fort included two two-story corner blockhouses of heavy timbers, powder and guard houses, a lookout accessible by ladder, extending along the entire ridge, and officers' quarters. Numerous barracks and other facilities were added in succeeding years.

During the Civil War regular troops were withdrawn and the fort was manned by volunteers that included a number of former Confederate soldiers, called Galvanized Yankees. In 1865 Pawnee were enlisted to help hold the Sioux in check, and they continued to serve during the building of the railroad. When the railroad displaced the wagon trains, the fort was no longer needed. It was abandoned in 1871, and a few years later the military reservation was thrown open to settlement.

Section 3. Kearney to Ogallala, 145.4 m. US 30.

West of KEARNEY, **0 m.**, US 30 follows Watson Boulevard through an archway of trees so dense that it is almost like a tunnel.

At **2.3 m.** is the STATE INDUSTRIAL SCHOOL (R), which occupies 11 buildings and is equipped to care for 210 boys.

It was in this area that the Mormon Pioneers saw their first herds of buffalo, an event always eagerly anticipated by emigrants. For several days before the animals were seen, the travelers had noted buffalo tracks and on April 30, 1847, had started using dried buffalo dung—chips, in emigrant parlance—for fuel. Brother Heber Kimball immediately invented an efficient method of obtaining the maximum heat from the chips by burning them in the middle of three pits with ventilating holes between them to create a draught. On the first of May the company sighted three buffalo through their telescopes, and three of the Pioneers started off on horseback in the hope of augmenting the dwindling food supply. After proceeding a few miles farther the travelers saw a herd "about eight miles away." Clayton said he counted 72 through his glass and Orson Pratt 74. Another and larger herd was seen later in the day. Clayton noted that the view of the animals "excited considerable interest and pleasure in the breasts of the brethren, and as may be guessed, the teams moved slowly and frequently stopped to watch their movement." Clayton's *Journal* was fat for several days thereafter with details of the hunts.

There was one other exciting event for the Pioneers in this area. Three wagons were observed on the south bank of the broad, shallow Platte River. Though the Mormons did not dare attempt to cross the river, a member of the other party came to talk with the Mormons. He said that the wagons carried nine fur traders on their way back from Fort Laramie. The Pioneers inquired eagerly about the condition of the road ahead and then requested that he carry letters back to the Missouri for them.

At **4.8 m.** US 30 passes the former 1733 RANCH HOUSE, now a roadhouse with an electric sign, "1733." At one time there was a marker on the section line at this point reading, "1733 miles to San Francisco, 1733 miles to Boston"; hence the name of the farm. The original 1733 Ranch, which contained eight thousand acres, has been broken up into many smaller farms since the death of its owner, H. D. Watson, who was the first promoter of alfalfa as a Nebraska crop.

By May 6 the excitement over buffalo hunting was beginning to impede Pioneer progress. Appleton Harmon recorded that "about 8 o'clock the camp was called togeather by Pres^t Young . . . he also instructed the captains of tens to Stay by their teams in times of traveling. . . . He also said that thair should be no more game killed until such time as it should be needed for it was a Sin to waste life & flesh."

ELM CREEK, **15.8 m.** (2,266 alt., 708 pop.), settled by a few families in 1873, has had a history marked by misfortune. Blizzard followed blizzard in the eighties, killing many cattle and sweeping away most of the possessions of the inhabitants. The town was rebuilt, but it was almost wiped out again in 1906 by a fire that destroyed every building along the main street.

The town is now a shipping point for prairie hay. It lies in an irrigated region producing alfalfa, corn, sugar beets, potatoes, livestock, and dairy products.

On May 8, as the Mormon Pioneers moved westward, Harmon wrote: "had to drive the buffalo out of the way whare we halted the buffalo seemed to form a complete line from the river their watering place to the bluffs as far as I could se which was at least 4 m. they stood their ground appurently amased at us until within 30 rods of the wagons when their line was broken down by some taking fright & runing off others to satisfy thar curiosity came closer within gun shot of the camp snuffing and shaking their Shaggy heads, but being pursued by the dogs ran off, at this time I could stand on my waggon & see more than 10,000 Buffalo from the fact that the Plain was purfectly black with them on both sides of the river & on the bluff on our right which slopes off gradualy."

LEXINGTON, **34.9 m.** (2,385 alt., 2,962 pop.), a market town, is the successor of a Pony Express station and trading post called Plum Creek that stood on the Oregon Trail, south of the river. After the coming of the railroad the inhabitants of the settlement moved across the river, and the name was changed to one commemorating the Battle of Lexington. Plum Creek was once a rendezvous for gamblers, thieves, and hold-up men, who preyed upon miners having gold or silver. Even after legal bodies had been established, they were ineffective against the well-organized outlaw gangs; eventually the citizens formed a vigilante committee that drove out most of the lawbreakers.

In 1867 the Cheyenne—aroused by the building of the railroad through their hunting grounds and the patrolling activities of Maj. Frank North and his Pawnee scouts—led by their chief, Turkey Leg, tore up a culvert four miles west of this place and wrecked the train, a west-bound freight. They scalped the crew, broke open the boxcars, and stole the contents; some of them took bolts of bright-colored calico, which they tied to the tails of their ponies to make a brave display as they fled across the plains.

In the early days, travel on railroads was quite as dangerous as travel on steamboats had been and even more hazardous than flying was to be. Most cars, locomotives, roadbeds, and bridges were jerry-built and were likely to fall apart with or without unusual strain. The engineers treated the locomotives as personal possessions, decorating them to suit their fancies and speeding them up, backing them, and stopping them as they pleased. One early Mormon autobiography tells how the engineer of a train carrying a group of emigrants to the point where they were to start westward in oxcarts "swore he would drive the Mormons to Hell and opened the throttle to verify his threat. The train was roaring across the plains . . . when someone noticed the baggage car was aflame. The engineer stopped the train, put it in reverse and backed seven miles to the nearest watering station where the fire was extinguished. The baggage car was a charred mass of wreckage."

Such fires, caused by sparks from the locomotives, were common and not confined to the baggage cars, for both they and the coaches were made of wood. The railroad death toll was frightful until well after the Civil War, when the increasing number of damage suits moved the companies to adopt safety measures and devices. A typical cartoon in *Harper's Weekly* of 1859 depicted a frightened traveler in a berth listening to a conversation between a brakeman and a conductor: "Jim, do you think the Millcreek Bridge safe tonight?" The answer was, "If Joe cracks on the steam, I guess we'll get the Engine and Tender over all right. I'm going forward."

COZAD, **48.7 m.** (2,486 alt., 1,813 pop.), a hay-shipping center, is in a region where in summer the acres of alfalfa and fields full of haystacks line the highway. Several alfalfa mills and feed-making plants are near US 30 in this town.

Whereas the Mormon Pioneers seldom traveled more than 10 or 15 miles a day even in this level country, later emigrants were sometimes able to do 20, provided the weather was dry. The rate of travel of the Mormon handcart brigades was painfully slow. An emigrant who drove past them wrote: "We met two trains, one of thirty and the other of fifty carts, averaging about six to the cart. The carts were generally drawn by one man and three women each, though some carts were drawn by women alone. There were about three women to one man, and two-thirds of the women single. It was the most motley crew I ever beheld. Most of them were Danes, with a sprinkling of Welsh, Swedes, and English, and were generally from the lower classes of their countries. Most could not understand what we said to them. The road was lined for a mile behind the train with the lame, halt, sick, and needy. Many were quite aged, and would be going slowly along, supported by a son or daughter. Some were on crutches; now and then a mother with a child in her arms and two or three hanging hold of her, with a forlorn appearance, would pass slowly along; others, whose condition entitled them to a seat in a carriage, were wending their way through the sand. A few seemed in good spirits."

At **59 m.** is GOTHENBURG (2,561 alt., 2,322 pop.), in whose park stands a FUR TRADING POST HOUSE (*adm. free*) that was erected in 1854 on the Oregon Trail four miles east of Fort McPherson. In 1860-1 it was the Fred Machette Pony Express station; later it was an Overland Stage station, and after the coming of the railroads became a ranch building.

Left from Gothenburg on State 47, a graveled road that crosses the Platte and passes the GOTHENBURG GUN CLUB GAME PRESERVE (L); at **2.7 m.** is (R) an Oregon Trail marker.
Left from the marker to the first dirt road; L. here to the LOWER 96 RANCH, **6 m.** (*visitors welcome*). A lean-to of the tree-shaded black and white ranch house is a former Pony Express station, a log cabin in good condition; the crevices between the logs have been cemented. This old house was known as the Pat Mullaly station. There is a black "96" painted on the big concrete silos of the ranch.
Right from Lower 96 Ranch to the SITE OF THE GILMAN RANCH HOUSE, **10 m.**, where stage riders used to stop and Pony Express riders came when off duty. Mark Twain stopped here on the trip across the plains described in *Roughing It*.

The story of the western migration has usually been told in terms of those who made mistakes—of those who suffered Indian attack because they chose to travel in small groups or failed to maintain guards at night; who made unsuccessful attempts to short-cut the well-known routes; who started with inadequate equipment and supplies; or who set out on the journey in advanced stages of ill health. But for every person who became a symbol of pioneer tragedy there were thousands who thoroughly enjoyed the overland journey. One emigrant who became wealthy remarked wryly in his later years that he suffered more and had less enjoyment on de luxe hunting trips than he had on his oxcart journey across the plains. A Utah woman who had crossed the country about 1850 remembered the trip as a picnic from beginning to end; how she ran beside the slow-moving cart with her arms full of wild flowers; how she and her playmates played hide-and-seek around the wagons; how her mother knitted placidly, day in and day out, and

always had time to tell stories; how in the evening the children ran
from one campfire to the other while their parents gossiped and sang.
People quarreled, made love, played cards, danced, wrote poetry and
letters, honeymooned, joked, and carried on other normal activities
under conditions that gave them added zest.

The migrant was able to indulge his passion for writing or chipping
his name on every available surface—the old-fashioned equivalent for
the postcard writing of the modern tourist—even on the plains; in this
area he smeared names and messages with axle grease on the skulls and
long bones of the buffalo skeletons lining the routes.

C. S. Abbott, who traveled overland to California shortly after the
gold rush started, wrote of the reason for the prevalence of buffalo
skeletons: "There were wagon-trains all along the road and everybody
was banging away at the buffalo, scaring them away, or killing them
and cutting out choice pieces and leaving the rest to rot, while the Indians were starving. It was the most flagrant injustice this Government
ever permitted its people to practice. The lines between the different
tribes were as distinctly marked as the boundaries between the different States of the Union, each of these tribes claiming the ownership of
all the game within its borders, and they looked upon the emigrants as
a white tribe infringing upon their rights. . . . We shudder at the
massacre of the whole nation of Armenians by the Turks, but no pen
can describe the misery and despair of a Pawnee village,—of men,
women and children dying of hunger,—while the white tribe was killing, or scaring their game off into the mountains, and I say that our
Government here caused as much misery by negligence as the Turks
have by savagery."

At **72.5 m.** is BRADY (387 pop.).

Left from Brady on a graveled road that crosses the river to a junction at
4 m.; R. to the UPPER 96 RANCH, **9 m.**, now the property of V. H. Davis. A
monument here commemorates the Pony Express riders. The blacksmith shop,
built of red cedar logs, belonged to the Fred Machette Pony Express station; the
station itself has been moved to the Gothenburg City Park (*see above*).

The highway crosses the North Platte River near its confluence with
the South Platte at the eastern end of NORTH PLATTE, **94.7 m.**
(2,821 alt., 12,061 pop.), seat of Lincoln County.

The Sioux, Cheyenne, and Arapaho occupied this territory; the forks
of the Platte were near the border line between the hunting range of
these tribes and that of the Pawnee.

In the 1860's William Peniston and Andrew J. Miller were running
a trading post at Cold Water, some 30 miles east of this point. While
in Omaha, Miller learned that the Union Pacific R.R. was going to
establish a station at the Fork of the Platte. The men opened a post
here on November 9, 1866, with merchandise fitted to the needs of the

railroad builders, after Gen. G. M. Dodge had established North Platte for the Union Pacific. The population increased to more than two thousand during the winter of 1866-67. By June, 1867, the railroad had reached Julesburg, Colo., and construction headquarters was moved to that point, leaving behind it a settlement of only three hundred people. Everything had been moved—business houses, barracks, even the town's newspaper. Only 20 structures remained. But that same year North Platte was made a division point on the line, and the Union Pacific built machine shops, a 20-stall roundhouse, and a hotel. Thereafter the increase in population was steady; the city is the leading trade center of western Nebraska.

On April 7, 1893, a prairie fire struck the city, destroying many houses, barns, outbuildings, fences, farm implements, and stock. Other prairie fires wrought damage in 1910 and in 1915.

A tense period in local history was reached in 1902, when machinists and boilermakers employed by the Union Pacific struck in opposition to the introduction of the piecework system. The machinists quit on June 30, joining the boilermakers, who had struck the week before. The company brought in carloads of strikebreakers; the boiler shop and several boxcars were fitted with bunks and utilized as living quarters for them, and they were protected by armed guards. A request that the Governor send troops was denied. The strike lasted for nearly a year, and workmen looked for employment elsewhere. The pickets grew lax and finally gave up. Local sympathy was with the strikers from the beginning; merchants would sell nothing to the strikebreakers, barbers would not shave them, and landlords refused to rent houses to them. After a time, however, they were accepted by the town and the strike seemed lost. But on June 8, 1903, the strike was settled; the question of piecework was ignored, and the strikers returned to their old jobs with a small hourly pay increase. A request that all strikebreakers be discharged was denied, but within three months nearly all of them had left.

Following the drought of 1890, I. A. Fort of North Platte converted Congressman William Neville of North Platte to his plan of "enlarged homesteads" as a way of settling this region. Estimating that it would take two square miles for a rancher to support a family and not let his stock overgraze the land, Fort advocated two-square-mile homesteads. Although Neville introduced a bill to this effect in 1900, it was not enacted into law until Congressman Moses Kinkaid of O'Neill brought it forward again in 1904. The Kinkaid Act was successful in its purpose and the homesteaded land was used mainly for cattle raising. Irrigation, which was begun in 1866, makes possible some crop raising, especially of sugar beets.

On the second floor of the LINCOLN COUNTY COURTHOUSE are many relics of pioneer days, among them a battered chariot presented to "Buffalo Bill" Cody by Queen Victoria.

North Platte lies at the tip of a long narrow delta between the mouths of the North and South Platte Rivers; the bluffs that line the Platte more than halfway across Nebraska here spread somewhat apart. From this point the Mormon Pioneers continued west along the north bank of the North Platte. Travelers of early days who had followed the trail on the south bank of the main stream to this point usually continued westward for some distance on the south bank of the South Fork before crossing the stream, though some forded it near the confluence.

(At the western limit of North Platte the time changes from Central Standard to Rocky Mountain.)

At **96.7 m.** is the junction with a dirt road.

Right on this road to SCOUTS' REST RANCH, **0.5 m.** *(adm. free)*. This was the home of "Buffalo Bill" Cody, who entertained many notables here. William Frederick Cody (1846-1917) spent his boyhood in Leavenworth, Kans., headquarters of the freighting line of Russell, Majors, & Waddell. Young Cody first appeared in the Platte country as an outrider for this company—an office boy on horseback —and is believed to have been a Pony Express rider for a short time. He served in the Civil War and afterward, when the Kansas Pacific (now part of the Union Pacific) was building westward from Kansas City, he contracted to furnish buffalo meat for workers on the Kansas route. Within 17 months he is said to have delivered 4,280 animals.

Later he went on the stage and toured the United States in a production called the *Prairie Waif*. Out of this experience he conceived the Wild West shows that made him famous. His collection of Indians, covered wagons, bronco-busters, cowboys, stagecoaches, and marksmen did much to build up the popular, romantic misconceptions of early western history.

At Scouts' Rest Ranch, where the Wild West show was rehearsed, are a solid ranch house, rebuilt since Cody's day, and an immense barn, shaded by cottonwoods. The eaves of the ranch's main corral, built in 1887, are hewn in the shape of gunstocks, and the cattle-stall partitions are shaped like horses.

The plat of the ranch resembled the map of Nebraska.

West of O'FALLONS, **111.6 m.**, the bluffs again draw near the stream and here the early Oregon Trail, like a branch of the Union Pacific R.R. today, crossed the stream to the south bank of the North Platte, reaching it at Ash Creek. After the establishment in 1864 of Fort Sedgwick *(see SECTION 4)*, near the present Julesburg in northeastern Colorado, many trains following the route of the Overland Stage, dipped down to the fort before striking northwest to Fort Laramie, the next point providing protection and supplies. The trail was on the south bank of the South Fork.

SUTHERLAND, **114.6 m.** (2,959 alt., 753 pop.), was named for an official of the Union Pacific R.R. in 1869, when the town was laid out.

Left from Sutherland on a marked, graveled road crossing the South Platte to a junction at **1.7 m.**; L. here to the SUTHERLAND RESERVOIR, **3.5 m.**, a natural depression of five thousand acres, walled off with dikes. Its design provides for a maximum height of 80 feet, and the impounding of two hundred thousand acre-feet of water. A tunnel of reinforced concrete, 14 feet in diameter and 7,800 feet long, conducts the water from the Kingsly Diversion Dam under the South Platte River.

PAXTON, **127 m.** (3,054 alt., 507 pop.), was named for W. A. Paxton of Omaha.

At **136 m.** is a marker (L) indicating that the ALKALI LAKE PONY EXPRESS STATION was south of the South Platte at this point.

OGALLALA, **145.4 m.** (3,211 alt., 1,631 pop.), the seat of Keith County, was named for the Oglala (also spelled Ogallala, *scatter one's own*) tribe of the Teton Sioux.

After the Civil War disruption of the cattle market, the ranchers of Texas were very anxious to find new markets. As soon as the Government-financed railroads had been carried across the plains the cattlemen started roundups of the herds on the vast unfenced range and sent the animals north to the railroads for shipment to eastern markets. Ogallala became an important cattle-shipping point of the early years; the first herd arrived in June, 1867, in charge of yippi-shouting cowpunchers who had been fighting Indians and stampedes for many hundreds of miles. In later years there were sometimes 15 outfits camped along the South Platte by the middle of July. The physical demands of such cattle drives were great and the punchers, who sometimes had to ward off sleep by plastering their eyelids open with wet tobacco, felt that they had a right to celebrate the end of the drives as long and as loudly as they desired.

Five blocks west of the main street of Ogallala is a plot of ground that rises 80 to 100 feet above the river level. This is BOOT HILL CEMETERY, one of many so called because those interred in them died and were buried with their boots on their feet. The graveyard, a relic of the old lawless, gambling, gun-blazing town, has not had a burial since the eighties. Though the hill bears a sign with the name, no mounds are visible and there are no tombstones.

In a park at the western edge of town (R) is an OREGON TRAIL MEMORIAL, and next to it is a round yellow CHISHOLM CATTLE TRAIL MARKER. Chisholm was the most famous of the cattle trails from Texas to Kansas, running in the neighborhood of US 81, but it never reached Nebraska.

At Ogallala is the junction with US 26, which closely parallels the Oregon and Mormon Trails through Fort Laramie (*see ALTERNATE ROUTE*).

Section 4. Ogallala to Wyo. Line, 124.3 m. US 30.

West of OGALLALA, **0 m.**, is BRULE, **9 m.** (3,287 alt., 329 pop.), named for the Brulé (Fr., *burned*) tribe of the Teton Sioux. The South Platte River bank here is a mass of tangled undergrowth, sand, and trees.

US 30, westbound, here leaves the South Platte, which turns southward into Colorado. Travelers following the Oregon Trail detour that
ran through Julesburg crossed the river at several points between Brule
and Julesburg. These were the Lower and Upper California Crossings.

At **10 m.** (R) is a marker calling attention to the SITE OF THE
DIAMOND SPRINGS PONY EXPRESS STATION, which was eight miles south
of this point.

At **13 m.** (R) is CALIFORNIA HILL, where the Oregon Trail in
the early Julesburg days turned northwest to reach the North Platte
near Courthouse Rock (*see SIDE ROUTE C*). This was before the route
that followed the South Platte and then turned north on the Cherokee
Trail into southern Wyoming was developed by the Overland Stage.
Holladay in July, 1862, abandoned the trail by Fort Laramie and
through South Pass largely because of the hostility of the Indians, and
many emigrants followed his lead.

At **18.2 m.** is a junction with US 138.

Left on US 138, through BIG SPRINGS, **2.2 m.** (595 pop.). JULESBURG,
Colo., **11.8 m.** (3,468 alt., 1,467 pop.), is a respectable successor to three former
towns of the same name, each of which was important in its day because of its
position on the trail to the West and to Denver and the Colorado mines. The
present town was founded in 1881 when the Union Pacific branch to Denver was
projected. Viewed today among the broken hills in a curve of the South Platte
River, the quiet town gives no evidence that it sprang from the ashes of "the
Wickedest Little City East of the Rockies."

Left from Julesburg **1 m.** on State 51 to the junction with a side road (R)
that leads to the ITALIAN'S CAVE, **1.5 m.** (L), a natural fissure running back
into a hill, open at both ends and artificially enlarged. Broad shelves for mangers
and storage rooms have been cut in the rock. At the mouth of the cave are the
ruins of a two-story stone building whose walls, more than two feet thick, are
pierced with loopholes. A primitive but effective water system served the house.
Many maintain that this was once the hide-out of Jules Reni, founder of Old
Julesburg. The truth seems to be that the house was built by Uberto Gabello, an
Italian miner, reputed to have amassed a fortune in the gold fields at Cripple
Creek. A strange man was Gabello, who dwelt in solitary state in his fantastic
castle, and repulsed all the well-meant overtures of his neighbors. In time he
came to be regarded as a madman by some, and feared as a sorcerer by the more
superstitious. After his death, his house was found to be a temple to the sun;
prayers and esoteric symbols were carved on the walls. Unfortunately, the searchers
considered these finds of insufficient importance for preservation, so no traces
remain today to give a clue to the exact nature of Gabello's one-man cult.

The dirt side road continues past the SITE OF THE SECOND JULESBURG,
4 m. (R), which sprang up immediately following the destruction of the first
town (*see below*), but was short lived, because when the Union Pacific was extended into Colorado in 1867 this town was off the route. Of the three early Jules-
burgs, it was by far the least notorious, having, in fact, no particular history.

West of the second town is the SITE OF OLD JULESBURG, **8 m.**, the first
of that name. It developed as an important Overland Stage station and was a
station of the Pony Express. Old Julesburg was the rendezvous of traders, Indian
fighters, buffalo hunters, and adventurers of the most devil-may-care kind, as well
as of desperados and bandits who came to divide their loot and squander it in
riotous celebrations. Jules Reni, the French Canadian who was first stage station

master here, was himself reputed to have been the leader of a band of outlaws; this may have been merely ill-natured gossip, however, because Jules was disliked by those who were jealous of his influence among the French Canadians of the area. At the time wagon trains were frequently looted and burned and solitary travelers murdered in this area. The outrages were naturally blamed on the Indians, but the presence of white men among the raiding parties was testified to by more than one survivor. Released prisoners told of white men who came and went freely in the Indian camps and shared the loot. Rumor grew that Jules himself was at the bottom of the business; it was remarked that the richest trains were almost invariably attacked and burned after leaving Julesburg.

Jack Slade, who was one of the most fearless men on an extremely tough frontier, was division superintendent of the early stage route. Slade distrusted Reni, and Reni resented Slade's methods of punishing his (Reni's) cohorts. The feud came to a head when Jules suddenly and without warning filled Slade with enough buckshot to have killed an ordinary man. But Slade lived and from his sickbed warned Jules that he would cut off his ears and wear them as watch charms. Slade had to go to St. Louis for treatment and when he returned to this place Jules had disappeared.

After Slade returned to his post he was told of repeated boasts by Reni that he would come back to finish the killing he had attempted unsuccessfully. Slade was at Pacific Springs, at the western end of his division, when he was told that Reni was hunting him. At each station, as he traveled back to Julesburg, Slade received a fresh warning. Slade did not meet him on the route and at Fort Laramie he talked over the situation with army officers because, in spite of many stories to the contrary, Slade was not a vicious man and the punishments he had dealt out were merely those of a man protecting his employers' interests in a lawless country. The army men advised Slade to catch Jules and kill him, because there would be no peace for the stage company until he was put out of the way. Slade acted on the advice in a way that made him a symbol of border ruthlessness for many decades. (*See ALTERNATE ROUTE.*)

The operations of the white renegades and desperados have led to search for treasure in this area. Even today there are many who firmly believe that the trail robbers buried much of their loot in some secluded place near the old town. Slade himself was of the opinion that there was a treasure cache nearby, and was untiring in his search for it. None has ever been found, and it is likely that the spoilers squandered their wealth. Old Julesburg passed out of existence in 1865, when it was completely destroyed during an Indian attack.

At **9 m.** on this road is the SITE OF FORT SEDGWICK (R), a military trading post established to protect travelers from marauding Indians and white robbers. The post was built in 1864 and garrisoned until 1871, when the efforts of the late sixties resulted in the subjugation of the Plains Indians. A few traces of sod buildings remain, but most of the fort, constructed of wood, has disappeared.

CHAPPELL, **39.3 m.** (3,697 alt., 1,061 pop.), was named in honor of Charles Chappell, a division superintendent of the Union Pacific, who assisted in laying out the townsite. It is a trade center for the chief wheat-raising area in Nebraska.

West of Chappell the highway follows Lodgepole Creek, so named because several Indian tribes procured poles for their tepees near the headwaters of the stream. The gradual rise in the land that takes place steadily as the route runs westward from Omaha becomes more apparent in this area. The growing season here is short but conditions are favorable for the raising of winter wheat. Some corn is also grown. Irrigation is carried on in the valley to a limited extent.

Soapweed grows on the hillsides; its ivory, bell-shaped blossoms rise above the green spike leaves in May or June. Cactus is also seen, and occasionally a coyote; but prairie dogs, prairie owls, and rattlesnakes are not found in the numbers that once existed here.

LODGEPOLE, **48.7 M.** (3,832 alt., 436 pop.), is the scene of the Cheyenne County Old Settlers' Reunion, held annually on Labor Day. Such events are held in many western towns, though their original character has changed because the great majority of the participants cannot be considered old settlers.

Numerous fossils found in the Ogallala formation of this area indicate how great a change has taken place in its physical condition. Several million years ago this high arid country was swampy lowland harboring now extinct animals such as three-toed horses and rhinoceroses.

SIDNEY, **66.5 m.** (4,085 alt., 3,306 pop.), seat of Cheyenne County, was named for Sidney Dillon, New York agent of the Union Pacific R.R. The town is surrounded by high rolling plains, broken here and there by imposing cliffs. High bluffs on the north protect it from winter winds.

The town grew up around Fort Sidney, which was originally a sub-post of Fort Sedgwick in Colorado and was called Sidney Barracks; in 1870 it was made an independent post. The fort was built for the protection of the railroad workers and of the wagon trains passing through the area. Near the highway is a 20-foot grassy mound that formed part of the rifle range. A small hexagonal structure, built of limestone, that was the Fort Sidney ammunition storehouse, is now part of a residence. Two old barracks are now used as dwellings. A large well-preserved building opposite them was the officers' quarters. A stone structure now serving as a sales pavilion and barn is said to have been the stable. The post was abandoned in 1894.

Most of the gold prospectors on their way to the Black Hills in 1876 bought their supplies in this town, which was the nearest railroad point to the New Eldorado. In those boom days the dance halls, gambling houses, and saloons seldom closed their doors. There were 23 saloons in one block at the time when approximately 1,500 people were passing through daily. The town boasted of introducing the all-night theater to the world.

Gun fights were daily events that caused little excitement. One night during a dance one of the participants was shot to death; someone propped him up in a corner and the dancers continued to whirl past his feet. Later another man was shot and his body was placed beside the first. It was not until the third corpse joined the group that the party came to an end.

Lynchings were also common and the townspeople were exceedingly critical of the conduct of the victims. One who gained approval was

Charlie Reed. He had been living with Mollie Wardner. One day in the spring of 1879 several citizens, among them Henry Loomis, were walking past Mollie's house; Mollie called to Loomis, "Come in, darling, and bring your friends along." Loomis, feeling that she had betrayed her position as Reed's consort, shouted at her indignantly, telling her to go back into the house; he then apologized for speaking in such manner to a lady. Gossips eagerly carried word of the rebuke to Reed, but apparently neglected to clarify the cause of Loomis' rebuke. Reed immediately hunted up Loomis and shot him. By the time Loomis had died, after acute suffering, public opinion against Reed had mounted and a mob went to the jail with a rope. Reed accepted the situation and generously confessed that he had previously killed five other men in Texas; he added, however, that three of the shootings had been in self-defense. Western Union telegraph poles were popular hanging trees in the treeless country; as Reed was taken to a ladder that had been placed against one he was asked whether he preferred to jump from the ladder or to have it pulled from under him. "I'll jump off, gentlemen, and show you how a brave man can die," he said. "Goodbye, gentlemen, one and all." His body was cut down two or three days later and put in Boot Hill Cemetery. Reed's reply became a popular exit line that was used later by others.

There is a legend that, during the peak of the boom, the Union Pacific R.R. would not allow its passengers to risk their lives by getting off the train during a stop here.

Opposite the Union Pacific depot is the UNION PACIFIC HOTEL, built at the time the railroad was under construction. Near it is a frame building that was a FREIGHT HOUSE, erected in the days when this was the distributing point to the forts and Indian agencies to the north.

West of Sidney the highway is level and nearly straight. In former days railroad passengers welcomed such flat stretches of country not only because the trains crossing them moved with fewer bounces and jerks and there was less danger of a wreck, but also because there was less chance of a train robbery. Such robberies were almost daily events in the early days of the West. The hold-up men sometimes wrecked trains in order to loot the mail cars and rob the passengers, but more often they merely flagged them at night in lonely spots and took what they wanted at the point of a gun. Trains carrying large quantities of gold to the mints were particularly marked for attack.

At **80.5 m.** is POINT OF ROCKS (R), which provides a good view of the craggy and pine-dotted country. From this point the Indians are said to have rolled rocks down on Union Pacific trains. Air currents in this area cause trouble for planes flying between North Platte and Cheyenne, Wyo. An airplane beacon is on top of the rock.

POTTER, **85 m.** (4,389 alt., 515 pop.), was named for a General Potter who at one time commanded troops in western Nebraska. Nearby,

LODGEPOLE CREEK disappears underground and reappears several miles downstream.

KIMBALL, **103.2 m.** (4,709 alt., 1,711 pop.), a wheat- and potato-shipping center, was the southern terminus of the old stage route that passed through the Wild Cat Range to Gering on the North Platte River.

BUSHNELL, **115.2 m.** (4,871 alt., 341 pop.), was named for a civil engineer of the Union Pacific R.R.

At **124.3 m.** is the Wyoming Line.

Wyoming

Neb. Line—Cheyenne—Laramie—Rawlins—Rock Springs—Granger—
Kemmerer—Idaho Line; 459.4 m. US 30 and US 30N.

Union Pacific R.R. parallels route throughout. Union Pacific Stages and Burlington
Trailways follow route between Cheyenne and Granger.

Oiled roadbed, occasionally closed for brief periods during severe blizzards.

Accommodations chiefly in towns.

US 30 in Wyoming runs through a land often referred to as "the
last frontier." The stages that in the first months followed the Oregon
Trail (*see ALTERNATE ROUTE*) through central Wyoming were in
1862 rerouted. In March, 1862, the Sioux, Cheyenne, and Arapaho, in
a united movement, had attacked all the stage stations between the
Platte and Bear Rivers, burning many and capturing every horse in the
service. Stage passengers were not molested in this period, but many
were left stranded in the coaches from which the horses had been taken.

By the middle of 1862 the coaches, after leaving Julesburg (*see
SECTION 4*), continued to follow the South Platte until they reached
the Cherokee Trail; after Overland stages were transferred to this route,
it was called Overland Trail. The Cherokee Trail came north from Fort
Smith on the Arkansas River and in Colorado followed Cherry Creek
to the point where it emptied into the South Platte, gradually swinging
northwestward to cross Laramie Plains and then westward to round
the northern flank of the Medicine Bow Mountains; it crossed the Divide
through Bridger Pass.

The Cherokee Trail was a natural route well known to trappers.
It received its name because the first large groups to follow it were the
Cherokee on their way to California in the gold rush of 1849-50. The
remnants of this intelligent and able tribe of the Southeast, which had
attempted to adopt white men's ways and forms of government, set-
ting themselves up as an autonomous nation, had been forced out of
Georgia after the discovery of gold on their lands. Even though the
U. S. Supreme Court had recognized their sovereign autonomy, Presi-
dent Andrew Jackson in 1838 refused to restrain white land-grabbers
and permitted the natives to be herded west by military force. The
Cherokee were segregated in the territory that is now the States of
Arkansas and Oklahoma.

Section 5. Nebraska Line to Laramie, 92.4 m. US 30.

US 30 crosses the Wyoming Line, **0 m.,** just east of PINE BLUFFS,
0.7 m. (5,047 alt., 670 pop.), whose name is descriptive of its sur-
roundings. This was near the center of the hunting grounds over which

the Arapaho, Cheyenne, Ute, Sioux, Blackfeet, and other tribes wandered.

West of Pine Bluffs US 30 runs through semi-arid rolling plains and short-grass country. In this vicinity are grown seed potatoes, many carloads of which are shipped annually, particularly into Texas and the Southwest.

At ARCHER, **33.8 m.**, is a STATE EXPERIMENT FARM (L) that specializes in dry farming and in growing altitude grains.

CHEYENNE, **41.6 m.** (6,062 alt., 17,361 pop.) (*see WYO. GUIDE*).

Railroad Stations. Union Pacific R.R., 15th St. and Capitol Ave.; Chicago, Burlington & Quincy R.R. and Colorado & Southern R.R., Capitol Ave. between 15th and 16th Sts.

Accommodations. Good hotels.

Points of Interest. State Capitol, State Supreme Court Building, Fort Francis E. Warren, Frontier Park, U.S. Horticultural Field Station, and others.

West of Cheyenne US 30 rises 1,773 feet in 31 miles to cross the Laramie Mountains. Colorado snow peaks, 60 miles away, are plainly visible (L); rugged pine-topped ridges and mountains form the background (R).

GRANITE CANYON, **60.5 m.** (7,315 alt.), has springs of exceptionally pure water.

BUFORD, **68.8 m.** (7,862 alt.), is a loading point for Sherman granite, used for railroad construction and other purposes.

At **71.9 m.** (R) is an old PINE TREE growing out of a large granite rock. It was kept alive in early days by firemen of the Union Pacific R.R., who drenched the tree daily with a bucket of water.

At **73.7 m.** is the junction with the Tie Siding road.

Left on this dirt road to the AMES MONUMENT, **1 m.**, built in 1881-2 at a cost of $80,000 to honor Oliver and Oakes Ames, promoters who played a large part in financing the construction of the Union Pacific R.R. It is a pyramid 60 feet square at its base and 60 feet high, surmounted with an oval cap. In the center of one side is a medallion of Oliver Ames, and on another one of his brother. The monument was erected about six hundred feet from the original railroad bed and marked the highest elevation (8,235 feet) reached by the Union Pacific in the Laramie Range. The Ames brothers were the manufacturers of Ames shovels, the most popular implements of their kind in the days of the gold rush. In the 1860's the brothers became heavily involved in the financing of the first railroad to the West. Oliver was later involved in the Credit Mobilier scandal, and received heavy public censure, though his practices differed little from those of other railroad financiers of his day.

Near the monument is a small graveyard, the sole remnant of old Sherman Station, a construction terminus and military camp in 1868 during the building of the railroad.

ARAPAHO (c. 1868)

GREEN RIVER VALLEY

F. S. A. Rothstein

Nearby are several large piles of granite. Soon after the monument had been completed, some of these stones were used for advertising purposes; inscriptions were painted on them, such as "Plantation Bitters" and "S.T. 1860." An ambitious agent of one patent medicine manufacturing concern contracted with a Wyoming newspaper correspondent to have an advertisement put across the face of the monument itself. When the job was done, the newspaper man was to furnish the Associated Press with a story severely censuring the vandalism, thus insuring the wide distribution of an advertisement of the nostrum. One morning the whole country read of the disfigurement of the monument. The newspapers denounced the so-called outrage, naming the patent medicine as the agent had planned. But the campaign of indignation was short-lived; the correspondent had not had the sign painted, reasoning that if people merely read that it had been done, the same result would be achieved.

The monument was again the subject of publicity when a Laramie justice of the peace named Murphy learned that the monument had been placed on public land instead of on railroad property; he hastened to file a homestead claim on the site, then notified the railroad company to take the pile of stone from his property. A railroad representative tried to arrange a settlement with Murphy, who insisted that the company remove the monument or pay an exorbitant price for his homestead. An agreement was eventually reached whereby the company gave the "homesteader" several lots in Laramie in exchange for his claim to the land.

A FOREST SERVICE SHELTER HOUSE (*open to public*), **74.7 m.** (R), is equipped to render aid during storms. (*Blizzards frequent in this vicinity October to April; usually come very suddenly; seek shelter at once.*)

At **81.6 m.** the highway crosses the crest of the Sherman Range (8,835 alt.). Near the highway at this point are bridle paths and a ski course. Near Summit Tavern is a wooden OBSERVATION TOWER maintained by the Forest Service; it is on the summit of Crow Creek Hill (8,877 alt.) in the Pole Mountain District of the Medicine Bow Forest. The tower commands a view of the Laramie Plains to the west, and of most of the drainage area of the Cache La Poudre River in Colorado.

West of this point US 30 drops quickly down the western slope of the range, descending about 1,670 feet in nine miles. (*Steep grade and almost blind curves; keep cars in gear.*) The highway traverses picturesque TELEPHONE CANYON.

KIWANIS SPRING is at **86.3 m.,** where drinking water can be obtained.

In early autumn this canyon and the upper hillsides in the Laramie Mountains are brilliant with the gold of the aspens, which stand out against the dark green of the lodgepole pines.

Emerging from the western end of the canyon, the highway runs across a stretch of sagebrush-covered land.

LARAMIE, **92.4 m.** (7,165 alt., 8,609 pop.), seat of Albany County, lies at the eastern edge of an extensive plateau known as the Laramie Plains. It is an outfitting point for hunting and fishing excursions into the nearby mountains and valley, and a trade center for cattle and sheep ranches and oil fields. The town was named for Jacques

La Ramée, a French-Canadian free trapper who in the early 1800's operated in the territory that is now Wyoming. He is said to have been killed by Arapaho Indians in 1820 or 1821. His name appears frequently in the American Fur Company correspondence.

The Indians of various tribes that formerly roamed over this area left many artifacts behind them; in the city are a number of extensive private collections of primitive weapons found in the neighborhood.

By 1866, when Ben Holladay's stages were running over the Cherokee Trail on fairly regular schedules, increasing numbers of emigrants followed the ruts worn by the swaying vehicles, and a military post, Fort Sanders, was established not far south of this point for the protection of travelers.

When, early in 1868, the Union Pacific R.R. tracks were nearing the big Laramie River, a small settlement appeared at his place, the inhabitants living in tents, sheds, and shanties, or in the open.

In April the Union Pacific R.R. Company began the sale of lots; within a week more than four hundred were sold or contracted for. Ten days later more than five hundred structures had been erected; some were built of logs, some of crossties with canvas tops, and some of rough lumber.

On May 9 the rails were laid through the town. The next day the first train clanked in and iron rails, crossties, ploughs, scrapers, tents, lumber, and provisions were unloaded. Peddlers also arrived with packs of notions, cooking stoves, crockery, tinware, and liquor. On the same train, riding on flatcars with their household goods, came men, women, and children.

Within three months Laramie's population was about five thousand. A temporary town government had been organized in May and a mayor and trustees elected. After three weeks, however, the mayor had resigned and the rest of the government disintegrated, leaving the inhabitants free to settle their difficulties with revolvers and knives. By August, 20 law-and-order citizens had formed a vigilance committee, which within a week hanged a young desperado called "The Kid." The hanging merely served to stimulate the ruffians to new endeavors; they boasted that they would run the town to suit themselves. Violence increased and a new vigilance committee with three or four hundred members was formed. They planned a complete cleanup, to be accomplished by simultaneous raids on all the notorious hell-holes and by the hanging of the leaders of the peace-breakers. On October 18, 1868, the members of the squads began to gather, one by one, in the saloons and dance halls to which they had been assigned. Unfortunately, an impatient vigilante in the group sent to care for a dance house called the Belle of the West fired a shot prematurely; the alert ruffians immediately grasped the significance of the presence of those who ordinarily shunned their company. In the ensuing affray three men—one from each faction and a neutral— were killed and 15 were wounded. Three of the leading ruffians were captured and immediately hanged from telegraph poles; the next day Big Steve, another badman, received the same treatment. After this affray many of the desperados moved on to other places, but a few allied themselves with the forces that wanted order and became blatant advocates of public virtue.

Out of the vigilance committee was evolved another local government. Late in 1868 the Legislature of Dakota Territory, of which Wyoming was then a part, approved a charter for Laramie and appointed a mayor. But the first legal government was no more successful than its predecessors, and in 1869 the legislative assembly of the new Territory of Wyoming revoked the charter and placed the town under the direct jurisdiction of the Federal Government. Under this regime order was established. On December 10, 1869, the Wyoming Territorial Legislature enacted a law granting suffrage to women, and in March, 1870, the first jury panel in the Territory containing women members was drawn here. Many important newspapers and periodicals of the day sent correspondents and special artists to cover the event. Five women served on the grand jury and six on the petit. The latter jury convicted a man of manslaughter.

In 1873 Laramie was re-incorporated under an act of the Wyoming Territorial Legislature. The town's position aided its development from a terminal camp to a trade and industrial center of importance in the area. Four oil fields are operated within a radius of 50 miles. Today Laramie is a city having many comfortable homes and attractive gardens.

At the corner of 3rd and Garfield Sts. is the SITE OF THE *BOOMERANG* PLANT, now occupied by a warehouse. The office of this newspaper, which was founded in 1881 by Bill Nye, was in the former hayloft of a livery stable; at the first-floor entrance was a sign with the direction: "Twist the Tail of the Gray Mule and Take the Elevator." Nye, whose given names were Edgar Wilson, came to Laramie in 1876 and opened a law office. In the course of his life in this town he served as justice of the peace, superintendent of schools, councilman, editor of the *Sentinel*, and postmaster. The *Boomerang* was founded as an organ of the Republican Party in the State, but it soon became nationally known because of Nye's brand of humor. In time Nye went to work on the New York *World* and later formed a lecture and writing team with James Whitcomb Riley. In 1886 the two men produced *Nye and Riley's Railway Guide*. The authors announced: "What this country needs is a railway guide which shall not be cursed by a plethora of facts or poisoned with information. In other railway guides pleasing fancy, poesy, and literary beauty have been throttled at the very threshold by a wild incontinence of facts, figures, and references to meal stations. For this reason a guide has been built at our own shops and on a new plan. It will not permit information to creep in and mar the reader's enjoyment of the scenery."

The UNIVERSITY OF WYOMING occupies a 96-acre landscaped campus on a rolling hill in the northeastern section of town. It is the only institution of higher learning in the State; all colleges are on this campus. The university, coeducational from the beginning, was established in 1887, largely through the efforts of Col. Stephen W. Downey, a Laramie attorney. (*See also WYOMING GUIDE.*)

Section 6. Laramie to Rawlins, 117.2 m. US 30.

US 30 runs almost due north from LARAMIE, **0 m.** Near the city limits is an excellent view of the surrounding country, with snow-capped Medicine Bow Peak (*see above*) in the Snowy Range 30 miles distant (L), Corner Mountain to the north, and Sheep Mountain to the south. Pine-covered PILOT KNOB tips the Laramie Mountains, just east of the city. It was a landmark for those crossing the Laramie Plains in the days of migration on the Cherokee and Overland Trails. In summer the fields north of Laramie are red with loco weed and, in spots, blue with lupine.

BOSLER, **19.2 m.** (7,074 alt., 75 pop.), on the Laramie Plains, bears the name of a ranchman who formerly owned the Diamond Ranch (R). The ranch was for some time the headquarters of Tom Horn, who was hanged in Cheyenne in 1903, charged with the killing of little Willie Nickell near Iron Mountain, Wyo. Horn, one of Bosler's range riders, was alleged to have shot the Nickell boy and to have wounded the boy's father during a range war between the cattlemen and sheepmen. It was believed that Horn was paid by some of the big cattlemen to keep the range clear of sheepmen.

US 30 crosses the Laramie River at Bosler and swings northwest past Cooper Lake (L).

At ROCK CREEK, **37 m.,** in 1865 Indians attacked a camp occupied by members of a train of 75 wagons with which an English family named Fletcher was traveling. The Fletchers were camped on the banks of the stream a short distance from the main party; the Indians killed the mother and wounded the father. The two daughters, Mary, 13, and Lizzie, 2, were captured by the Indians, while the three sons escaped. Mary, who had been wounded by several arrows, saw an Indian seize Lizzie and ride off with her. Mary was carried off to the mountains, where the squaws were waiting; from the Indian camp she watched the burning of the wagons in the valley below. The girl was given Indian garments and, like other prisoners, had to care for ponies and gather firewood for the squaws of her captors.

In the spring of 1866 the band came to a white trading camp in charge of a man named Hanger. Despite the fact that she had been ordered to keep out of sight of white men, Mary Fletcher walked into Hanger's tent and asked in English if he had any soap. An Indian who overheard her knocked her to the floor and carried her away; but the squaws, who were jealous of her, aided her in communicating with Hanger. He gave the Indians a large amount of cash, a good horse, and a gun to obtain her release and placed her in the charge of an Indian agent who took her to Fort Laramie. She was soon sent to friends in Illinois. In later years, while on a trip to Salt Lake City, she found her father, who had recovered from his wounds.

Thirty-five years after the Rock Creek raid, some Indians from the Wind River Reservation came to Casper, Wyo. With them was a white woman wearing Indian garb, and speaking only the Arapaho language. She attracted the attention of some Casper citizens, who learned from the reservation authorities that the woman had been captured by Indians when she was two years old, and was married to John Brokenhorn, an Arapaho. This story, published in a Casper newspaper, came to the attention of Mary Fletcher, who went to the Arapaho reservation and identified Mrs. Brokenhorn as her sister; the white woman refused to leave her Indian home.

Over the railroad tracks, (L) north of Rock Creek, are large concrete snow sheds that were erected by the Union Pacific R.R. after a severe blizzard in 1916 had tied up overland trains at this point for several days.

ROCK RIVER, **39.2 m.** (6,892 alt., 260 pop.), is a livestock-shipping point and a trade center for many ranches. Here in 1916 two cowboys, while excavating a caved-in cellarway on property owned by a man named Taylor, unearthed glass jars containing several thousand dollars' worth of old gold coins. Taylor claimed the money and recovered it through legal proceedings that were carried to the Wyoming Supreme Court. According to one theory, the money had been hidden in the cellar by an innkeeper who had occupied the place and who was not seen after he was reported to have left for a visit to his homeland, Germany. Another theory was that the coins were loot from a stagecoach robbery.

At **42 m.** (L) is the SITE OF THE WILCOX ROBBERY of a Union Pacific train. On June 2, 1899, two men flagged an express train, pointed revolvers at the engineer, and ordered him to take the train across the bridge beyond Wilcox and stop. The men blew up the bridge with dynamite in order to prevent the arrival of the second section of the train, which was due in 10 minutes. They then forced the engineer to run the train two miles farther west, where they looted the cars, blew open the express safe, and escaped with $60,000 in unsigned bank notes. More than a hundred pounds of dynamite were found near the scene on the following day. Though pursued by a posse, the robbers made their escape on horseback into Montana. "Flat Nose George" Currie was supposed to have been responsible for the crime.

West of Rock River US 30 runs through rolling, short-grass country where great herds of buffalo once roamed. Some of the old buffalo wallows can be seen from the highway.

At COMO BLUFFS, **52.2 m.**, is the CREATION MUSEUM, in a store. Many fossils and relics are on display.

Right from Como Bluffs on a dirt road to the COMO BLUFFS FOSSIL BEDS in the bluffs, **1.3 m.**, from which in 1877 was taken the first complete dinosaur skeleton; two others were discovered in Colorado the same year. The largest herbivorous dinosaur skeleton found here was, when assembled, 70 feet long. Fourteen complete skeletons have been recovered here since 1880; they have been sent to the leading natural history museums of the world.

MEDICINE BOW, **58.1 m.** (6,563 alt., 264 pop.), provided the experiences that enabled Owen Wister to write *The Virginian*. Wister had ridden the range with the Two Bar outfit at one time. The first scene in the book was laid in Medicine Bow; here the narrator stepped off the train and was met by the Virginian. Later in the day he witnessed the first clash between the Virginian and Trampas, when during a card game Trampas called the Southerner a name that, according to the custom of the day, was omitted from the book, but which caused the spectators to look anxiously for cover. The Virginian stared at his enemy for a moment and then drawled, "When you call me that, smile," a remark that entered the popular speech during the days of the book's great popularity.

The town has grown little since the days when Wister knew it but local life is now quieter.

1. Right from Medicine Bow on a dirt road to the PETRIFIED FOREST, **30 m.**, covering 2,560 acres and judged by scientists to be 50 million years old.

2. Right from Medicine Bow on a dirt road to the EPSOM SALT BEDS, **11 m.**, one of the natural wonders of the State.

West of Medicine Bow US 30 runs through country occasionally dotted with bands of sheep and sheepherders' wagons.

HANNA, **78.2 m.** (6,777 alt., 1,500 pop.), is owned by the Union Pacific R.R., for which it supplies coal. The coal deposits of the area, discovered by Frémont in 1843, were a decisive factor in determining the course of the railroad in this area; early plans routed the railroad along the Oregon Trail. The coal is sub-bituminous and burns so freely that locomotives using it throw out cinders that have frequently set the grass of the plains on fire.

Many fossils, including the bones of dinosaurs, are found in the rocks west of Hanna; they belonged to the last of the species.

Left from Hanna on a partly graveled road to the town of ELK MOUNTAIN, **17 m.** (7,100 alt., 54 pop.), on the Medicine Bow River. The town is picturesquely situated at the base of ELK MOUNTAIN (11,162 alt.), a landmark of the covered-wagon days. What is said to have been the first band of sheep brought into Wyoming was trailed from California to the Sederlin ranch south of the town.

a. Right from Elk Mountain **6 m.** on an improved dirt road to the Quealey ranch, the SITE OF FORT HALLECK, established in July 1862; it was named for Maj. Gen. Henry W. Halleck, who was appointed commander of the Missouri Department of the U. S. Army in 1861 and became General in Chief in 1862. The post was a stage and express station of the Overland stages. It was situated at a strategic point and consisted of several substantial buildings. The post was constructed when the mail route was transferred (*see Section 5*). Escorts were furnished from the fort for the surveyors of the Union Pacific R.R. route. In February 1864, the post store was turned into a hospital to care for a party of 28 soldiers who had been caught in one of the worst blizzards of the area's early history. Two of the men died, and many of them had frozen hands and feet.

b. Left from Elk Mountain about **1 m.** on a rough road to a point near the CABIN OF JOHN SUBLETTE, an early settler believed by some to have been a nephew of William L. Sublette. Hand-made furniture and other old relics remain in the cabin. (*Specific directions for reaching cabin obtainable in Elk Mountain.*)

At **87 m.** is the junction with a dirt road.

Left on this road to DANA, **0.5 m.**, a small station on the Union Pacific R.R., near which in 1934 an attempt was made, by an ex-convict named Lovett, to rob the Portland Rose Overland Limited. Lovett succeeded in derailing the locomotive, a baggage car, and one coach; but owing to the fact that the coach was filled with marines, who swarmed outside as soon as the wreck occurred, he beat a hasty retreat without robbing the passengers. The fireman on the train, who was almost totally buried under the coal, was quickly extricated by passengers. Lovett was subsequently captured.

At **102.6 m.** is the junction with a graveled road.

Right on this road to FORT FRED STEELE, **1 m.** (6,480 alt., 139 pop.), a village that bears the name of a military post established during the construction of the Union Pacific R.R. The post was occupied from June 20, 1868, to August 7, 1886. On Sept. 14, 1879, Major Thomas F. Thornburg led a party from the post to rescue Nathan C. Meeker, Indian agent for the White River Utes in northwestern Colorado. When within about 24 miles of the agency the relief party was attacked by Indians; Major Thornburg and 12 of his men were killed and 47 others were wounded. The Utes set fire to the brush along Milk River, and destroyed all supply wagons. A scout, Joe Rankin, escaped, crawled through ravines, and, obtaining a horse, carried the news of the disaster to Rawlins; he made the 164-mile trip in 24 hours. More troops were sent but meanwhile Meeker had been killed, and the women and children from the agency had been carried off by the Indians.

Here US 30 again crosses the North Platte River and continues across rolling plains.

At **107.9 m.** (R) is the SITE OF BENTON, perhaps the most notorious mushroom town that sprang up during the construction of the Union Pacific. It was the first terminus established west of Laramie; within two weeks the place was occupied by about three thousand people. According to Beadle's *Undeveloped West:* "There were regular squares arranged into five yards, a city government of mayor and alderman, a daily paper, and a volume of ordinances for the public health. It was the end of the freight and passenger, and the beginning of the construction division; twice every day immense trains arrived and departed, and stages left for Utah, Montana, and Idaho; all the goods formerly hauled across the plains came here by rail and were reshipped, and for ten hours daily the streets were filled with Indians, gamblers, 'Cappers', and saloon keepers, merchants, miners, and mulewhackers. The streets were eight inches deep in white dust as I entered the city of canvas tents and polehouses; the suburbs appeared as banks of dirty white lime, and a new arrival with black clothes looked like nothing so much as a cockroach struggling through a flour barrel. The great institution of Benton was the 'Big Tent', sometimes called the 'Gamblers' Tent. This structure was a nice frame building 100 feet long and 40 feet wide, covered with canvas and conveniently floored for dancing, to which and gambling it was entirely devoted. It was moved successively to all the mushroom terminus cities."

PARCO, **110.9 m.** (6,592 alt., 727 pop.), is variously known as "the million-dollar town" and as "an oasis in the desert." It is completely modern from its waterworks to its 80-room Spanish-type hotel, which occupies an entire block. The principal buildings of the town are grouped around three sides of a large expanse of lawn, the plaza.

RAWLINS, **117.2 m.** (6,755 alt., 4,868 pop.), seat of Carbon County, is a distribution and supply point for operators of sheep ranches, oil fields, coal mines, and lime and stone quarries. "Rawlins Red" paint, whose basic ingredient is a natural pigment found in the nearby hills, is manufactured here. The product is used particularly for painting roofs. In 1874 a carload of the product was shipped east for use on Brooklyn Bridge, then under construction.

Gen. John A. Rawlins, for whom the town was named, served with distinction during the Civil War and became Secretary of War in 1869, but died shortly afterward. The town came into existence with the arrival of the Union Pacific R.R. because the site had an excellent spring, a rarity in this arid region.

The usual tent town sprang up here; in the wake of the construction workers, and the settlers who hoped to profit by serving them, came the gamblers and badmen. Crimes of the neighborhood received a large amount of publicity. In June, 1880, George Parrott—"Big Nose George"—and Charlie Burris—"Dutch Charley"—with two other men attempted to derail a westbound Union Pacific pay car by drawing spikes that held some of the rails in place. A passing section boss noticed the loose rails, flagged the train, and then notified the sheriff's office. A posse, headed by Tip Vincent and Ed Widowfield, was quickly formed. The leaders became separated from the other men but found the trail of the bandits and followed it to a grove of willows, where they discovered a campfire. While testing the ashes to find whether they were still warm, both men were killed from ambush by the bandits, who seized the mounts of the officers and fled farther into the hills.

Four months later word was received from Miles City, Mont., that the robbers had been arrested on charges of murder and robbery in that State. "Big Nose," while under the influence of liquor, boasted of his Wyoming escape, and he and "Dutch Charley" were turned over to Wyoming authorities. The latter was taken off a train at Carbon by a group of local citizens and hanged to a telegraph pole.

"Big Nose George" was tried here and sentenced to death by hanging. Because of his desperate character his legs were shackled at all times. One day, however, he managed to file through one of the shackle bolts with a knife, and that evening used the shackles to fell the jailer. The jailer's wife closed the door on the bandit and gave alarm.

Before midnight a mob formed and took "Big Nose George" from the jail. The bandit was made to climb upon a big box beside a telegraph pole with a rope around his neck; when he would not jump, the box was kicked from under him, but the fall broke the rope. Another noose was applied and this time the bandit was ordered to climb a ladder; when he reached the top he wrapped his arms around the telegraph pole and hung on until he dropped in exhaustion. Dr. John E. Osborne, later Governor of Wyoming, officially pronounced him dead, and was permitted to retain patches of hide from George's body, which he had made into a pair of shoes. The Rawlins city records reveal that 24 ruffians were notified that night to leave town within a day if they did not want the same treatment. The next day the railroad agent reported that 24 tickets had been sold for the morning train west.

Owing to the presence of Rawlins Spring, the first settlements were made on the south side of the railroad tracks. Within a year, however, many people were living on the north side, where most of the city stands today.

The STATE PENITENTIARY, on the northern side of town, has landscaped grounds. Inmates of the institution formerly made brooms and shirts; they now manufacture woolen goods, including blankets, from wool produced on the surrounding ranches. The penitentiary has a lethal gas chamber for administration of the death penalty; the system was adopted by the legislature in 1936.

US 287 (R) leads north from Granger to a junction with the unnumbered dirt road running through South Pass (*see ALTERNATE ROUTE*).

Section 7. Rawlins to Idaho Line, 249.8 m. to US 30 and US 30N.

West of RAWLINS, **0 m.**, US 30 runs slightly southwest and climbs to CRESTON, **26.5 m.** (7,178 alt.), on the Continental Divide. The approach to the Divide is so gradual that it is difficult to recognize the highest point. For approximately a hundred miles west of Rawlins, US 30 runs through barren and, for the most part, uninhabited country. (*Few filling stations or other facilities available along this part of route.*) Bridger Pass, used by the Overland Stages after 1862, is about 25 miles southwest of Creston.

Left from Creston on State 87, which has an oiled gravel roadbed and runs due south through a land of sagebrush and cactus. BAGGS, **51 m.** (6,245 alt., 192 pop.), named for Maggie Baggs, an early settler in the valley, is on the banks of the Little Snake River near the Colorado Line.

Owing to its isolated position, Baggs, during the 1880's and 1890's, was a favorite rendezvous and hide-out for badmen of every description—train and stage robbers, horse thieves, bank robbers, and killers.

The notorious Powder Springs gang of outlaws, led by Butch Cassidy, came to the town to celebrate successful hold-ups in surrounding States. Their biggest haul, about $35,000 in gold taken in Winnemucca, Nev., caused a celebration lasting several days. The inhabitants, while not terrorized by the outlaws, nevertheless experienced considerable uneasiness until the event was over. Baggs, like other Snake River towns of the area, profited by the celebrations because the gang, even when engaged in amusing itself, took no unnecessary risks, including that of wearing out its welcome in the towns where it loafed. On reaching Baggs, the leaders would appoint one man to care for the horses and to keep them ready for a quick get-away, if that should be necessary; another would guard the arms and ammunition, which was stacked in an orderly fashion. The leaders took turns in remaining sober during the spree in order to prevent excesses that might cause innocent bystanders to suffer. And it was a rule that ample compensation must be made to the owners of local property destroyed by accident.

Powder Springs, the gang headquarters, was on a mountain side about 40 miles to the west. Cassidy and Longabaugh in time fled to South America, where they are said to have been killed after a pack-train robbery.

Visible west of Creston is the RED DESERT, where the colorings change hourly with the light. Although the desert seems barren and worthless, hundreds of thousands of sheep are wintered here annually.

WAMSUTTER, **40.5 m.** (6,709 alt., 150 pop.), ships large amounts of wool and has extensive shearing jugs (pens).

North of the highway, for nearly a hundred miles, is a great stretch of sand dunes, many of them a hundred feet high. They shift constantly with the prevailing winds in a direction a little north of east. Mirages are frequent. The region has great beauty in spite of its barrenness; every shade of red is here—russet, brick, vermilion—in addition to grays, browns, greens, and purples. Late in the afternoon the landscape is bathed in a purple haze.

Left from Wamsutter on a dirt road (*guides advisable*) to weird, eroded formations of gumbo clay called ADOBE TOWNS, **30 m.**

On the desert west of Wamsutter are still many traces of the early trails. Occasionally remnants of wagons, human and animal skeletons, Indian artifacts, and the like are found.

POINT OF ROCKS, **84.6 m.** (6,509 alt.), is a ghost town named for the rocks that rise 1,100 feet above the railroad tracks. In the vicinity are sulphur springs. In the 1870's Point of Rocks was the nearest railroad station to the South Pass and Sweetwater districts, and was an outfitting station for the mines. In 1870 a daily stage, mail, and express line operated between here and a point near the eastern end of South Pass. The Wells Fargo Overland Express Company maintained offices at the station and carried on a large business. The buildings, chiefly adobe, stood until the late 1880's.

1. Left from Point of Rocks, **25 m.,** on a dim, unimproved trail to the SITE OF THE BARREL SPRINGS STAGE STATION of 1862. The trail that carried the Overland Stage dipped slightly south in the area because of the springs.

Beadle wrote of the region: "For sixty miles on Bitter Creek, Wyoming, the soil is a mass of clay, or sand, and alkali—a horrible and irreclaimable desert which has made the place a byword. . . . On the stage routes across such tracts the animals labor through a cloud of dust and the coach drags heavily, the wheels often causing a disagreeable cry in the sand and soda, while the passengers endure as best they can the irritation to eye and nostril, and the slime formed upon the person by dust and sweat. This penetrating alkaline dust sitts in at the smallest crevice, and even the clothing in a close valise is often covered with it." A popular local phrase describing such desert areas was: "A jack rabbit can't cross it without a haversack, while an immigrant crow sheds tears at the sight."

2. Right from Point of Rocks on a trail that nearly parallels US 30 to the REMAINS OF THE ALMOND STAGE STATION, **4 m.**

3. Right from Point of Rocks on a dirt road (*sometimes impassable; carry ropes*) that leads to large SAND DUNES, **30 m.**

ROCK SPRINGS, **110.6 m.** (6,271 alt., 8,440 pop.), is the railroad station and United Airline stop nearest to the Jackson Hole recreational region (*planes to area available at municipal airport*). It is also an outfitting point for big-game hunting and fishing expeditions.

The Rock Springs, for which the town is named, were discovered by a Pony Express rider while making a wide detour to avoid a band of Indians. The water, which is impregnated with minerals, comes from a rock at what is now known as No. 6 mine, just northwest of the town. There are few sources of potable drinking water between Rawlins and Green River. An Overland Stage station was established northwest of the place and in 1866 Archie and Duncan Blair, the founders of the town, built a rock bridge and a stone cabin opposite the stage station for the accommodation of travelers and emigrants. The REMAINS OF THE BLAIRS' TRADING POST, which was surrounded by a stockade, still stand. Becky Thomas, the station master here, charged 10 cents a head for watering horses, and the Blairs served venison steak and coffee to hungry travelers. Back of the station is a great rock that was the usual emigrant register.

The first settlers built their shacks in whatever spots suited their fancy and the early town looked as though it had been scattered from a pepperbox. Though the original lack of design has been corrected the town is still picturesque, with Parisian bakeries, Greek candy shops, and Jewish markets to emphasize its international character.

Rock Springs is primarily a coal-mining town. Most of the males in the population, which is made up of people of 47 nationalities, work in the mines; these have been owned and operated by the Union Pacific R.R. since 1868.

The valuable coal beds of Wyoming were the cause of considerable scandal between 1903 and 1906 because of collusion between railroad agents, General Land Office agents, and local officials to turn over public lands rich in coal to the railroad corporations.

As the result of a miners' strike in 1875, Chinese workmen were brought into the area. In 10 years Chinatown contained ten or twelve hundred people, chiefly men, and was much larger than the white settlement. At this time San Francisco had become a center of anti-Chinese agitation, which spread throughout the West wherever the Chinese offered labor and business competition because of their willingness to accept wages lower than those demanded by the whites. In 1885 a mob of white miners attacked the Chinese here, burned their buildings, including a large clubhouse, killed 30, and attempted to drive them all out of the area. A detachment of troops, rushed in to preserve order, remained here for some time. Chinatown was later rebuilt and the Chinese Government called on the U. S. Government to pay indemnities to the relatives of those killed in the riot.

About 1886 two old prospectors "salted" some nearby sagebrush country with rough diamonds. They interested a group of financiers in the property, led blindfolded inspectors to the place, and later succeeded in fleecing several people, including Horace Greeley and one of the Tiffanys; they obtained about half a million dollars before the fraud was discovered by a cook with a Government surveying party, who kicked from an anthill a diamond that plainly showed traces of a cutter's tool.

An annual International Night, first held about 1924, is given here in May; in addition to a program conducted by people of various nationalities, there is an exhibition of relics and examples of handicraft.

At Rock Springs is the junction with US 187 (*see SIDE ROUTE A*).

Southwest of Rock Springs, PILOT BUTTE (R), a trail landmark called "the Sphinx of the Desert," can be seen from the highway. US 30 continues westward, crossing Green River Valley, in which, to the north, is the site of the first big Rocky Mountains rendezvous of white traders and trappers; employes of William Ashley's company met him here in July, 1825. This valley played an important part in the history of the fur trade of the West, being in an area that was a popular hunting and trapping ground of both Indians and whites.

Small truck farms and sheep ranches are widely scattered in Green River Valley. The ranches with their barns and corrals are typical of those in the West. Oats, alfalfa, corn, and a variety of other vegetables, cultivated with the aid of irrigation, are the chief products of the farms. In the valley wild flowers are numerous, the more common varieties being Indian paintbrush, rock and sand lilies, and bluebells. Wild currants are the only edible berries growing in abundance along the riverbanks. Cactus, greasewood, sagebrush, mesquite, and grama grass are found on the hills and in canyons. The region near the river is arid, rocky, and sparsely wooded. Cottontail and jack rabbits, prairie dogs, gophers, chipmunks, coyotes, badgers, weasels, beavers, deer, and antelope are seen in the region. Trout, grayling, whitefish, and squawfish are found in the river.

GREEN RIVER, **125.7 m.** (6,100 alt., 2,589 pop.), seat of Sweetwater County, is on the east bank of the river of the same name. It is surrounded by picturesque cliffs and strange formations, the most prominent of which, CASTLE ROCK, rises a thousand feet above the river. A path beginning at the edge of the city (R) leads to the summit and circles the rock. TOLLGATE ROCK, just north of Castle Rock, was named for the tollgate established in a passage widened by the Mormons.

The Overland Trail crossed Green River at a point south of the city.

The site for the town was selected by speculators in April, 1868; in July it had been platted, lots had been sold, and houses were being built; by September there was a population of two thousand people.

When the Union Pacific tracks reached the town, however, the railroad company did not do what the promoters had naively hoped it would—show interest in the supposed strategic position of the place and buy the townsite at inflated prices; the company already had plenty of land to be exploited for townsites. Nor did the company establish a rail-end camp here, which would have produced a temporary boom. Nonetheless, the town grew gradually in importance, justifying the first settlers' faith in its position.

Here is the small HUTTON MUSEUM (*private; visited by appointment*), containing fossils and relics of the Indians and early settlers.

Green River, although reported by Bancroft to have been named for a partner of William Ashley, was so named because of its apparent color, which comes from the green shale over which it flows. The name is a translation of that given by the Spanish. The Crow called the stream the Seeds-ke-deé-agie, or Prairie Hen.

While calm enough here, farther down stream the river is rapid and dangerous, a fit feeder of the Colorado, into which it drains. The Green and the Colorado Rivers run through canyons for most of their course; in 1,100 miles there is a drop of 5,000 feet, as a result of which there are 365 major rapids and quite as many minor ones. The stream, be-

tween the town of Green River and Boulder Dam, has been continuously traversed only a few times—the first in 1869 by an elaborately
equipped party under the leadership of Maj. J. W. Powell. Two pho-
tographers, Ellsworth and Emory Kolb, made the journey in 1911. On
October 3, 1936, a young filling-station attendant, Buzz Holmstrom, left
this town in an attempt to reach Boulder Dam alone; he arrived at his
goal on November 25.

Green River was usually forded by travelers using South Pass at
some point near the mouth of the Sandy, north of US 30 (*see ALTER-
NATE ROUTE*).

Left from the town of Green River on a dirt road to FIREHOLE BASIN,
0.5 m., whose rugged and picturesque beauty is reminiscent of that of the Grand
Canyon.

At **152.6 m.** US 30 divides into US 30N, leading northwest, and
US 30S, leading southwest.

Left here on US 30S. CHURCH BUTTES, **10 m.** (L), composed of blue and
black sandstone, rise 75 feet above the level of the surrounding hills and resemble
a cathedral.

LYMAN, **27.6 m.** (6,693 alt., 377 pop.), whose population is predominantly
Mormon, has a successful co-operative marketing association.

At **32.6 m.** is FORT BRIDGER (6,657 alt., 100 pop.), a settlement on Black's
Fork of the Green River.

On the grounds of old FORT BRIDGER (L), now owned by the State, are several
well-preserved army post buildings and a PONY EXPRESS STABLE. In the little
museum (*free*) are such relics as ox yokes, wagon bows, old maps, Indian trophies,
furniture, books, and rifles.

Fort Bridger was established as a trading post by Jim Bridger, one of the most
picturesque figures in the history of the American fur trade. He was born in Virginia in 1804, was apprenticed to a St. Louis blacksmith for a period, and in 1822
went west as a trapper with the Andrew Henry party. From then on until his
death in 1881, Bridger was constantly in view; the vast range of his wanderings
and the speed with which he moved were amazing. Everyone who traveled between
the Missouri and the Pacific Northwest seemed to meet him. After the fur trade
had declined—in part with the substitution of silk hats for beaver—Bridger became
a scout and guide. Every post commander desired his services because he never
forgot the features of any region he had traversed, and he had visited most of
the West. He had, moreover, acute sensitivity that enabled him to see, smell, or
feel the presence of Indians when no one around him did. In time no officer dared
to disregard his warnings on the subject. As he became the oldest white inhabitant
of the Rockies he acquired an increasing scorn for tenderfeet, perhaps because
his stories of the wonders of the Great Salt Lake and Yellowstone regions were
disregarded in the early days; he in time mingled fact with tall tales to the utter
confusion of newcomers.

In the course of his life Bridger handled enormous quantities of furs and at
various times announced his intention of retiring with a fortune; but he was not
a businessman and lived his final years in poverty. Like most other men who had
tasted wilderness life even for a brief time, he was unhappy away from it and
could never settle down in any spot. He had an Indian wife and lived as the
Indians did, eating and sleeping when he felt like doing so, without regard to
conventional hours for such activities.

One of Bridger's business ventures was the founding of a trading post at this key spot. In a letter written in December 1843, probably dictated since Bridger was practically illiterate, Bridger told Pierre Chouteau, Jr., the St. Louis merchant: "I have established a small fort with a blacksmith shop and a supply of iron in the road of the emigrants on Black's Fork of Green River which promises fairly. They, in coming out, are generally well supplied with money, but by the time they get there are in want of all kinds of supplies. Horses, provisions, smith work, etc., bring ready cash from them, and should I receive the goods hereby ordered will do a considerable business in that way with them. The same establishment trades with the Indians in the neighborhood, who have mostly a good number of beaver among them."

But Bridger could not stay at home long enough to run his post, so he took a partner, a Mexican named Louis Vasquez. Vasquez seems to have been little more satisfactory than Bridger as a post trader—at least from the standpoint of travelers on the Oregon Trail. The emigrants would count eagerly on collecting news of road conditions ahead of them and on supplying their needs at this post, the first west of Laramie; but frequently, in the midst of the migration seasons, trains would find no one here when they arrived. The blacksmith shop, which could have had plenty of business, was nearly always without a smith. The partnership continued, however, until 1854 and additions were sometimes made to the facilities. Meanwhile other trappers settled in the neighborhood.

In July 1847 the first Mormon caravan, led by Brigham Young, camped here for two days of rest and repairs before proceeding to the Great Salt Lake, where, as J. W. Gunnison wrote, they were to "endure perils and tribulations for a time, before their final triumph over fear."

Bridger had none of the contemporary prejudices against polygamy and for a time he had friendly relations with the Mormons. The causes of the feud that culminated in the Mormon occupation of Fort Bridger are obscure. There are stories that the Saints captured the place because they were jealous of the flourishing business done at Fort Bridger; this, however, does not seem in line with Mormon procedure. There are other stories to the effect that they took it because they believed that Bridger was selling ammunition to the Indians to be used against the Saints.

The relations between the Federal Government and the Mormons had become strained; the Saints had "left the United States" to settle in Mexican land but had arrived in the Great Salt Lake basin to find that the United States was taking over the territory. Eastern enemies continued their persecution of the Mormons because of their non-orthodox customs and beliefs and were determined to force "gentile" government on the territory.

The discovery of gold in California brought a rush of non-Mormon emigrants through the territory that Young had chosen because of its isolation; while the Saints profited by catering to these travelers, the President and the Twelve, as the church council was called, soon saw the demoralizing effects of the influx of non-Mormons, some of whom insisted on settling in the area. Utah Territory was established in 1850, to the dismay of the Saints who had dreamed of an independent State of Deseret; settlement on the land became subject to Federal control, and a tactless non-Mormon Territorial judge was appointed. Friction between the Federal Government and the Mormons increased rapidly.

In the meantime the Mormon Church had been pushing its plans for filling up the territory with Mormon converts from abroad and was establishing way stations to provide aid and provisions for its emigrant trains. In the fall of 1853 the Annual Conference of the Church commissioned Orson Hyde to lead a company to this neighborhood to establish such a station. Hyde and a small group left on November 2 and selected a place of settlement nine miles upstream from Bridger's post, naming it Fort Supply. Behind them came a second company bringing horses, mules, cattle, and wagons loaded with seed, farming implements, and other supplies. A two-story log building with wings, large enough to house the entire population, was immediately erected.

In 1853 or 1854 Bridger moved away from the post and the primitive buildings were burned. Bridger said the Mormons drove him out; he asserted that he had held the land under a Mexican grant, but the Mormons insisted that they had paid for the land.

In 1857 President James Buchanan appointed a Governor and other Federal officers for Utah Territory, and a military force was assigned for their protection in taking office. The troops proceeded west under Col. Albert Sidney Johnston. When Johnston and his forces arrived here they found little but ruins in the valley. The Mormon colonists had been recalled to Utah, and had burned all the buildings and such goods as could not be moved. Colonel Johnston established winter quarters on Black's Fork about a mile and a half south of the former trading post, calling the place Camp Scott. In June 1858 a detachment of Johnston's troops took possession of the Bridger site and built a military post. The tact of the new Governor, and Brigham Young's sensible acceptance of the inevitable, had quieted the Utah situation; but suspicious enemies of the Mormons wanted a military post in the area as a threat. It was maintained almost continuously until 1890. Bridger later filed claims against the Federal Government for having taken possession of his land; the Mormons did also, but neither of the claims was allowed.

It was at Fort Bridger, in July 1846 that the Donner party left the established Oregon and California Trail to take the route advised in an open letter addressed "To all California Emigrants now on the Road." They had seen this letter, written by a man unknown to them, near South Pass; the writer, L. W. Hastings, said that he had found a shorter and safer route to California across the desert around Great Salt Lake. George Donner, leader of the party of 81 people, had sold his large fertile farms east of the Mississippi and was taking his family to California to settle; with him were friends, neighbors, and some emigrants who had joined the group on the road. Half the members were less than 20 years old. Donner had excellent equipment for the undertaking and carried about $10,000 in cash in a secret pocket. Only Mrs. Donner opposed taking advice on this serious subject of routes from a stranger. Hastings had promised to be at Fort Bridger to conduct emigrants, but when the Donner Party arrived they found that he had already gone and had left word for late comers to follow the tracks he was making with the first party.

The message said that pasturage ahead was good and that there was only one stretch where an unusually long journey must be made to find water at the end of the day. The emigrants set off from Fort Bridger in high spirits, but before long ran into difficulties. They lost the tracks left by Hastings' party but pressed on, each day hopeful that they would soon find the wonderful new short cut. By the time the leaders were convinced that they were in serious trouble, the season was so late that they dared not turn back to the beaten road. One calamity after another overtook them—murder, illness, and dissension. Donner was seriously injured and the minds of some of the emigrants broke under the strain. At the end of October, when they were near the summit of the pass through the Sierra, they were caught in blizzards and had to stop. Windbreaks were erected and dugouts made. Supplies gave out completely. At length a small, hardy group managed to reach the Sacramento Valley and summon help. The story of the winter will never be completely known. Some members of the party finally ate the flesh of those who had died; the survivors (33 left the camp but 3 of these died on the way to the valley) were either too young or were too much afraid of public opinion to give details of what occurred.

It was in the neighborhood of the post in the fall of 1843 that the mysterious Indian woman believed by some historians to have been Sacajawea, who had fled from the neighborhood of St. Vrain's Fort after her husband had been killed, left Frémont's party, with which she had been traveling, in the hope of finding her

THE SAND HILLS

THE LONELY TRAIL

BUILDING THE UNION PACIFIC

relatives nearby. This woman was often near the post in later years. (*See ALTER-NATE ROUTE.*)

Beyond Fort Bridger, for a few years after 1842, the Oregon Trail turned northwest, crossed to Little Muddy Creek, crossed the northern end of the Bear River Divide, and then followed Bear River toward Fort Hall. Later travelers omitted the dip down to Fort Bridger and took the Sublette Cut-off, which went due west from the Big Sandy (*see ALTERNATE ROUTE*). (*For the Mormon and California Trails beyond this point see THE CALIFORNIA TRAIL, American Guide Series.*)

US 30 swings northwest from the junction with US 30S.

At **154.6 m.** (R) is GRANGER (6,240 alt., 135 pop.), the trade center of a large sheep- and cattle-growing area. The OVERLAND STAGE STATION established here is still standing.

The stage stations of the early days were rough-and-ready affairs. The owners, lacking competition, made little effort to satisfy the guests who were forced to depend on their services. Richard Burton's account of his trip to Utah in 1860 is a series of diatribes against the accommodations—or lack of them—at the halting places and against the miserable substitutes for food he managed to buy from the agents and their indifferent wives. Some coaches drove day and night with the passengers eventually sleeping upright from exhaustion. Other coaches halted at night and the passengers were allowed to stretch out in dormitories having tiers of bunks, usually covered with filthy quilts and buffalo robes. Flies swarmed everywhere. Under the circumstances it is not surprising that whiskey was the chief commodity sold at the stage stations.

Just north of Granger on US 30N is the junction with the South Pass unnumbered dirt road, part of an alternate route between Ogallala, Neb., and this point (*see ALTERNATE ROUTE*).

US 30N here runs through long stretches of open country used chiefly for livestock grazing.

OPAL, **182.2 m.** (6,668 alt., 147 pop.), is a trade and shipping point, so named because of the fact that opals have been found in the vicinity. There are large wool-shearing pens here.

DIAMONDSVILLE, **195.8 m.** (6,885 alt., 812 pop.), a coal-mining town, is virtually a suburb of Kemmerer. In 1868 Harrison Church, a trapper who became a prospector, discovered coal on the Hamsfork, and built a cabin a mile below the site of the present town. Later a company was formed to develop the mines. Coal mining was for a time the only industry in the vicinity, but now oil production and sheep raising are important. The nearby valleys are dotted with farms and cattle ranches.

KEMMERER, **197.4 m.** (6,927 alt., 1,884 pop.), is the Scranton of the area. The town was named for M. S. Kemmerer, who invested money in developing the coal of the region. Kemmerer is an important outfitting point for fishing and big-game hunting expeditions.

Right from Kemmerer on graveled US 89 to EMIGRANT SPRINGS, **26 m.**, used by travelers on the Oregon Trail. Nearby are the graves of several emigrants, marked by stone slabs. Sagebrush five or six feet high covers the graves.

At **40 m.** is the SITE OF A MORMON FERRY on Green River used largely by travelers on Sublette's Cut-off.

NAMES HILL, **42 m.** (L), has the names of trappers and emigrants dating back to 1820, when the first white men entered the area. Even Jim Bridger's is among those inscribed in early days.

FOSSIL, **207.2 M.,** is a small post office.

Left from Fossil on a dirt road to the FOSSIL FISH BED, **2 m.** (*guides available*), one of the largest known deposits of fossilized fish in the world. The formation is Tertiary.

West of SAGE, **221.4 m.** (6,332 alt.), US 30N turns north and runs through a rolling country that is used chiefly for grazing; the highway follows Bear River.

At Fort Bridger (*see above*) the Oregon Trail swung northwest toward this stream, which one branch of the trail followed in this area.

At **240.6 m.** (L) is COKEVILLE (6,191 alt., 430 pop.), on Smith's Fork of the Bear River. The town is the trade and shipping center of a sheep-raising district. Coke ovens for filtering illuminating gas were put into operation here at an early date.

At **249.8 m.** US 30N crosses the Idaho Line.

Idaho

Wyo. Line—Montpelier—Pocatello—Burley—Twin Falls—Boise—Ore.
Line, 451 m. US 30N and US 30.

Union Pacific R.R. parallels route throughout. Bear Lake Stages follow route between Montpelier and Pocatello, Union Pacific Stages between Pocatello and Boise.

Surfaced highway.

Accommodations chiefly in larger towns.

US 30N runs through the southeastern part of Idaho, an area of lakes, rivers, creeks, and small valleys. The valleys are farmed and the uplands used for grazing. West of Pocatello the route roughly parallels the Snake River; it traverses a dry-farming belt and also large arid sections.

Section 8. Wyoming Line to Pocatello, 120 m. US 30N.

US 30N runs through Bear Lake Valley. Little of the area lies at an elevation of less than six thousand feet; winters are severe and summers cool. In the Caribou National Forest (R) and the Cache National Forest (L) most of the old-growth timber has been exhausted, and the somewhat denuded watersheds offer the same problems in erosion and overgrazing that exist in many other parts of the State.

BORDER, **0 m.** (6,100 alt.), is a small village practically on the Wyoming Line.

MONTPELIER, **22 m.** (5,941 alt., 2,436 pop.), is the largest town in this area. Founded in 1864, it was first known as Clover Creek and later as Belmont; but when Brigham Young visited the town, he renamed it in honor of the capital of Vermont, his native State.

Left from Montpelier on State 35 into one of the chief recreation areas of eastern Idaho. PARIS, **9 m.** (825 pop.), has finer buildings than any other small town in the State. Here (L) is a typical TABERNACLE of the Church of Jesus Christ of Latter-Day Saints (Mormon). The dominant sect in eastern and southeastern Idaho is Mormon, and the most attractive structures throughout this region are the tabernacles.

At **12 m.** on State 35 is the junction (R) with a road that goes up a canyon **9 m.** to lovely BLOOMINGTON LAKE (*camp sites available*). This clear, deep lake, lying under huge cliffs, covers 12 acres and is fed by innumerable springs. In season the lake is framed by an unusually luxuriant growth of wild flowers, including larkspur, columbine, dogwood, and mountain ash. The lake is stocked with the rare California glacial or golden trout.

US 30N between Montpelier and Soda Springs follows circuitous Bear River, which, west of Soda Springs, turns sharply and weaves its way south to the Great Salt Lake.

103

At **46 m.** is the junction with a poor road.

Right on this road, which leads **2 m.** up a canyon to the SULPHUR SPRINGS. The rock around these springs is so nearly pure sulphur that it will burn with a steady flame.

SODA SPRINGS, **51 m.** (5,777 alt., 831 pop.), at the northern bend of Bear River, is one of the oldest settlements in the State.

Fort Connor, the southwestern part of the present town, was established in 1863 by Gen. Patrick Edward Connor and a little band of Morrisites, dissenters from the orthodox Mormon creed. According to the diary of John Bidwell, who promoted the first sizable emigration to the West, Soda Springs was "a bright and lovely place. The abundance of soda water . . .; the beautiful fir and cedar covered hills; the huge pile of red or brown sinter, the result of fountains once active but then dry—all these, together with the river—lent a charm to its wild beauty and made the spot a notable one." Some of the trappers called the place Beer Springs, imagining that they experienced alcoholic stimulation after drinking the bubbling water.

Beadle in *The Undeveloped West* says: "The springs on the soda mounds are mere tanks, but a few inches wide, sending out such faint streams that all the solid contents are precipitated and the water quite evaporated before reaching the plain. Thus it is easily seen how these mounds were built by the water; and many of them have risen so high that they have no springs, the water having broken out at some other place."

Many springs, highly charged with carbonic acid gas and most of them cold, gush out in this area. Some of them, however, including STEAMBOAT SPRING two miles west of town, now emerge at the bottom of an artificial lake created by a dam. Steamboat still boils up through 40 feet of water and explodes at the surface; the name of the spring derives from the sound made by the explosions. Among the mineral springs the HOOPER, a mile north of town, is popular with visitors. Close by is the CHAMPAGNE SPRING, and to the north is the MAMMOTH SODA SPRING, which is almost precisely the same size as the Mammoth Hot Springs in Yellowstone Park.

Just south of the town, where Little Spring Creek crosses the road, is the spot where a family of seven was killed by Indians; the cemetery in which these persons were buried, with their wagon box serving as a coffin, is west of the town.

At Soda Springs the oldest California trail branched from the Oregon Trail to follow the course of Bear River to the Great Salt Lake. It was at Soda Springs that 32 of the Bidwell party of 64 people, afraid to attempt the little-known route to California, decided to go on to Oregon. The party that turned south, which included one woman and an infant, reached California only after great hardship. Many other emigrants changed their minds on destination in this area. (*See FORT HALL, SIDE ROUTE B.*)

Right from Soda Springs on a country road to STAMPEDE PARK, **2 m.**, where an annual stampede and rodeo are held in August. This park is a natural amphitheater, bordered by peaks and flanked by peculiar stone formations and rock crystals. The road to the park winds through cedar and pine woods and is known as the Red Road because of the brightly colored rock formations nearby that were sculptured long ago by the springs. Flowing into the park is EIGHTY PERCENT SPRING. There was formerly a bottling plant at NINETY PERCENT SPRING, near Stampede Park; though the plant no longer operates, thousands of persons come here annually to drink the waters. Of this spring Beadle, the gossip, reported: "The Ninety-per-cent. Spring, which Gentiles call the Antipolygamy Spring, is some two miles west of Hooper's, and about the same distance from the river. Of the solid contents ninety per cent. is soda, and the rest of some peculiar mineral which has a remarkable effect on the male human. Many ridiculous stories are told of its anti-Mormon properties, but fortunately the specific effect lasts but a few weeks."

Visible from the highway at **57 m.** (L) is SODA POINT, which Frémont in 1842 called Sheep Rock because of the great number of mountain sheep seen on it. It is an important lava formation inasmuch as it caused Bear River to turn southward and eventually enter Utah instead of following the natural watershed of this region.

At **58 m.** is a junction with State 34.

Left on this road is GRACE, **6 m.**, where there is a large hydroelectric plant. At **8 m.** is VOLCANO HILL, a few hundred yards east of which is ICE CAVE. The entrance hall pitches down for 50 yards, but thereafter the floor is fairly level. About halfway through is a skylight. The remarkable thing about the cave is its structural symmetry: 50 feet in width and about 25 in height, it runs in an almost perfect corridor for half a mile and looks like the upper half of an enormous barrel. Because this was once a volcanic outlet, the walls and ceiling look as though they had been plastered with hot lava. The far end, which terminates in piles of lava, once molten, is known as the DEVIL'S KITCHEN. Though there is not much ice in it, this has been known as an ice cave since its discovery many decades ago.

LAVA HOT SPRINGS, **85 m.** (544 pop.), is situated on the lovely Portneuf River at the base of great cliffs. The river, so named for a Canadian trapper who was murdered nearby by Indians, has a rare feature: low rocks dam it, forming quiet pools that are separated by cascades of unusual beauty. The town has springs that are remarkable in volume and mineral content. Even in prehistoric times the Indians visited the hot springs because of their curative properties and set the spot aside as neutral ground to be shared by all tribes. The daily flow from the hot springs, each with a different mineral content, is 6,711,000 gallons. Natatoriums have been established here, two by the State and one by the town, and there is a fully equipped sanatorium.

Both the State and city natatoriums have established large indoor pools. The State also maintains an outdoor pool called the Mud Bath, which has varying degrees of temperature in its waters, which are fed by 30 springs. It is not a large pool, but a swimmer can stroke from almost cold water into hot water, through various degrees of cold and warmth between the two extremes. Just below the balcony of the Riverside Inn runs the clear cold water of the Portneuf River with hot springs steaming almost at its edge.

To the south of Lava Hot Springs is a great mountain that is almost a solid pile of unquarried building stone, which because of its strength and lightness is valued by construction men. It has been used in building two cabins across the river from the Mud Bath. Interesting, too, are other rock formations of limestones, shales, sandstones, and quartzites. Upon the river within the radius of a mile are 50 small waterfalls; and the smoke holes of old volcanoes are within hiking distance. The canyons and glens offer camping retreats.

At **97 m.** US 30N turns north and follows the Portneuf River and Canyon. With its abrupt walls and innumerable crevices cut in limestone and shales, the canyon was formerly a favorite hide-out for bandits as well as Indians. It was here in 1865 that a stage carrying several passengers and $60,000 was betrayed by its driver to a gang led by Jim Locket, a notorious bandit. Two passengers were killed and their bodies buried in a gulch near the scene of the crime. Another robbery of the period occurred not far south of Pocatello in a grove of trees near the Big Elbow of the river; ten robbers held up the Wells-Fargo stage, murdered six of the seven passengers, and escaped with $110,000 in gold dust.

INKOM, **107 m.,** has the largest cement plant in Idaho. For its materials the factory draws on the limestone mountain that stands behind the village.

POCATELLO, **120 m.** (4,464 alt., 16,471 pop.) (*see IDAHO GUIDE*).

Railroad Station. Oregon Short Line, end of W. Bonneville St.

Bus Station. Union Pacific Stages, Fargo Building, S. Main St.

Pocatello is the seat of Bannock County, and the second city in size in Idaho. It was named for a marauding Chief Paughatella (Ind., *he who does not follow the beaten path*) of the Shoshone tribe.

Standing at the northern end of Portneuf Canyon and upon a bed of the ancient Lake Bonneville, of which the Great Salt Lake is the remnant, the city began as a collection of tents in 1882, when the Union Pacific branch was completed to this point. It is now an important junction and repair and maintenance point of the Oregon Short Line R.R. The city is bisected by the network of railways, and the mountains flanking it are denuded and formidable. West of the black tangle of rails is most of the business area; beyond this and against the mountains are many of the most attractive homes. East of the tracks is also a residential section.

There are a number of Basque and Greek families here, as well as a colony of Negroes.

MEMORIAL BUILDING, overlooking Memorial Park and Portneuf River, was erected to Idaho veterans of all wars. It has a spacious ballroom and a terrace that opens upon the river.

The SOUTHERN BRANCH OF THE UNIVERSITY OF IDAHO is in the eastern part of the city at the base of Red Bluff. It is housed in seven buildings, scattered over 225 acres of land, and has an enrollment of about 850. Its HISTORICAL MUSEUM contains old records and journals, Indian handicraft, and fossils that have been gathered in various parts of the State.

ROSS PARK, just south of the city, has a nine-hole golf course, a small zoo, and a delightful rock garden. Of greater interest are the lava rocks above the park, which carry Indian petroglyphs recording a part of the legends and histories of the Bannock and Shoshone tribes.

West of the city, highly tinted Cambrian quartzite is overlain with rhyolite, a light-colored volcanic rock that flowed to the surface before the basalt. Across the bare plateau of the Snake River country the Twin Buttes are dimly visible.

Above the city in the west is KINPORT PEAK, which offers a far-reaching view. Stretching westward as far as the eye can see is Snake River Valley, which in times past was deluged with overwhelming outpourings of molten lava.

At Pocatello is the junction with US 91 (*see SIDE ROUTE B*).

Section 9. Pocatello to Twin Falls, 124 m. US 30N and US 30.

US 30N goes northwest from POCATELLO, **0 m.** At **6 m.** (R) is the municipal airport, MCDOUGALL FIELD.

SNAKE RIVER (R), not visible from the highway, is tributary to the Columbia, but larger. It is a thousand miles in length and the extreme breadth of its basin is 450. For more than half its distance it flows through a gorge, and already upon it and its feeders are 80 huge reservoirs, and 70 hydroelectric plants that use less than one-tenth of its potential power. Most of its waters are unnavigable.

In the earliest geologic period most of the Snake River basin was covered by a shallow sea in which were deposited great quantities of sand and mud. These have hardened into quartzites. After the sea receded there were tremendous upliftings of granitic materials, which were consolidated into the Idaho batholith and its smaller but related masses of rock. Following this there was an epidemic of volcanic upheavals and explosive eruptions accompanied by flows of lava and ash. Erosion came next and slow sculpturings by glaciers, but the region was not yet ready to accept its alluvial deposits, and tremors and gigantic quakings shook the area from time to time, and basaltic uplifts rose like black monuments on the landscape. Within recent centuries earthquakes have been infrequent and never severe, but there are still deep and troubled rumblings. After peace came, Snake River settled down to the business of eroding its gorge. In the upper valleys here it flows too lazily to achieve much, but beyond Milner it gathers speed and has been impressively busy.

The Snake River area was the most trying one traversed by early travelers on their way to Oregon. The west-bound Astorians, who attempted to go down the stream in canoes, were finally forced to travel along the rim of the gorge (*see below*). The land, now irrigated in a number of places and under cultivation, was formerly barren. Game was so scarce that the area was shunned even by the Indians who were forced from the Great Plains by the powerful tribes dwelling there. Though the Oregon Trail ran near the river, it was often difficult for travelers to find water for themselves and their animals; with the river constantly in sight they sometimes traveled a day or two without finding any place where they could descend into the gorge and drink.

At **20 m.** (R) is the AMERICAN FALLS RESERVOIR, one of the largest of many along the Snake that are making farming possible. The dam is a mile wide and has a maximum height of 87 feet. The reservoir it creates is 12 miles wide, 26 miles long, and covers an area of 56,000 acres. The cost of the dam was $3,060,000, of the entire project three times that sum.

The former site of AMERICAN FALLS, **25 m.** (4,330 alt., 1,280 pop.), was a favorite camping spot on the trail in this area; an elevator in the artificial lake marks the area where the early settlement stood. The new town is the trade center of a huge dry-farming wheat belt; reclamation projects reach for 170 miles westward.

Close by the Idaho Power Company's hydroelectric plant is the TRENNER MEMORIAL PARK, dedicated to an engineer who helped to develop this region. A rocky terrace made of lava from the Craters of the Moon, a fountain and a landscaped lawn, a lava monolith, and a miniature power station make this park a pleasant oasis. The park is illuminated at night. Nearby is one of the State's large fish hatcheries, with a capacity of 2,500,000 fingerlings a season.

A part of the Oregon Trail can still be seen in the town and for a short distance south.

At **27 m.** is the junction with an unimproved road.

Left on this road are the INDIAN SPRINGS, **1 m.**, where pools and baths are available. This resort is one of the most popular of the mineral hot springs of the State, not only because of its reputed therapeutic properties but also because it is easily accessible.

At **35 m.** is a monument commemorating an emigrant tragedy; the site is called MASSACRE ROCKS.

By 1862 the western Indians had reached a point of desperation. They had been misled and coerced into signing agreements that confined them to lands far too small and quite unsuitable for the ways of life to which they had been accustomed. Promised payments in goods were either not being made, or were inadequate to support them. Game on which they depended for food was being destroyed recklessly by the invaders. Faced with starvation they were easily influenced by the medicine men and other leaders who urged them to fight. When the Civil War broke out, word spread that the whites, quarreling among themselves, could be attacked successfully and driven away.

In the Pacific Northwest there had been trouble ever since the settlement of the boundary question; the Hudson's Bay Company, which had maintained order until 1846, had become merely a trading firm without power to reward or punish the Indians. The new territorial government, established by the United States, did not inspire the Indians with respect because its agents neither understood the Indians nor treated them with the fairness and kindness exercised by the Chief Factor of the Hudson's Bay Company's Department of the Columbia. Whereas earlier travelers had journeyed with a fair degree of safety on the Oregon Trail, by 1862 small groups were in constant peril of attack.

On August 10 of that year a train of 11 wagons drawn by ox teams and carrying 25 families from Iowa was winding over the sagebrush-covered plain at this point. A hot luminous haze covered the landscape. The ox teams moved slowly, covering only a mile or so in an hour. Thirst, weariness, and the monotonous sameness of earth, sky, and sun had far diminished the adventurous spirit of the pioneer. The journey was beginning to seem endless, with the fabulous valleys of Oregon as remote as ever.

The driver of the first wagon, sitting high on the seat, was doubtless looking ahead, trying to distinguish between the blue gray of the desert and the gray blue of the sky. Behind him in the crawling wagons, reaching back for a quarter of a mile, were men, women, and children sitting in a half stupor. The yellow earth was turned up by the wheels in lazy blinding clouds that rolled back from wagon to wagon and settled upon freight and travelers in thick layers. When the first wagon came to the crest of the slight rise, the driver could see a long slope with great piles of stone on either side of the trail. For 15 minutes the wagons plowed down this hill toward the bluffs, and it was not until the leader had passed into the small gorge, with its refreshing shadow, that a sudden movement in the stones above threw terror into the emigrants; they realized that they had been ambushed by Indians. The confusion and panic, the awful horror of the next few minutes, are imaginable. The chronicle relates that nine whites were slain, six were scalped, many were injured, and a few miraculously escaped. Wagons were plundered and burned and the beasts were driven off; on the following day another wagon train reached this spot and buried the dead.

At **38 m.** is the junction with an unimproved road.

Left on this road to EMIGRANT ROCK, **3 m.**, a stone 20 feet high on which early travelers left their autographs. Some of the names carved into the rock and even some of those painted with axle grease as early as 1849 are still visible.

For eight miles US 30N continues to follow the river, then climbs to arid plains that have not been reclaimed by irrigation. On a clear day the Lost River Mountains are visible in the north, and on the south is a spur of the Goose Creek Range. The hilltops here offer a broad panorama of the Snake River Valley and the haze of the Burley and Twin Falls areas. At **49 m.** the highway crosses Raft River.

RUPERT, **73 m.** (4,200 alt., 2,250 pop.), is one of the few towns in Idaho that were not allowed to grow aimlessly. Laid out by the engineering division of the Bureau of Reclamation and named for the engineer who planned it, Rupert looked ambitiously into the future and arranged itself around a central plaza. Like many of the towns along the Snake, it is of recent origin, and sprang up almost overnight. At the beginning of the present century the whole area between American Falls and Buhl was a domain of sagebrush and coyotes, bunch grass and bromegrass, cheat grass and lizards. Swiftly, section by section, it is being transformed into a huge irrigated garden. Today the long sweep down the valley to the west is one of the State's three principal agricultural areas.

Right from Rupert an unimproved road leads to the MINIDOKA DAM, **15 m.** The Minidoka Reclamation Project involved the construction of a dam across Snake River, a main canal and tributaries, and an elaborate pumping plant. This last has three units, each lifting water 20 feet. The diversion system irrigates about 116,000 acres. The body of water impounded, now called LAKE WALCOTT, has a capacity of 107,000 acre-feet.

BURLEY, **82 m.** (4,240 alt., 3,826 pop.), is the center of reclamation project covering 121,000 acres. It is a thriving little city of recent origin. It has an alfalfa-meal mill with a capacity of 125 tons, a beet-sugar factory with a capacity of 800 tons, and a large potato-flour mill. West of Burley US 30N and US 30S became US 30.

Left from Burley on a graveled road is OAKLEY, **24 m.**; thence L. over a dirt road to the SILENT CITY OF ROCKS, **38 m.**, which covers an area of 25 square miles. Because the California Trail ran through it and the Lander Cut-off ended here, its walls bear thousands of names and dates, as well as messages left for persons who were presumably soon to follow; it is evident that some of the more ambitious and foolhardy scribes must have suspended themselves by ropes from the tops of the cliffs, so high and remote are the records they left.

This formation has been carved by erosion from an enormous dome of granite that was anciently pushed up here. Because the weathered granite has become indurated or case-hardened on the surface, while its inner structure has often more rapidly disintegrated, the rocks form not only bizarre mosques, monoliths, and turrets, but also bathtubs, hollow cones, shells, and strange little pockets and caverns. BATHTUB ROCK towers two hundred feet, and can be climbed to its summit whereon is a large depression that catches rainfall; in this depression, according to Indian legend, a bath before sunrise restored youth to the aged. Near the southern end of the formation are the gleaming turrets and fortresses, which stand on a low saddle against the road. North of these are spires that rise two hundred and fifty feet from the floor of the basin and from a distance suggest the sky line of New York City. Still others, fantastically grouped, look as if heathen temples had been rocked with dynamite and had rearranged their structure but refused to fall. Many so closely resemble one thing and another as to have been named; there are the OLD HEN WITH HER CHICKS, the DRAGON'S HEAD, the GIANT TOADSTOOL, ELEPHANT ROCK, and the OLD WOMAN.

It is believed that treasure is buried here. When a stage from Kelton to Boise was held up in this city in 1878, $90,000 in gold is said to have been taken. One of the bandits was slain, and the other subsequently died in prison; but before his death he revealed that he had buried the treasure among five junipers. Five cedars growing in the shape of a heart were found in the city long ago, and frantic excavations were undertaken, but the treasure has never been found.

At **96 m.** on US 30 is the junction with an improved road.

Right on this road to MILNER DAM, **4 m.,** a structure of earth and concrete. Less impressive than some other dams in the State, it marks, nevertheless, the most successful large reclamation project in Idaho. Undertaken by the Twin Falls Land and Water Company in 1903, it was completed in 1905, and impounds enough water to irrigate 240,000 acres on the south side of the Snake and 32,000 on the north. The storage of 80,000 acre-feet is supplemented by a right to 98,000 acre-feet in the Jackson Reservoir in Wyoming and 155,480 acre-feet in the American Falls Reservoir. The number of acres actually farmed under the South Side Milner Project is 203,000, and the number under the North Side is 128,000.

The town of MILNER is just below the dam. Here in the Snake River is CALDRON LINN, where the Astorians in October, 1811, experienced a disaster that finally convinced them that the Indians were right when they warned them against attempting to navigate the Snake (*see SIDE ROUTE 3*). "The leading canoe," wrote Irving, "had glided safely among the turbulent and roaring surges, but in following it Mr. Crooks perceived that his canoe was bearing toward a rock. He called out to the steersman, but his warning voice was either unheard or unheeded. In the next moment they struck upon the rock. The canoe was split and overturned. There were five persons on board. Mr. Crooks and his companions were thrown amid roaring breakers and a whirling current, but succeeded, by strong swimming, to reach the shore. Clappine and two others clung to the shattered bark, and drifted with it to a rock. The wreck struck the rock with one end, and swinging round, flung poor Clappine off into the raging stream, which swept him away, and he perished."

After this event the party camped on the border of Caldron Linn (lin, Scotch, *ravine*) and held council to determine a course of action. Exploring parties reported that for nearly 40 miles westward the river foamed, roared, and twisted through a steep canyon where access to the stream from the rim was rarely possible. But the prospect of carrying the luggage through the rough arid country was so discouraging that the members of the party determined again to attempt

navigation, entering the river six miles below the caldron. One canoe with its
contents was swept away while being launched and three others were caught on
the rocks. Even the *voyageurs* were now willing to admit that the river route
would have to be abandoned. To add to the distress the food supply was reduced
to an amount sufficient for only five days. The party was divided into four groups,
which were to make their ways as best they could toward the Columbia. Hunt,
left with 31 men and the squaw of Dorion—far advanced in pregnancy—and
her two children, made a cache for the luggage that had to be abandoned, a
process that required three days. During this period one party, which had attempted to return to Fort Henry (*see SIDE ROUTE B*), arrived and reported that
it was impossible to go back by land.

The Hunt party, having no other recourse, set out on foot to follow the Snake
westward across the terrifying wasteland. Hunt led the majority along the north
bank while the minority traveled on the south bank.

US 30 continues to follow the general course of the Snake, which
in this area takes a relatively direct route. For most of its length the
Snake winds and twists convulsively; old-timers say that the river was
formed the night Paul Bunyan started out from Idaho Falls for Seattle,
with his Blue Ox, after drinking nine kegs of rum. It was a wet, black
night and Paul's wandering trail filled up with water.

Because of varying degrees in the hardness of the stone through
which the river runs and the consequent variations in the ease and
speed of erosion, the river has sculptured several waterfalls, including
Dry Creek, Twin, Shoshone, Pillar, Auger, and the Upper and Lower
Salmon.

At HANSEN, **115 m.**, are the junctions with country roads.

1. Left on a country road is the SITE OF A TRADING STATION, **7 m.**, that was
for years the first west of Fort Hall. It was a camping site, a Pony Express station,
and then in 1863 a settlement. The old store still stands.

2. Right from Hansen on a country road that leads to the HANSEN BRIDGE,
4 m., which spans the Snake River gorge. It is 345 feet high and 688 feet long
and is suspended on enormous cables. The gorge here is narrower than below
and offers from the bridge a beautiful summary of what time and a mighty river
have been able to do with lava rock.

TWIN FALLS, **124 m.** (3,492 alt., 8,787 pop.), is the largest city
and the metropolis of south-central Idaho. Three miles south of Snake
River and on the bank of Rock Creek, it stands on gently rolling
terrain that was covered long ago by lava flows. The overlain soil in
the surrounding country is uncommonly deep, and its richness has made
this part of Idaho notable in crop yields. Twin Falls is one of the
towns that have risen suddenly and swiftly after water reclaimed the
arid valley. It was settled chiefly by families from the Middle West and
was carefully planned.

There are several small museums in the city. The CRABTREE (*adm.*
25¢), 211 Addison Ave. W., has an excellent collection of Indian

artifacts, including arrowheads from many parts of the United States; there are also a few fossils and archeological relics. The WEAVER MUSEUM (*free*), 149 Main Ave. W., has a collection of guns, fossils, and curios. WHITAKER'S TAXIDERMIST SHOP AND MUSEUM (*free*), 216 Second Ave. S., has, in addition to Indian artifacts, an interesting group of mounted game animals, wild birds, moths, and butterflies. The GASKILL BOTANICAL GARDEN (*adm. 15¢*), 266 Blue Lake Blvd., is a beautifully landscaped spot. Surrounded by trees, shrubs, and vines, the concrete pools within are stocked with water plants and fish. The GARDEN OF YESTERDAY (*adm. 25¢*), just southeast of the city, is noteworthy for its miniature reproductions of frontier structures, including a tiny log house, and a gristmill operated by water from a ditch.

A natural CAVE in the wall of Rock Creek Canyon (R) was the first jail in Twin Falls County, and prisoners were incarcerated here until a Federal statute made it illegal to keep persons below the surface of the earth. Just south of the depot is a private fishery where rainbow trout can be bought fresh from the ponds.

Right from Twin Falls on US 93, which turns L., following Blue Lakes Blvd. (*The roads beyond this point are unmarked and confusing; inquiry should be made locally.*)
There is a toll-gate at about **3 m.**, on the rimrock (*adm. to the area and its attractions 25¢*). From the rim there is a magnificent view of the gorge, which here is seven hundred feet in depth and almost sheer, and of the Twin Falls-Jerome Bridge. Far below, by the river, is the PERRINE RANCH, which Douglas Fairbanks, Sr., considered buying before he decided to settle in England. A narrow but safe road leads down to the ranch through a corridor of poplars. The PERRINE MUSEUM contains Indian artifacts, fossils, and old relics. The Perrine orchard is noted for its rare fruits. The road leaves the ranch and crosses the river on a bridge to small, lovely BLUE LAKES, **4.3 m.**, which are as blue as the sky.

On US 93 is the junction with a country road.
Right on this road to a second road (L) leading to SHOSHONE FALLS, first described by Wilson Price Hunt in 1811, and for many decades thereafter the chief scenic attraction in Idaho for the thousands of emigrants passing through on their way to Oregon. During years of light snowfall upon the watersheds, only about enough water goes over this wide escarpment in August to fill a teacup. After heavy winters the reservoirs are soon filled, and the full flow of the river is delivered downstream. In May, 1936, Shoshone Falls was roaring mightily in unusual splendor. The river here plunges in a sheer drop of 212 feet over a great basaltic horseshoe rim nearly a thousand feet wide.
At **6 m.** on the up-river road TWIN FALLS are seen. They are no longer twins; the larger one was taken over in 1935 by the Idaho Power Company, whose plant here is notable for its compactness and beauty. The larger of the twins was a plunge of 180 feet, with more than half the river poured over a narrow escarpment in a terrific column. The diversion dam has now produced a series of cascades that are an appropriate prelude to the falls below. The great plunge is against the south wall, where the water goes down like a tumbling mountain of snow with a part of its body rolling in pale green veins. At the farther-side the flood spills in an enormous foaming sheet over a wide and almost perfect arc.

Section 10. Twin Falls to Boise, 144 m. US 30.

US 30 runs west from TWIN FALLS, **0 m.** There is an unob-structed view (R) of the Sawtooth Mountains beyond Snake River.

At **8 m.** is FILER, the home of the well-known Idaho white bean; nine bean plants are operated here.

Right from Filer on a country road to AUGER FALLS, **5 m.,** on Snake **River.** The water here pours through a partly obstructed channel over a series of **escarp-**ments, and twists and spirals strangely in its descent.

BUHL, **18 m.** (3,792 alt., 1,883 pop.), flanked on the east by roll-ing country that in June looks like Iowa, is one of the most attractive towns in the State.

North from Buhl on US 30; at **26 m.** (R) Snake River Canyon is visible. At **28 m.** some of the Thousand Springs can be seen on its wall in the distance. At **32 m.** (R) is the Thousand Springs (sometimes called the Minnie Miller) Farm, known for its blooded Guernsey cattle.

Just west of the farm are the THOUSAND SPRINGS, many of which have been hidden by a power development. Though long a source of mystery to both laymen and geologists, the Thousand Springs, it is now believed, are the outlets of buried rivers that are lost in the lava terrain 150 miles to the northeast. In this stretch occur a group of springs having a combined discharge of more than five thousand second-feet. The whole of central Idaho seems to be an area of subterranean rivers and possibly cavernous lake beds; at various points in this valley a person can put his ear to the ground and hear deep and troubled rum-blings as of a mighty ocean rolling far beneath the surface of the earth. Opposite Thousand Springs is a ghost town, AUSTIN, marked by a cellar, a chimney, some stone walls, and fruit trees that bloom in a forgotten orchard.

HABERMAN, **40 m.,** is a small hamlet in the valley.

At **40.5 m.** is a tablet commemorating Dr. Marcus Whitman, **the** missionary who in 1836 traveled along the Snake on his way to Oregon. With Whitman were his bride, Mr. and Mrs. Henry Spalding, and two other men; they were led by Thomas McKay and John McLeod, experi-enced Hudson's Bay Company men who knew the route well. Nonethe-less they had an unusually difficult time because Whitman was bent on demonstrating that wagons could be used in reaching the Columbia River. The missionaries had started from St. Louis with two wagons and the fur traders with whom they traveled on the first part of their journey had had seven. The traders left their wagons at Fort William (Fort Laramie), but Whitman had insisted that he and Spalding con-tinue with one wagon. After they had had endless trouble and delays on account of the wagon, other members of the party attempted to persuade him to leave it. He persisted in spite of them. Two or three days before reaching Fort Hall one of the axletrees broke and even the bride rejoiced at what seemed the deathblow to her husband's plan. But she was not yet acquainted with Whitman. He contrived a cart of the rear wheels and lashed the other pair to it. At Fort Hall the trader endeavored to dissuade Whitman from attempting to take the cart farther and one man in the missionary party said that he would not go on if the cart went. Whitman took the cart. As the little group passed over the route at this point the cart was still vexing Spalding, the women, and the Hudson's Bay Company men. It was finally abandoned at Fort Boise.

In the high cliffs above Thousand Springs and in other places throughout Haberman Valley, marine fossils are abundant. Besides remains of luxuriant tropical vegetation, there are also survivals of mastodons, wild hogs, and a rare species of ancient horse that seems to have been the immediate forebear of the present animal.

Between Hagerman and Malad River US 30 crosses the Snake in whose canyon wall is a cave containing Indian petroglyphs that have been interpreted as a story of an Arapaho massacre. MALAD RIVER, **43 m.**, is only a few miles long. In springtime it is a wild torrent of considerable size. The main source of Malad River is a huge spring that plunges down a precipice in a chain of cascades. The subterranean nature of central Idaho is demonstrated by the fact that this is the only stream in the southern part of the State west of Henrys Fork that, rising in the mountains in the north, reaches Snake River in the summertime.

The highway leaves the rim of the canyon. At the foot, just before the ascent begins, is the old Bliss Ranch where B. M. Bower wrote *Good Indian.* The evolution of the winding grade from a crude pack trail through different eras of travel is still discernible. At the top of the ascent is the village of BLISS, **49 m.**, which was named for an old-timer and not because its settlers regarded it as an especially felicitous haven.

1. Right from Bliss on a fair road to lakes, **11 m.**, in which the water is so astringent that it will take the hair off a hog. These small lakes occupy old crater beds. They are known under various names, but one of them is sometimes appropriately called LYE LAKE. The hot springs were held in high esteem by Indians, who often journeyed far to bathe in the waters. The story is told of one buck who gambled so expertly that he left the others destitute. He was denounced in angry council, but allowed to accompany the tribe on its pilgrimage to the spring. When he fell ill of spotted fever, he was thrust into the hot waters to effect a cure and was dragged out dead.

2. Right from Bliss on State 24; at **4 m.** R. over a smooth road to the MALAD GORGE, **14 m.** No gorge in the State excels this one with its ragged chasms, and none is more picturesque. Near its head is a blue lake fed by a waterfall, and below it is the river, cascading and bursting forth in springs and turning through all shades of pale green and blue.

West of Bliss US 30 traverses one of the chief grazing areas of the State, from which seventy thousand cattle and two hundred thousand sheep are shipped annually.

Just northwest of KING HILL, **66 m.**, at the foot of the hill, stood an Overland Stage station that was burned by Chief Buffalo Horn in 1878. On a flat above the village is the Devil's Playground, a picturesque area of round smooth stones.

At **74 m.** is THREE ISLAND FORD where the Oregon Trail crossed the Snake. An Indian trail still leads down to the river. Indians used to lie in ambush by the crossing; just south is DEAD MAN'S GULCH. With his band, Buffalo Horn, an Indian scout having an honorable discharge from the U. S. Army, killed three miners on DEAD MAN'S FLAT.

It was in this area that Hunt's Astorians found a small Indian village and bought some salmon and a dog for food.

Near the ford US 30 turns abruptly northwest from the Snake and the route of the west-bound Astorians. The men of that party stumbled along over the rough land near the river, galled by the loads they were carrying and weakened by lack of food. At one Indian village a pack horse was obtained in exchange for an old tea kettle after payment with articles of more value had been refused. Two days later Hunt unfortunately accepted the advice of Indians and turned inland, away from the river; the men almost went mad with thirst before they reached a pleasant stream. Dorion, at a nearby Indian camp, was able to buy a horse to carry his wife and children. Another man also acquired a horse but a few days later the starving party killed it for food.

MOUNTAIN HOME, **100 m.** (3,124 alt., 1,243 pop.), is on a great sagebrush-covered plateau.

West of Mountain Home US 30 traverses prairie with typical flora.

The highway here follows a section of the Oregon Trail that is associated with many tragedies. The one most frequently related concerns the Sager family; how much of the story is true and how much pure legend is unknown. The family had left the Missouri with a wagon train but in western Wyoming, where the parents became ill with dysentery or cholera, the train moved on without them. They managed to reach Fort Hall before the parents died. Of the five children, John, aged 14, was the eldest; the youngest was a four-months-old infant. There were no women at the Hudson's Bay outpost, so John determined to press on toward the Whitman mission near Walla Walla. In the confusion around the post the children slipped off into this region that taxed the endurance of the hardiest adults. It was many weeks later, according to the story, that John approached the gate of Fort Boise, carrying the baby and followed by his little sisters. A month later the forlorn children arrived at the mission; John still carried the youngest and behind him perched on the back of an emaciated cow, were his

UNION PACIFIC WORKERS (1867)

WAGON TRAIN (c. 1871)

sister of eight, with a broken leg, and his sister of five, who had supported the leg mile after mile to keep it from swinging. Shortly after she was lifted from the cow's back, the injured girl died. The children had traveled five hundred miles, subsisting on the cow's milk and on wild fruits and roots. John and Francis were slain three years later during the Whitman mission massacre.

At **111 m.** (L) is CLEFT, a few deserted shacks by the railroad tracks.

Left from Cleft over cow trails (*hazardous*) to the CRATER RINGS, **3 m.** (L). These two great volcanic cones look like ancient amphitheaters from which all benches have been removed. The rings were doubtless caused by two gigantic eruptions of such force and volume that a cubic mile of lava was hurled into the air and blown into dust. Here also is an earthquake fissure; for five miles the surface was split open by some tremendous tremor in the past, and the crack, from five to ten feet in width, is of unknown depth in places.

BOISE, **144 m.** (2,741 alt., 21,544 pop.) (*see IDAHO GUIDE*).

Railroad Station. Union Pacific, on the Bench.

Bus Station. Union Pacific Stages, 929 Main St.

Accommodations. First-class hotels.

Boise, the capital of Idaho and its largest city, stands on the bank of the Boise River. It is a city of trees and homes, protected by great mountains on the north and lying in a belt of prevailing westerly winds. Its summers, though often hot, are nearly always dry, and its nights are usually cool. Its winters are mild. The city is supported by a few factories, and by the trade from a fertile agricultural area chiefly producing hay, grain, vegetables, and fruits.

Boise has a large Basque colony. Its midsummer festival is a genuine *romeria*, similar to fiestas in Spain, with Basque food, costumes, dances, and music. Like many other Idaho towns, it has an abundance of natural hot water, with wells that flow 1,200,000 gallons daily at a temperature of 170 degrees F. Many of the homes, especially in the eastern part, are heated from these flows; the chief avenue, Warm Springs, is named for them. The large NATATORIUM and its playground are on this avenue at its eastern end.

The domed STATE CAPITOL is reminiscent of the Capitol in Washington, with Corinthian columns supporting a Corinthian pediment. It is faced with Boise sandstone. It is most impressive when viewed from the head of the long boulevard leading from the railroad station on the Bench. In the rotunda is an equestrian statue of George Washington, the work of Charles Ostner, a soldier of fortune sojourning in Idaho; it was carved by hand from a yellow pine tree with the crudest of tools and with only a postage stamp bearing Washington's head as a model. It was completed in 1869, after four years' work; when the carving was completed, the statue was scraped with glass, sandpapered, gilded, and overlaid with gold leaf. In one crowded room in the basement of the capitol is the STATE HISTORICAL SOCIETY MUSEUM (*free*); many valuable gifts and collections are being withheld until a suitable building is erected to house them. On the capitol grounds is the FRANK STEUNENBERG MONUMENT, designed by Gilbert Riswald and cast by Guido Nelli. Steunenberg, Governor of the State (1897-1901), was killed by a bomb in December, 1905, during the mine labor troubles of the period. The trial of those accused of causing his death was a court duel between William E. Borah, acting for the State, and the late Clarence Darrow for the defense.

At the southern end of Capitol Boulevard, and facing the capitol, is the beautiful UNION PACIFIC STATION. Set upon a hill, it overlooks the city as well as the landscaped Howard Platt Gardens with their flowers and Norway maples, blossoming catalpas, and weeping willows. These gardens, particularly lovely when lighted at night, were designed by Richard Espino of Los Angeles. ST. JOHN'S ROMAN CATHOLIC CATHEDRAL, 8th and Hays Sts., was designed by Tourtellotte and Hummel of Boise, the architects of the capitol. It is Romanesque in design and the interior is elaborately adorned with stained-glass windows and marble altars. ST. MICHAEL'S EPISCOPAL CATHEDRAL, 8th and State Sts., is of the English Gothic type.

In JULIA DAVIS PARK, lying upon the north bank of the river just east of 8th St., is the COSTON CABIN. Built in the spring of 1863 by I. N. Coston, it was fashioned of driftwood gathered from the river, and put together with pegs. Its original site was on the river seven miles above Boise; there it served as a rendezvous for Indians, prospectors, freighters, and packers. In this park, too, is the PEARCE CABIN, built by Ira B. Pearce in the fall of 1863 of logs brought from the mountains by ox team. On the south side of the river near the Holcomb school is the BLOCKHOUSE, a two-story stone structure, built in 1869, that served as a refuge against Indian attacks; it is now locally regarded as haunted.

The DELAMAR HOUSE, 8th and Grove Sts., was, in its heyday, the largest and most modern in the town. It had the first mansard roof in the State. In 1892 Capt. J. R. DeLamar, the "silver king," bought it for $35,000 and converted it into an expensive club; in 1905 it became the home of Boise's first beauty parlor; today it is a Basque rooming house.

The O'FARRELL CABIN, 6th and Fort Sts., was built in 1863, and now has a tablet above the door declaring that this was the first home in Boise to shelter women and children. Within it are the fireplace and tea-kettle used by the first occupants.

CHRIST'S CHURCH, 15th and Ridenbaugh Sts., was erected in 1866 in another part of the city.

Opposite the Statesman Building on Main Street is the SITE OF THE OVERLAND STAGE STATION.

A saloon operating on Main between 8th and 9th Sts. half a century ago, managed by James Lawrence and known as the Naked Truth Saloon, advertised itself in the following fashion:
"Friends and Neighbors:

"Having just opened a commodious shop for the sale of liquid fire, I embrace this opportunity of informing you that I have commenced the business of making:

"Drunkards, paupers and beggars for the sober, industrious and respectable portion of the community to support. I shall deal in family spirits, which will incite men to deeds of riot, robbery, and blood, and by so doing, diminish the comfort, augment the expenses and endanger the welfare of the community.

"I will undertake on short notice, for a small sum and with great expectations, to prepare victims for the asylum, poor farm, prison and gallows.

"I will furnish an article which will increase fatal accidents, multiply the number of distressing diseases and render those which are harmless incurable. I will deal in drugs which will deprive some of life, many of reason, most of prosperity, and all of peace: which will cause fathers to become fiends, and wives widows, children orphans and a nuisance to the nation."

The URGUIDES LITTLE VILLAGE of 30 one-room cabins, 1st and Main Sts., was erected in 1863 by Jesus Kossuth Urguides, a frontiersman from San Francisco, as a freighting station. Built to house packers and wranglers, the cabins today are occupied by old-timers who can still remember how the generous Urguides cared for them in sickness and in health.

Boise has a large playground in JULIA DAVIS PARK, with an art museum, picnic grounds, boating facilities, and tennis courts.

Right from Boise on Warm Springs Avenue (State 21) to a junction at **19 m.**; L. here on State 20 to IDAHO CITY, **45 m.** (187 pop.), in the Boise Basin. In its heyday this former mining city sheltered daily almost as many people as Boise has today as permanent residents. But they constantly moved in and out as news came of gold strikes, first here, then there. The best index of the tempo of former Idaho City life is found in the graveyard; old-timers say that of the 200 people buried there in 1863, only 28 died of natural causes. This cemetery apparently inspired the vigilantes of the locality because it was one of their favorite meeting places. The town jail, first in the Idaho region, was on an acre of ground surrounded by a stockade. The most notable siege this fortress withstood was from a mob, armed with a cannon, in an attempt to take Ferd Patterson from the sheriff's custody and lynch him. Patterson was a gambler who had scalped his ex-mistress and killed the captain of a Columbia River boat. He brought himself to the attention of Idaho City by a gaudiness of attire that included plaid pants, high-heeled boots, a fancy silk waistcoat spanned by a heavy chain of California gold nuggets, and a frock coat of beaver cloth trimmed with otter; he further attracted public odium by killing the Idaho City sheriff. A thousand men waited

to intercept the deputy who was bringing him to the jail, but the deputy outwitted them by placing his man behind the bars—and the stockade—and defending his stronghold with a cannon thrust through portholes in the protecting fence.
It is said that the deputy almost died of chagrin when Patterson was later ac-
quitted at the trial.

Left from Idaho City about **10 m.** to PLACERVILLE, another mining town
that is almost a ghost. Facing the weed-covered plaza is the Magnolia Saloon,
known the length of the Rockies in the days when gold dust was legal tender
and a glass of whiskey was worth a pinch of it. Because of the numerous mice,
a cat was as valuable as a whole jug of whiskey until one enterprising fellow
broke the market by carting a load of cats into town. Before 1864 mail was brought
to Placerville on horseback at 50 cents or a dollar a letter, the price fluctuating
according to the number of thugs along the road. Placerville began to decline in
importance by 1870.

Section 11. Boise to Oregon Line, 63 m. US 30.

US 30, westward, follows Main Street in BOISE, **0 m.** MERIDIAN,
10 m. (2,650 alt., 1,004 pop.), is shipping point for a fertile agricultural area and has one of Idaho's largest creameries.

NAMPA, **20 m.** (2,482 alt., 8,206 pop.), seventh city in size in the
State, is said to have been founded by a wealthy old-timer who, falling
into a fury with Boise one day, strode out of it swearing that he would
make grass grow in its streets. Neither his rage nor his wealth enabled
him to fulfill his threat, but he did help to bring into existence a town
that has been thriving ever since. Nampa was named for Nampuh, a
leader of the western Shoshone who was one of the most notorious
thieves and murderers that ever broke the back of a pony. Nampuh was
so huge that the vest of John McLoughlin, the giant Chief Factor of the
Department of the Columbia of the Hudson's Bay Company, failed by
15 inches to reach around him.

This city is the trade center of an agricultural and dairying area.
Lakeview Park, 70 beautiful acres at the eastern border of the city, has
golf course, playgrounds, and a large swimming pool supplied with
hot artesian water. On the north side of town is a Spanish colony; just
northwest of the city is a Bohemian settlement; and there is a scattered
Scandinavian colony, largest of all.

Left from Nampa on State 45, which leads into Owyhee County, a picturesque
and little-known area that has a population of fewer than four thousand, but an
area larger than Connecticut and two Rhode Islands. Old-timers here declare that
anything can be found in this county, including, they suspect, the lost tribes of
Israel. Just north of the bridge across Snake River, about **8 m.**, a road branches
R. and follows the north bank **10 m.** to an unusually large Indian Pictograph.
Upon a great stone close by (R) is carved a great crude map that roughly defines
not only the Snake River Valley but also Jackson Lake in western Wyoming and
a few areas adjacent to both. Vandals in recent years have broken off chunks of
the rock and carried away parts of the map.

The bridge on State 45 is at the Site of Walters Ferry, which for 58 years
was an important link in the Boise-San Francisco stage route. A few adobe huts

remain on the bank. When building the bridge, workmen found arrowheads, rifle balls, and a hidden poke of gold dust.

MURPHY, **12 m.,** is the present county seat.

Right here to SILVER CITY, **44 m.** (6,000 alt.), patriarch of the State's ghost towns. It sprang up after gold was discovered in 1863 in Jordan Creek, on whose headwaters it stands. Ore from the nearby Poorman mine assayed four to five thousand dollars a ton. At the height of its prosperity the city had a newspaper; a Roman Catholic church, Our Lady of Tears; a barber shop advertising baths as a specialty ("Call and be convinced"), with a photograph of the tub; and bar-rooms with impressive mirrors and polished interiors. The area became notorious because rival mining companies, setting an example later followed þy urban indus-trialists, hired thugs to further their interests. The mountain metropolis had two hotels, the Idaho and the War Eagle, but they were crazy aggregates of buildings ranging from one to three stories in height. Though its glory had departed by 1898 it was still a thriving place; by 1935 it had lost importance to the point that the county seat was moved to Murphy.

CALDWELL, **29 m.** (2,367 alt., 4,974 pop.), has in the College of Idaho, visible at the eastern edge of the city, the oldest institution of higher learning in the State; it was founded in 1891 and has approxi-mately four hundred students. Opposite the college is an unusually large livestock feeding and shipping station. In Memorial Park (L), beyond the campus, are playgrounds, a large outdoor pool fed by artesian water, and the Johnson Cabin, in which three bachelor brothers lived in early days. The town, with 19 churches and somewhat monastic quiet, is quite unlike any other in the State.

At the northwestern edge of Caldwell is Canyon Ford Bridge over Boise River, which US 30 crosses. Near the northern end of the bridge is the Marie Dorion Monument, honoring the Indian woman who traveled with the Astorians.

Left along the northern bank of the Boise River on State 18, which follows the old emigrant trail, to ROSWELL, **14 m.** Near this small town is the SITE OF FORT BOISE, established on Boise River, about eight or ten miles from the Snake in 1834 but later moved down to this point near the larger stream. The Hudson's Bay Company erected this trading post as an answer to Wyeth's Fort Hall, established in July, 1834. It became an important point on the Oregon Trail as the first white settlement reached after the dreary trek from Fort Hall. By the time the emigrants arrived here many were practically destitute, having mis-calculated the amount of foodstuffs necessary to carry them to the Columbia and possessing scanty means. From a trading standpoint this was not a highly suc-cessful post, the surrounding country having relatively few beaver.

US 30 goes north through the Payette Valley, the only part of the State that has more water available for irrigation than is needed. The valley, like the river, was named for Francois Payette, who arrived at Astoria on the ship *Beaver,* and was later in charge of Fort Boise. NEW PLYMOUTH, **54 m.,** was conceived in the Sherman House in Chicago by the chairman of a national irrigation congress. FRUITLAND, **61 m.,** is the center of one of the most prolific fruit areas in the State.

At **63 m.** is the junction with US 30N.

Right on US 30N at **2.9 m.** is PAYETTE (2,147 alt., 2,618 pop.), with a well-known shade-tree nursery, which has developed a pink flowering and a purple-bloom locust tree that blossoms every month. An apple blossom festival is an annual event here when the orchards burgeon. Just west of the town are the SHOWBERGER BOTANICAL GARDENS, an inventory of which in 1934 showed 132 native plants that had been identified, 100 that were still unnamed, and 1,500 wild and cultivated varieties. From these gardens Hyde Park in London was supplied with wild hollyhock after a long search had been made in Weiser Canyon to find it. Fifty species of pentstemon are grown here.

WEISER (*pron. Wee'-zer*), **17.9 m.** (2,119 alt., 2,724 pop.), stands at the confluence of the Snake and Weiser Rivers. It was the "river Wuzer" described by Alexander Ross, and the "Wazer's" River of Peter Skene Ogden in 1827. Lewis and Clark, whose knowledge of the stream's existence was limited to information obtained from Indians, called it the "Nemo." One tradition has it that the river was named for Peter Wiser, a private in the Lewis and Clark expedition; another that it was named for Jacob Wayer or Wager, a North West Company trapper with Mackenzie in 1818, but this is contradicted by the fact that the river was known as "Wisers" to Robert Stuart in his overland trip eastward from Astoria in 1812-3.

By 1890 the town, for a time called Weiser Bridge, had several stores, hotels, and six saloons; but in that year a man who tried to take in all the saloons in a day's stride knocked over a lamp in a hotel, and the subsequent fire destroyed most of the structures. A new Weiser one mile westward was founded, and what remained of the first settlement was moved there.

At the eastern end of town is the old EMIGRANT CROSSING where wagon trains forded the river in early days. An old ferryboat still stands here.

It was in this neighborhood that the westbound Astorians reached a point of almost inhuman desperation. December had arrived and snows impeded their progress. The party led along the south bank of the Snake had fared even worse than the party on the north bank. When finally sighted they had given themselves up to death. The men on the north bank, who had stolen a horse from the Indians and killed it for food, were so apathetic to the fate of the members of the other party that they made no effort to share the meat until Hunt forced them to do so. Small groups set out to explore north and south in this area and Hunt finally determined to leave "the accursed mad river" and cut across to the Columbia; this was done on the day before Christmas.

US 30N crosses the Oregon Line at **20.7 m.** and almost immediately unites with US 30.

US 30 leads west to the SNAKE RIVER, **63 m.,** which forms 217 miles of the boundary line between Idaho and Oregon. Clark called it the Lewis River in honor of his partner. Its present name was derived from the Snake (Shoshone) Indians, who lived near it.

Oregon

Idaho Line—Baker—La Grande—Pendleton—The Dalles—Portland—
Astoria; 522.7 m. US 30.

Union Pacific R.R. roughly parallels US 30 between Idaho Line and Portland;
Spokane, Portland & Seattle R.R., between Portland and Astoria. Union Pacific
Stages follow US 30 between Idaho Line and Portland; Spokane, Portland &
Seattle Stages between Portland and Astoria.

Paved route, passable except in severe snow and ice storms, when Columbia River
Gorge and Blue Mountain sections are sometimes temporarily blocked.

All types of accommodations; improved campsites.

US 30 in Oregon closely follows the Oregon Trail, traversed by
explorers, fur traders, missionaries, spies, settlers, and adventurers in
early days. The members of the Lewis and Clark expedition were the
first white men to travel through the Columbia River Valley; they went
down the river, which the highway follows closely for more than half
its course, but had to make many portages. The Astorians were the next
to use the river, for many years the main highway of travelers in the
region. Nathaniel Wyeth was the first who attempted to take wagons
overland to Oregon, but it was not until 1846 that a pass was opened
around Mount Hood, and wagons went from the Missouri to the Willamette Valley.

Every mile of the trail is filled with memories of the multitude that
passed over it. The smooth modern highway of today was then a crude,
dangerous thoroughfare providing the climax to the journey requiring
five months from the Missouri River to the lower Columbia Valley.
Over sculptured hills and parched plains, through cultivated valleys
and orchard slopes, the highway passes scenes that vary from the
monotonous to the magnificent. It winds up pine-covered ridges of the
Blue Mountains and, descending, crosses miles of rolling grain fields.
It wedges between basaltic cliffs and rugged gorges. Along a route of
scenic splendor, named in part the Columbia River Highway, it reaches
the wide estuary of the old River of the West, and at last the Pacific
Ocean, where Lewis and Clark terminated their historic journey in 1805.

Section 12. Idaho Line to Pendleton, 187.7 m. US 30.

US 30 crosses the Oregon Line, **0 m.**, in the middle of the Snake
River.

ONTARIO, **1.4 m.** (2,153 alt., 1,941 pop.), platted in the 1880's,
is in the midst of a 300,000-acre irrigation district. Served by the Union
Pacific branch lines, the town is the shipping point for the Owyhee and
Malheur Valleys, and for a region with vast cattle ranges. Cereals, hay,
and vegetables are shipped in large quantities. Cattle and sheep are

crowded into loading pens before being driven into the long freight trains that constantly fill the sidings. The annual Malheur County Fair and Rodeo is held here during September. The glamor of the Old West still lingers about the town, which has a background of barren hills and distant rimrock.

At **3.9 m.** US 30 crosses the Malheur River, whose banks in spring are overgrown with fragrant tangles of wild syringa, or mock orange, found many places in the Northwest and described by Lewis and Clark in their *Journals*. From its straight shoots the Indians fashioned their arrows, giving the bush the local name of arrow-wood.

The highway leads north, with the Sawtooths of Idaho visible (R), changing color with the changing light, from deep purple to rose. Volcanic dust in the air results in unusually beautiful sunset colors over these barren hills. After a brief rain the sage-scented air becomes so clear that the distant mountains seem unbelievably near.

Mountain mahogany and gnarly juniper are scattered over the hills. Deer and larger game abound in the wilder regions, while coyotes and rabbits lurk in the nearer coverts. Antelopes formerly ranged the plateaus; attracted by the sound of the bells on the wagon tongues, they often followed for miles the careening stagecoaches and lumbering wagon-trains. Pheasants, quails, and sage-hens live in the sage and greasewood, and geese and brilliantly colored ducks feed near the streams. At intervals small migratory birds with vivid plumage brighten the drab landscape. The desert lark is an ever-exuberant inhabitant of these waste spaces.

For ten miles northward from **25.5 m.** the highway, flanked (L) by sheer hills, roughly parallels Snake River (R).

At **31 m.** (R) is the village of OLD'S FERRY; a ferry established in 1862 is no longer operated.

Here at FAREWELL BEND the Oregon Trail left the Snake River and ran northwest over the ridges to Burnt River; at this point the pioneers bade farewell to water, not knowing how soon they would find some again. The ferry at Farewell Bend is said to be the locale of *Buckskin's Fight with the Wolves* by George H. Waggoner, whose parents brought him overland by ox-team in 1852.

VANTAGE POINT, **32.8 m.**, is a hill on which the Indians sometimes lay in ambush for emigrants who camped in the vicinity before starting inland; near this place several small emigrant trains were completely annihilated.

(*A marker at 36 m. indicates the change between Rocky Mountain and Pacific Standard time.*)

HUNTINGTON, **36.5 m.** (2,108 alt., 803 pop.), with its sun-parched houses, black train sheds, and smoke-stained trees and hills, is in a canyon of the Burnt Mountains. It was founded as a stage stop and maintained that role until 1884, when the Oregon Railroad & Navigation Company line was linked with the Oregon Short Line, connecting Oregon with the Atlantic seaboard. Huntington is now an important railroad division point and freight station, with sidings and loading pens to accommodate the Hereford herds from the nearby ranges.

North of Huntington US 30 follows the canyon of Burnt River, which it crosses 15 times in 12 miles. This stream was first mentioned and probably named by Peter Skene Ogden of the Hudson's Bay Company; either charred timber or the burned appearance of the volcanic rocks along its banks suggested the name. In April and May the spring grass relieves the somber tones of the rock and the sage-covered hills. Small side valleys hold irrigated farm land and large herds of cattle, though few are seen from the highway.

The highway runs through the forbidding country traversed by the desperate, half-starved Astorians seeking a short cut between the Snake and the Columbia Rivers, after the dreadful two months in which they had attempted to navigate the "cursed mad river."

At LIME, **41.3 m.,** a large conveyor passes over the highway, connecting two units of a cement plant. Lime deposits were formerly worked and burned in concrete kilns, the remains of which now crumble beside the road. Tunnels in the hills adjacent to Burnt River indicate small-scale attempts to obtain gold.

The stark walls of the Burnt Mountains canyons have been grotesquely carved by the snow-fed rivulets that in spring flood the river and fill small irrigation reservoirs. Occasionally a lone juniper clings to the rocks.

The highway winds through lands alternately arid and irrigated, and characterized by surprising contrasts created by green alfalfa fields and the gray of the sagebrush, to a widening valley.

At **55.7 m.** the route crosses a ridge known locally as an "iron dike." Car radios have no reception when stopped on the dike.

DURKEE, **57.9 m.** (2,654 alt., 100 pop.), is a weather-worn cattle-shipping point retaining the aspect of a frontier town of the buckboard era. Nearby, along Burnt River, are found fire opals rivaling the Mexican stones in quality.

Junipers appear in small clumps on the hills, and cottonwood and willows grow in profusion at PLEASANT VALLEY, **68 m.** (3,819 alt.), which served as a resting place for the emigrant train of 1878 that named it.

BAKER, **82.2 m.** (3,440 alt., 7,858 pop.), the seat of Baker County, was named for Col. E. D. Baker, who was a friend of Abraham Lincoln while both were practicing law in Illinois, and who was later for a few months U. S. Senator from Oregon; he left the Senate for military services in the Civil War and died in action. The city is on Powder River, between the Elkhorn Range and the Eagle Spur of the Blue Mountains, whose white peaks form an imposing background. It was neglected by the early emigrants, who were intent on reaching the greener Willamette Valley.

Born as the result of the discovery of gold in eastern Oregon, Baker is one of the few cities in the State that has kept its importance as a mining center. From the crude settlement of the grubstake and shovel days, it has evolved into a graceful, modern city, with enough of the old mining-town atmosphere lingering about its streets to give it flavor. Gold was discovered October 23, 1861, in Griffin's Gulch, and since that day the surrounding mines have produced $150,000,000 worth of gold. The FIRST NATIONAL BANK maintains a bullion department and has on display an exhibit of quartz, gold dust, and nuggets, one of which weighs 86 ounces and is valued at $2,500.

In Baker is the HEADQUARTERS OF THE WHITMAN NATIONAL FOREST (*maps, information*). Farming, stock raising, and lumbering in the county contribute to the town's prosperity.

Left from Baker on State 7, a graveled road, to GRIFFIN'S GULCH, **3.2 m.,** where Henry Griffin discovered gold in April, 1861. At **7 m.** is a junction with a dirt road; R. on this road, which leads through Blue Canyon. BLUE CANYON CREEK (L) is still placer mined to some extent.

At **8.4 m.** ELKHORN PEAK can be seen directly ahead, 12 miles to the north-west, its distant wooded slopes offering a sharp contrast with the sagebrush and stubble along the roadside. Lodgepole pine and juniper become more frequent as the route reaches the SITE OF AN INDIAN BATTLEGROUND, **9.6 m.** (L), where many spear and arrow heads have been found.

From the crest of a hill, **10.3 m.,** can be seen the SITE OF AUBURN (*see below*), once the seat of Baker County but now marked by a group of weeping willows. There were only about 40 houses, nearly all built high on the hillside, in the town of more than 5,000 population. In true mining-camp fashion, most of the floating population rolled in blankets before fires at night or lived in tents. Two cemeteries are still visible, one for whites and the other for Chinese. The bones of many of the latter were sluiced away in the insatiable search for gold.

At **10.8 m.** (L), easily identified by its grove of cottonwoods, is the SITE OF THE DAVID LITTLEFIELD HOME, the first in what was to become Baker County. Littlefield was one of the men who discovered gold here in 1861. A few of the outbuildings still stand.

At **12 m.** (R), directly opposite across the canyon, is a second view of the site formerly occupied by Auburn. Beyond the bare area is Frenchman's Gulch.

In the vicinity are CALIFORNIA and POKER GULCHES (L), and FREEZE-OUT GULCHES NOS. 1, 2, AND 3. Gold to the value of millions of dollars has been taken from this district but the rich veins have been exhausted; the streams are still panned to some extent.

At **83.4 m.** is a junction with a graveled road.

Left on this road is the SITE OF POCAHONTAS, **6 m.,** now a field with one gray shack. The town once received 11 votes to make it the capital of Oregon.

HAINES, **93.6 m.** (3,334 alt., 431 pop.), is the center of a rich farming district. The ELKHORN RANGE (L) is broken by a series of peaks; from south to north, Elkhorn Peak (8,922 alt.), Rock Creek Butte (9,097 alt.), Hunt Mountain (8,232 alt.), named for Wilson Price Hunt, Red Mountain (8,920 alt.), and Twin Mountains (8,920 alt.).

At **96.2 m.** is a junction with a road.

Left on this graveled road is CASTORVILLE, **6 m.**, with one stone building left to commemorate its former importance as a mining and milling settlement. The flood of 1914 washed away all other traces of the town.

Crossing the North Powder River, **101.7 m.**, near the point where it enters the main Powder River, US 30 enters NORTH POWDER, **102.1 m.**, which was a stage station on the Oregon Trail. The Powder River is so named because of the character of the volcanic soil along its banks.

At **105 m.** is a marker indicating the camp where Marie Dorion, the Indian wife of the half-breed interpreter, paused on the morning of December 30, 1811, to add another feeble life to the Wilson Price Hunt party. The main party went on but Pierre remained with his family; the next morning he came trudging into camp, leading his son and the skeleton of a horse, which bore the woman with the babe in her arms and her two-year-old son slung in a blanket at her side. The infant died within a week, while the party was crossing the Blue Mountains on the last lap of the journey to the Columbia. Dorion had managed to acquire this horse from the Indians along the Snake though other members of the party had failed in their attempts to make like purchases. Toward the end of the journey along the dreadful river, when the party was half dead from starvation, Hunt had determined to kill the horse for food. Dorion had resisted, finally leaving the party in order to protect his property. Hunt and two men started after Dorion, prepared to take the horse by force. Two days later they found the Dorions; Pierre still refused to give up the horse and, oddly, the men backed him in his stand.

This seemingly barren country is not without inhabitants. Long-tailed magpies circle above the thickets, and porcupines make regular forays on grain and haystacks. Badgers, jackrabbits, and ground-squirrels whisk in and out of their underground homes, and some beavers, once abundant, still dam the small streams. Hawks and bald eagles range the skies.

The highway now traverses GRANDE RONDE VALLEY, which the French-Canadian trappers called La Grande Vallée. The sight of this great green bowl, encircled by mountainous walls, brought delight to early travelers after their long journey across the alkali plains. Captain Bonneville, who saw it in 1833, reported: "Its sheltered situation, embosomed in mountains, renders it good pasturing ground in the winter time; when the elk come down to it in great numbers, driven out of the mountains by the snow. The Indians then resort to it to hunt. They likewise come to it in the summer to dig the camash root, of which it produces immense quantities. When this plant is in blossom, the whole valley is tinted by its blue flowers, and looks like the ocean when overcast by a cloud." Frémont spoke of the charm of the country when he traversed it ten years later.

UNION, **117.5 m.** (2,717 alt., 1,107 pop.), whose name, bestowed in 1862, shows the patriotic spirit of its first citizens, was once the seat of Union County. The first flag flown over the old courthouse was made in 1864 of red flannel, white muslin, and blue calico. Though early emigrants, bound for the Willamette Valley, passed through the fertile Grande Ronde, it was not until 1860 that the first claim was staked; Conrad Miller, the first settler, selected land a mile west of the present town. Union is the center of a large agricultural and stock-raising area. Catherine Creek, a good trout stream flowing from the western slope of the Wallowas, runs through the town. The 620-acre EASTERN OREGON STATE EXPERIMENT STATION is at the edge of the town; here experiments are made in growing and improving grains, grasses, and forage crops. Here also are a dairy unit, a poultry unit, a five-acre orchard, and truck garden plots.

At HOT LAKE, **123.2 m.** (2,701 alt., 250 pop.), water gushing from springs has a temperature of 208 degrees, the boiling point at this altitude.

LA GRANDE, **131.9 m.** (2,784 alt., 8,050 pop.), the seat of Union County, is a beautifully situated recreational center. It lies between the Blue Mountains and the Wallowas, at the western edge of the Grande Ronde Valley.

For 20 years pioneers came into the valley, camped here, then hurried on toward the Willamette. In 1861 a small group of men retraced their trail from the Umatilla River to stake claims in the valley. Ben Brown of this company built a house on a low bench above the river. Later he converted his house into a tavern, around which a small settlement sprang up, known variously as Brownsville and Brown Town, until the establishment of a post office, when the present name was adopted.

The discovery of gold in eastern Oregon turned the village into a thriving mining town, which declined as surface diggings played out. In 1884 the arrival of the railroad gave fresh life to the place. The railroad was laid straight across the valley, missing the town by a mile, but part of the inhabitants moved to spots near the railroad, creating New Town; the Old Town, as it is still known locally, is today an integral and populous part of the city. The industrial life centers about the railroad shops and the two large sawmills.

In 1864, when Union County was carved out of Baker County, the FIRST UNION COUNTY COURTHOUSE was erected on the site of the Brown cabin and hotel; the old building, which is still standing at 1st and B Sts., has successively been occupied as a store, church, and residence since 1876.

La Grande was the home of Blue Mountain University, a Methodist college that ceased to function in 1884. During an Indian uprising of 1878 the alarmed citizens of the valley took refuge behind the thick brick walls of the old institution. The EASTERN OREGON NORMAL SCHOOL, the leading educational institution of the area today, has a campus of more than 30 acres and several attractive buildings.

La Grande was the birthplace (1888) of Kay Cleaver Strahan, a writer of mystery stories. T. T. Geer, Governor of Oregon (1899-1903), lived 10 years of his young manhood near here and accumulated much material published in his volume of reminiscences, *Fifty Years in Oregon.*

By an Oregon Trail marker, **133.4 m.**, standing in GANGLOFF STATE PARK, is an impressive view of the Grande Ronde Valley. Dipping to the gorge of the Grande Ronde River, the highway crosses the stream five times, closely paralleling railroad tracks; the gorge is so narrow that its walls, streaked with red iron oxide, and the pines along the road are blackened by smoke.

Leaving the gorge, the highway begins to climb the BLUE MOUNTAINS. These mountains are Oregon's oldest land; when what is now the State was a waste of waters, they stood above the flood. During winter snows their precipitous slopes held the migrating pioneers helpless, and in summer exhausted them. The Blue Mountains have a quieter appeal than have the Cascades; seen from a distance, their blue haze has a shadowy, unsubstantial appearance.

At **141.7 m.** the highway enters BLUE MOUNTAIN TIMBER PRESERVE, which stretches for 18 miles along the crest of the Blue Mountains.

At **151.5 m.** is a junction with a road.

Left on this dirt road to the EZRA MEEKER SPRINGS, **0.2 m.**, named for the gray-bearded patriarch whose eagerness to mark the old trial made him a national figure. He traversed the Oregon Trail by ox-team in the emigration of 1852 and, as an old man, retraced it in the same manner; at 94 years of age he covered approximately the same route by airplane.

At **152 m.** on US 30 is a junction with Ruckle Road.

Right on Ruckle Road to the SUMMIT RANGER STATION, **14 m.** This road, constructed in the late 1860's by Thomas & Ruckle, was a stage route between La Grande and Weston. Beyond the ranger station it is now covered with underbrush.

KAMELA, **152.1 m.** (4,206 alt., 27 pop.), is in the highest railroad pass of the Blue Mountains. All trains take on an extra engine for the climb to it. The town is a starting point for camping and fishing trips. Deer are plentiful nearby, and trout swarm the numerous streams.

Northwest of Kamela the highway winds along the top of a wide ridge. The undergrowth of the evergreen forests here includes a small variety of the Oregon grape, whose bloom is the State flower of Oregon.

At **153.6 m.** is the summit of the Blue Mountains pass (4,337 alt.).

MEACHAM, **157.7 m.** (3,681 alt., 70 pop.), was named for Col. A. B. Meacham, a member of the Modoc Peace Commission. The ill-starred Hunt party, after its wanderings in the Snake River wilderness, passed this way. It was near here that the Dorion child, born a few days earlier, died. Across this region covered wagons creaked and men and women trudged, sustained by the nearness of their goal. Later, stage drivers cracked their long whips above plunging eight-horse teams to hurry them to the Meacham Tavern. So recklessly did they drive that passengers were often injured, and Meacham's coachmen figured in editorial diatribes of 50 years ago. Two large trees that formerly stood near Meacham sometimes concealed bandits, who preyed on the stage passengers. A series of bold robberies, including that of the Wells Fargo Express, occurred at this point.

At **161. m.** is EMIGRANT SPRINGS STATE PARK (*facilities for picnicking*). Near the entrance a stone shaft marks a spring said to have been discovered in 1834 by Jason Lee. The bronzed pine and green or gold tamarack of the park-like groves were inviting to the pioneers wearying of the long journey. Deep ruts made by the wheels of covered wagons are near the highway.

At **163.4 m.** the route crosses the eastern boundary of the UMA-TILLA INDIAN RESERVATION, now occupied by about 1,200 members of the Cayuse, Umatilla, and Walla Walla tribes, who engage in wheat growing and ranching. The reservation has no Government school, but missions are maintained by the Roman Catholic and Presbyterian churches. Graveled roads give easy access to almost all parts of the reservation.

The highway crosses a plateau where there is a wide view of the ranges receding to the indigo haze of the horizon. Nearer are harsh, broken hills suggestive of the Badlands of Dakota, relieved only by the scanty growth of wiry grass and scattered pines. An Oregon Trail marker, **66.9 m.**, is in DEAD MAN'S PASS, the site of an attack by Indians in 1878.

Winding along hillsides and broken cliffs, US 30 reaches the summit of EMIGRANT HILL, **168.6 m.** (3,800 alt.) ; the view here is one of the most impressive in the State on the old Oregon Trail. Beyond the ragged line of the nearer terrain rise ridge after ridge of wheatlands. Beyond the fields undulant sage plains fade to purple, and are lost in the distance. Snow fences are seen, strategically placed to prevent drifts over the highway during winter storms. The tall red or yellow sticks placed upright along the highway are traffic guides during heavy snows.

The route curves around hills colored in spring and early summer with the yellow of sunflowers, the scarlet of paintbrush, and the blue of desert lupine, campanula, and iris. At **173.4 m.** Mount Hood and Mount Adams, more than 100 miles distant, are visible (L). The highway climbs a lesser eminence, and from this height the hills slope gently downward to the Umatilla Valley floor, with its pattern of angular fields. These seemingly endless acres of grain lands are broken only by occasional shadows where cottonwood and willow mark the course of a wandering stream. Bands of horses, in silhouette against the sky, suggest the nearness of the range country.

At **181.6 m.** is a junction with a road.

Right on this graveled road is CAYUSE, **7.5 m.** (1,350 alt., 32 pop.), within the Umatilla Reservation. This scattered Indian village was named for a tribe that formerly dwelt in this region. The crude buildings, protected by brush and small trees, are for the most part along the Umatilla River and various creeks. In the summer many of the inhabitants leave their houses to dwell in tepees.

MISSION, **181.9 m.**, is the UMATILLA INDIAN AGENCY. At the STATE PHEASANT FARM, **182.6 m.**, grouse, quail, pheasants, and other game birds are bred for release on the plateaus and in the uplands of eastern Oregon.

185.6 m. US 30 leaves the Umatilla Indian Reservation and, following closely the tree-lined Umatilla River (R), passes a few Indian dwellings (L).

PENDLETON, **187.7 m.** (1,070 alt., 6,621 pop.), was named for George Hunt Pendleton, who was Democratic nominee for Vice President in 1864 and later a leader in the Greenback Party. In 1865 M. E. Goodwin traded a team of horses for a claim covering much of the land on which the city now stands and in the following year he built a toll bridge over the Umatilla River, which flows through the town. In 1869 Goodwin donated land for the site of a county courthouse and the place was made the Umatilla County seat. The settlement early became the base of supplies for cattle barons and an oasis for their employees; each Saturday the cowboys raced their ponies down the streets, clinked spurs over the board walks, and tilted glass after glass above the bar of the Last Chance saloon. The town grew haphazardly, its first school being held over the jail in the courthouse.

Some of the old cattle trails that led into Pendleton in the 1880's are now followed by modern highways; others have been obliterated by wheat fields. In Pendleton are flour mills, foundries, planing mills, creameries, and saddle factories. Sheep, once despised by the cattlemen, yield fleece for the town's woolen mills. Pendleton blankets are widely known.

The TIL TAYLOR STATUE here is a memorial to a Umatilla County sheriff who was killed in 1920 during a jailbreak. Taylor, one of the old-time sheriffs, served the county for 18 years.

The Pendleton Round-Up, produced first in 1910 and annually since 1912, attracts thousands of visitors during three days of mid-September. It is held in ROUND-UP PARK, which has a stadium seating 40,000; the park is at the western end of W. Court St. Stagecoaches, covered wagons, and some 2,000 Indians in full regalia preserve the pageantry of the Old West. Also in the park is an OPEN AIR THEATER, with a stage of natural basalt.

Section 13. Pendleton to Portland, 228.2 m. US 30.

West of PENDLETON, **0 m.**, at **1.8 m.** (L) is the EASTERN OREGON STATE HOSPITAL, a modern institution with facilities for 1,325 mentally ill patients.

US 30 runs straight ahead through the Umatilla wheatlands. The ranch buildings, often at considerable distance from the highway, are sheltered by groves of locust trees. Silhouettes of windmills are conspicuous against the skyline. In the fall great piles of sacked wheat dot the harvested fields, whose stubble alternates with the grays and duns of freshly plowed land. West of the wheat region the route passes through a sheep-raising country, where immense bands feed on the natural forage.

STANFIELD, **23.5 m.** (204 pop.), the center of a sheep-raising district, was named for the Stanfield family, owners of a nearby ranch.

HERMISTON, **29.2 m.** (459 alt., 608 pop.), a tree-shaded oasis, is in the center of the Umatilla Irrigation Project. Irrigation ditches run through the streets. These waterways have reclaimed the fields that produce grain, vegetables, and fruits, and that stand out conspicuously against a background of sagebrush and cactus. It was named for *Weir of Hermiston,* which Robert Louis Stevenson was engaged in writing at the time of his death in 1894.

At **35.2 m.** is a junction with US 730; W. of this point US 30, here called the Upper Columbia River Highway, runs on the south side of the Columbia River.

Right from the junction on US 730, which follows the south bank of the Columbia River. Sergeant Ordway of the Lewis and Clark expedition described the country on the westward trip as "in general Smooth plains then the barron hills make close to the River on each side . . . no timber along the Shores." The next day he said that the party "proceeded on pass'd high clifts of rocks on each Side of the River."

At **20.6 m.** the highway crosses the Washington Line.

WALLULA, **26.6 m.** (324 alt. 36 pop.), surrounded by sand and sagebrush near the mouth of the Walla Walla River, is now a railroad junction. Near the Columbia are a few adobe remnants, the RUINS OF FORT WALLA WALLA, first

UNION PACIFIC CONSTRUCTION TRAIN (1867)

BREAKING CAMP

Leslie's Weekly

METHODIST MISSION NEAR THE DALLES (1845)

known as Fort Nez Percés. This was established by the North West Company not long after it had bought out Astor's interests on the Columbia. The first post, built of wood and strongly fortified with bastions and a 20-foot palisade because of the constant hostility of the Indians in the neighborhood, burned down and was replaced in the 1840's by an adobe structure. The post was important to fur traders and other travelers because, while off the Oregon Trail, it offered a supply point in time of need after the always trying journey across the plains of the Snake. The Rev. Samuel Parker visited it in 1835 when seeking a site for the Whitman mission. Because of the dry, unpleasant character of the country he recommended a spot farther inland.

At the mouth of the Walla Walla is the point where the returning Lewis and Clark expedition, advised by Indians camping on the west bank of the Columbia, determined to take a short cut to the Snake. The leaders wished to cross the river at once but the Indians begged them to stay, having heard of the white men's skill as dancers. George W. Fuller in his *History of the Pacific Northwest* calls the party "the dancing explorers"; rather, they were a road show. Not a little of their success in obtaining supplies and in safely crossing the continent rested on their ability to entertain the aborigines. The star of the troup was York, Clark's servant, a big, good-natured Negro who was never so happy as when he was surrounded by wondering Indians who rubbed his black skin with moistened fingers and yanked his curly hair to test their reality. Another favorite entertainer was Peter Cruzat, who clung to his fiddle all the way across the country and back, preserving it even at times when every extra ounce was a burden. A third was Rivet, who, as Ordway wrote, "dances on his head." On some occasions the entertainment offered to the Indians had the character of a medicine show, Lewis giving out eye water, ointments, and Rush's pills to all who applied.

Ordway described the entertainment at this village: "they said they wished us to Stay with them to day as we lived a great way off, and they wished to see us dance this evening & begged on us to Stay this day. So our officers concluded to Stay this day. the head chief brought up a good horse & said he wished to give it to us but as he was poor he wished us to give him some kind of a kittle, but as we could not spare a kittle Capt Clark gave his Sword a flag and half pound of powder & ball for the horse. we took our horses across the river. our officers made another chief gave him a meddle &C. in the afternoon a number of Indians came to our officers who were diseased the lame and many with Sore eyes and lame legs & arms &C. our officers dressd their wounds, washed their eyes & gave them meddicine and told them how to apply it &C. the chief called all his people and told them of the meddicine &C. which was a great wonder among them & they were much pleased &C. the Indians Sent their women to gether wood or Sticks to See us dance this evening. about 300 of the natives assembled to our Camp we played the fiddle and danced a while the head chief told our officers that they Should be lonesome when we left them and they wished to hear once of our meddicine Songs and try to learn it and wished us to learn one of theirs and it would make them glad. So our men Sang 2 Songs which appeared to take great affect on them. they tryed to learn Singing with us with a low voice. the head chief then made a speech & it was repeated by a warrier that all might hear. then all the Savages men women and children of any size danced forming a circle round a fire & jumping up nearly as other Indians, & keep time verry well they wished our men to dance with them So we danced among them and they were much pleased, and Said that they would dance day and night untill we return. everry few minutes one of their warries made a Speech pointing towards the enimy and towards the moon &C. &C. which was all repeated by another meddison man with a louder voice as (so) all might hear the dance continued untill about midnight then the most of them went away peaceable & have behaved verry clever and honest with us as yet, and appear to have a Sincere wish to be at peace and to git acquaintance with us &C. &C."

Right from Wallula on US 410. Near TOUCHET, **36.1 m.**, the highway follows the former right-of-way of the Walla Walla & Columbia R.R., built in
1872. Part of the crew of this first railroad connecting towns in the Territory
was a collie whose job it was to run ahead of the locomotive and drive cattle off
the track.

At **49.1 m.** is the junction with a paved road. Right here **1 m.** to
WAIILATPU, site of the Marcus Whitman mission, founded in 1836. The buildings are being reconstructed. Whitman built his mission here in spite of the
warnings of the Hudson's Bay Company's Chief Factor of the treacherous nature
of the nearby Cayuses.

Myron F. Eells, a missionary from Massachusetts who visited the place in
1838, wrote: "It was built of adobe, mud dried in the form of brick, only
larger— There are doors and windows of the roughest material, the boards being
sawed by hand and put together by no carpenter, but by one who knows nothing
about the work. There are a number of wheat, corn and potato fields about the
house, besides a garden of melons and all kinds of vegetables common to a
garden. There are no fences, there being no timber with which to make them.
The furniture is very primitive; the bedsteads are boards nailed to the sides
of the house, sink-fashion; then some blankets and husks make the bed."

As long as Dr. McLoughlin retained his post at Fort Vancouver, the Indians
in his domain feared to attack white people. But their resentment against the
invaders had been growing and when, after McLoughlin's dismissal, a particularly
fatal epidemic of measles developed, they listened to the whispers of medicine
men that the whites were bringing in the disease to annihilate them, and that the
Indians must drive the whites out if they were to survive. On November 29,
1847, the Indians descended on the mission, killing Dr. Whitman, his wife, and
five other people. More men were slain in the following week while returning
to the mission, making a total of 14; 53 men, women, and children were taken
captive.

When news of the event reached Fort Vancouver, Peter Skene Ogden, of
the Hudson's Bay Company, set out for Walla Walla. On January 2, after paying
a ransom of 62 blankets, 63 cotton shirts, 12 guns, 500 rounds of ammunition, 12
flints, and 37 pounds of tobacco, he loaded the captives on boats bound down the
Columbia. Three years later five Indians were tried and hanged for the murders.

UMATILLA (Ind., *water rippling over sands*), **36.1 m.** (294 alt.,
345 pop.), at the confluence of the Umatilla and Columbia Rivers, was
formerly the shipping point for the output of the Boise, Powder River,
and Owyhee gold fields. It sprang up during the rush to the gold
diggings of Idaho and eastern Oregon. Oxcarts, stagecoaches, and
freight wagons passed along its dusty streets on their ways to the distant
mines. River boats, laden with supplies, crowded the wharves. When
the mining fever subsided, the town was beginning to ship quantities of
grain from the eastern Oregon fields. The building of the Oregon Railroad and Navigation Company road diverted traffic, and the place declined in importance.

US 30 traverses an irrigated district, its green, cultivated fields
contrasting with tablelands and soft beige hills. Narrow farmlands (R)
border the highway. Houses and gardens are sheltered by the fringe of
cottonwoods and poplars. The green of the farms (L) terminates
abruptly, the plateau beyond them being covered with gray cactus and
sagebrush. Beyond the river (R) stretch the brown hills of Washington. The chief event that Ordway found to note in this area was the

purchase of nice "fat" dogs; Captain Clark was the only one in the party who did not learn to smack his lips over this delicacy.

IRRIGON, **43.2 m.** (297 alt.), a former stopping place for travelers to and from the old Boise and Owyhee mines, derives both its name and its livelihood from the irrigation district of which it is the trading center. An experiment station demonstrates the agricultural possibilities of the rich silt. Vegetables and fruits are grown successfully. Cantaloups and other melons bear the Irrigon label to distant markets. Peach, cherry, and apricot trees cover the knolls. Conspicuous throughout the region are the lush growths of wild asparagus along irrigation flumes.

At **54.9 m.** on a slight knoll (R) is a concrete slab in which is embedded an excellent specimen of the picture writing of prehistoric Indians. The pictograph was brought here from a spot on the basaltic bank of the Columbia River a few miles east.

BOARDMAN, **55.1 m.** (250 alt., 100 pop.), lies in an area that holds many fossilized remains of prehistoric animals. Specimens taken from the vicinity include part of a mastodon tooth, bones of fishes, of the three-toed horse, and of the rhinoceros, and bits of turtle shell.

US 30 follows the river, a green band of water separating the grayness of the bleak, barren shores. The plateau rim (L) along the Oregon side rises almost sheer except where creeks break through to join the river. Occasionally a row of poplar trees serves as a windbreak in winter against icy gales that roar down the Columbia.

CASTLE ROCK, **60.8 m.**, was once a busy community. The editor of *West Shore* in his issue of October, 1883, wrote: "Castle Rock, in Umatilla County, bordering on the Wasco line, was laid out on the 15th of last May upon ground taken up only a year before for a sheep ranch. It now contains an express office, post office, saloons, dwellings, schools, etc. A large forwarding and shipping business for the Heppner region is its chief support, though many settlers are taking up land in the vicinity. The growth of western towns is wonderful."

HEPPNER JUNCTION, **70.3 m.**, is at the point where many early wagon trains turned south to cross Alkali Flats, avoiding the jagged scoria and sage-grown cliffs that US 30 follows along the river.

For 45 miles westward the highway crowds close to the river, in places climbing along the basaltic cliffs and affording views of the wild river gorge and the mountains in Washington. The emerald green of the water contrasts with the tawny hills and the rusty cliffs, colored by lichens and iron oxide deposits. These cliffs show the successive flows of lava that inundated what is now the upper Columbia Valley.

ARLINGTON, **81.4 m.** (224 alt., 601 pop.), a town not much wider than its one locust-shaded street, is wedged between two high and barren ridges. It was formerly called Alkali, but was renamed by a group of settlers for Arlington, Va. The town is a trading center for the country to the south. It is also headquarters for hunters of the wild geese that swarm the islands and gravel bars of the Columbia. It is estimated that from 20,000 to 25,000 geese use the vicinity as a feeding ground. Though there are strict limits on the number of birds that may be taken, the season, usually the month of November, finds eager hunters gathering here from all parts of the State. Hunting rights are frequently rented from the ranchers at fees ranging from $8 to $10 a day. The Arlington Ferry (*cars, $1; round trip, $1.50*) makes connections with Roosevelt, Wash.

West of Arlington the rolling lands recede and the valleys along the highway (L) are little more than canyons leading to confined ranches and irrigated farms. Saffron-stained patches of lava color the cliffs of the plateau rim. Passing through BLALOCK, **90.6 m.**, US 30 threads the narrow gorge through which the Columbia has cut a ragged channel.

At **105.3 m.** Mount Hood is seen, rising above the waters of the Columbia.

The JOHN DAY RIVER, **105.6 m.**, originally called LePage's River by Lewis and Clark for a member of their party, was named in honor of John Day of the Astorians. According to Washington Irving, Day was a Virginia backwoodsman who had hunted on the Missouri a number of years before joining Hunt's overland party. Day and Crooks fell behind on the Snake River, while Hunt went ahead (*see above*) with the main party in the winter of 1811-12. During the following spring Day and Crooks were robbed of everything they had and left naked on the banks of the Columbia. After reaching Astoria, Day decided to return with Robert Stuart's party. Before he reached Walla Walla, however, he became violently insane and had to be taken back to Astoria.

A swift, turbulent stream, the river has worn its way through stratum after stratum of rock. In its steep gorges are written successive chapters of Oregon's geological evolution.

Near RUFUS, **110.7 m.** (172 alt., 70 pop.), long breaks in the growths of poplars bear witness to the wind's severity. Gardens and orchards thrive between rows of closely grown trees or behind woven-willow shelters.

At **113.3 m.** is the junction with US 97.

Right on US 97 to the landing of the Maryhill ferry, **0.4 m.** (*fare $1; service as needed*). From the north bank ferry landing in Washington, US 97 continues to the junction with US 830, **1.2 m.**; L. here **2.9 m.** on US 830 to MARYHILL CASTLE, built by Samuel Hill, a road builder. The castle, dour and desolate, is visible from the Oregon side of the Columbia. It is a three-story rectangular structure of concrete, fascinating yet forbidding, set on a cliff 800 feet above the river. Though construction was begun in 1914, and Queen Marie of Roumania dedicated the structure in 1926 as an international art museum, for years its windows were barred, its doors padlocked, and its winding, concrete driveways a tangle of matted weeds and grass. Armies of rats scampered through its labyrinth of rooms. In 1937 the building was opened to visitors. Queen Marie gave a life-size portrait of her daughter, an ornate desk supposed to have been made by herself, a set of chairs, and other pieces of furniture. Other exhibits are being added.

After carefully comparing weather records, Samuel Hill chose this spot, midway between the damp coast and semi-arid southeastern Washington, as the perfect place in which to live. He lavished a fortune on the estate, and left a bequest of $1,200,000 for completing and maintaining it as a museum. Hill never lived at Maryhill. In a crypt constructed during his lifetime repose the owner's ashes, commemorated by a tablet bearing the inscription: "Samuel Hill—amid Nature's unrest, he sought rest."

Two abandoned fish wheels (L), half obscured by a poplar grove and now outlawed for use in Oregon streams, stand at the mouth of the DESCHUTES RIVER, 120.5 m. US 30 crosses the river on the CHIEF DUC-SAC-HI BRIDGE, a fine concrete structure named for a chief of the Wasco tribe, who operated a ferry across the river. The Deschutes has been important as a fishing and hunting stream for both Indians and whites. On early maps the Deschutes often bears its English name, Falls River.

Lewis and Clark found the river "divided by numbers of large rocks, and Small Islands covered with a low groth of timber." The Indians knew it as the Towahnahiooks River, although the explorers on their westward trip learned only that it was known as "the River on which the Snake Indians live."

CELILO, 123.4 m. (158 alt.), at CELILO FALLS, is a canoe portage as old as the fishing stations still held by the Indians under a treaty granting exclusive and perpetual fishing rights to them. Long before Lewis and Clark halted at this place, likely fishing stands on these rocks were handed down by the Indians from father to son.

When the explorers visited the vicinity they found ". . . great numbers of Stacks of pounded Salmon neetly preserved in the following manner, i.e. after (being) suffi(c)ently Dried it is pounded between two Stones fine, and put into a speces of basket neetly made of grass and rushes better than two feet long and one foot Diamiter, which basket is lined with the Skin of Salmon Stretched and dried for the purpose, in this it is pressed down as hard as is possible, when full they Secure the open part with the fish Skins across which they fasten th(r)o. the loops of the basket that part very securely, and then on a Dry Situation they Set those baskets. . . . thus preserved those fish may be kept Sound and sweet Several years." Here fish arè still speared, cleaned, and dried in the traditional manner, but they are no longer pounded into pemmican and stored in the woven baskets. Although this untidy and stench-ridden village has long been a joy to ethnologists, it is exceedingly unpopular with its neighbors. The bucks fish and the squaws prepare the catch for food, resorting to the primitive open-air methods of curing developed by their prehistoric forebears. Across the Columbia is the old village of WISHRAM, described by Lewis and Clark in their *Journals* and by Washington Irving in *Astoria.* This village furnished many fine studies of Indian life to Edward Curtis in preparing his *North American Indians.*

Sergeant Ordway said of the falls: "the hight of the particular falls in all is 37 feet eight Inches, and has a large rock Island in the midst of them and look Shocking the water divided in several channels by the rock. Some of the cooks at camp bought several fat dogs this day."

There is scarcely a traveler of the early days who did not speak of the settlement at the great falls of the Columbia. It was here that the tribes of the upper country met the down-river and coast tribes for barter, the vicinity being regarded as neutral ground. It was here that the westward-surging pioneers lowered their wagons over the rimrock by means of ropes and pulleys. Freight was transferred from the wagons to large canoes and barges. Wagon beds, resting on their own wheels and lashed to crude rafts, sheltered women and children from the fierce Columbia squalls on the perilous trip to Vancouver.

Lewis and Clark, finding 17 Indian lodges along here, "landed and walked down accompanied by an old man to view the falls, and the best rout for to make a portage which we Soon discovered was much nearest on the Star'd Side, and the distance 1200 yards one third of the way on a rock, about 200 yards over a loose Sand collected in a hollar blown by the winds from the bottoms below which was dis-agreeable to pass, as it was steep and loose. at the lower part of those rapids we arrived at 5 Large Lod(g)es of nativs drying and prepareing fish for market, they gave us Philburts, and berries to eate. we returned droped down to the head of the rapids and took every article except the Canoes across the portag(e) where I had formed a camp on (an) elegable Situation for the protection of our Stores from thieft, which we were more fearfull of, than their arrows." A portage railroad, 14 miles long, was opened in 1863. The construction of canals and locks here was started by the Federal Government in 1905; they eventually cost five million dollars. Below the falls the OREGON TRUNK RAILROAD BRIDGE spans the river, its piers resting on solid rock above the water.

On October 24, 1805, the day after making the arduous falls port-age, the Lewis and Clark party came to the Short Narrows of the Columbia, where the high walls of the gorge made portage so difficult that Clark "deturmined" to shoot the rapids, "notwithstanding the hor-rid appearance of this agitated gut swelling, boiling & whorling in every direction." Ordway merely commented that they went through "verry rapid and bad whorl pools, and went on verry well." He was much more interested in the "number of fat dogs, crambries and white cakes of root bread" bought from the Indians.

Passing under the railroad bridge, US 30 is sheltered by basaltic palisades (L), dusted with sulphur-colored lichen, which, like the sage, willow, and cottonwood of the section, is not true green, being grayed by the alkaline soil.

SEUFERT, 132.6 m., was named for the Seufert family, who established a large salmon- and fruit-packing plant at this point. Fish wheels, formerly operated by the cannery, stand along the river (R). Many Indian petroglyphs and pictographs are on the bluffs facing the Columbia; prehistoric as well as historic aborigines of the region came here to fish for salmon, and while some of the pictures of fishes, beavers, elks, water dogs, and men were doubtless made as primitive art expression, others were carved and painted to carry messages.

THE DALLES (Fr., *flagstones or gutters*), 136 m. (98 alt., 5,883 pop.), the seat of Wasco County, is the principal market town of a large agricultural area. The name was given by the *voyageurs* of the Hudson's Bay Company because the basaltic rock walls of the swift narrows of the Columbia River just above the present townsite resembled the stones confining the gutters of their native villages. The site of the city has numerous upthrusts of basaltic rock, which cause many dead-end streets. The retail business district, where ancient frame buildings shoulder modern brick structures, occupies a broad, low bench near the river. Behind it, in the terraced residential section, some houses stand 50 feet above their neighbors. There is a prevalence of stone houses of the type found in Italy and on the Dalmatian coast. These were erected by Italian workers, who were brought in to build the locks and decided to settle in the place.

A mission under the superintendency of Jason Lee was established here in 1838 by Daniel Lee and H. K. W. Perkins. Owing to their failure to interest the Indians, the Methodists sold the property in 1846 to the Whitman mission, but it was abandoned after the Whitman massacre. From the time of the mission's establishment the settlement that grew up around it became an intermediate goal to transcontinental travelers as the single place of white habitation in the area. Many travelers and would-be settlers found their supplies completely exhausted by the time they had reached this point and the unfriendly Indians early learned to exploit their needs, making exorbitant demands for goods in return for pounded fish and other foodstuffs. The Indians' values were peculiar, however; Father DeSmet, when passing The Dalles in the early 1840's, found the Indians proudly parading in odds and ends of clothing obtained from the whites. One man wore a G-string and a sailor's glazed cap, another a pair of pants much too small for him, a third a G-string and a pair of enormous brogans, and a fourth a gaudy vest and little else. The envied dandy of the party wore a lady's nightcap with wide flapping white frills.

In 1847 Fort Dalles was established to protect immigrants. The first store was established in 1850. The plight of the average newcomer reaching The Dalles is shown in George A. Waggoner's account of his family's migration experiences: "We left our wagon on the Umatilla. . . . We packed our bedding on Old Nig, the last ox left us, and started on afoot. . . . My father sold him (Old Nig) at The Dalles for $20 to buy food. We stopped two weeks at The Dalles. Father found an old stove and rigged up a table out of some old endgates and sideboards of an abandoned wagon and ran a lunch counter for the soldiers and civilians who were building the military post there."

The town grew as the gold rush of the Northwest developed in the 1860's.

H. L. Davis, who wrote *Honey in the Horn*, a Harper prize novel (1935) and winner of a Pulitzer prize (1936), was a resident of The Dalles for a number of years.

The second bluff above the town bears evidence of the eager desire of early travelers to register for the benefit of posterity; the sandstone face bears names, initials, and dates from 1841. Among them is the name of U. S. Grant, who was stationed in Oregon as a young man.

PULPIT ROCK, a basaltic formation at Twelfth and Court Sts., served as a missionary pulpit as early as 1837. Interdenominational Easter sunrise services are now held annually at this place. FORT ROCK, at the foot of Liberty St., was a camp site of the Lewis and Clark party. It is a natural depression in the basaltic cliffs, reached from the railway station by a marked trail.

The HORN (*visitors welcome*), 205 Second St., an old saloon, has hundreds of horns of mountain sheep, bison, deer, and elk. The OLD FORT DALLES HISTORICAL SOCIETY BUILDING, at 15th and Garrison Sts., is the only remaining structure of the old fort; it houses a remarkable collection of Indian arrows, stone bowls, baskets, and beadwork, and scores of articles brought across the plains in covered wagons.

West of The Dalles, scoria yields to pine-grown plateaus, confined by mountains (L), beyond which Mount Hood towers. Across the Columbia Gorge (R), Mount Adams rears its white peak. On both sides of the river, rocky benches rise above each other in irregular steps to lofty, weathered palisades.

West of the village of ROWENA, **144.6 m.,** the highway leaves the flatlands by a sharp climb over the Rowena Loops, a series of reverse curves hewn from solid basalt in places.

Opposite Rowena, near Lyle, Wash., is the burial place of the writer, Frederic Homer Balch (1861-1891). His sweetheart, Genevra Whitcomb, who is buried near him, was commemorated in his posthumously published novel, *Genevieve: A Tale of Oregon.*

ROWENA CREST, **147.2 m.** (706 alt.), is in MAYER STATE PARK, where a parking place is provided at the point offering the finest view.

It commands a majestic panorama of rugged country and miles of winding river.

US 30 rounds ROWENA DELL, **147.9 m.**, a deep canyon (R) with oakgrown walls cut through solid stone. It was infested with rattlesnakes until pioneers fenced the lower end of the canyon and turned in a drove of hogs. The animals soon cleared the dell, and the place was for a time thereafter known as Hog Canyon.

At **150.7 m.** Memaloose View Point overlooks the MEMALOOSE ISLAND, the "Island of the Dead," for hundreds of years an Indian burial ground, partly submerged since the completion of Bonneville Dam (*see below*). Many of the bleached bones of generations of Indians were moved to other cemeteries along the Columbia.

The MOSIER TUNNELS, **154.9 m.**, one 261 feet and the other 60 feet long, often referred to as the Twin Tunnels, penetrate a promontory more than 250 feet above the river. West of this point the contrast between the barren, semidesert contours of eastern Oregon and the lushness of the Pacific Slope becomes apparent.

US 30 crosses HOOD RIVER, **160.2 m.**, a picturesque stream descending from glaciers on the northern and eastern slopes of Mount Hood, and known in pioneer days by the unromantic name, Dog Creek. The name is said to have been inspired by the fact that a starving exploring party of early days began to eat dog meat here. Though such food was frequently used by early travelers in the area, Mrs. Nathaniel Coe, a well-known pioneer of the valley, objected to the name and forced a change. Lewis and Clark named the stream Labiche River for one of their followers. Its limpid, cascading waters have great beauty.

The town of HOOD RIVER, **160.6 m.** (100 alt., 2,757 pop.), is the center of a prolific apple and berry region, and is one of the entrances to the large recreational area about Mount Hood. Surrounded by evergreens and oaks, the town is beautifully situated. Its tiers of houses stand on the sharply rising land between the Hood River and Indian Creek gorges; the blue-gray waters of the Columbia River sweep in front of it through a channel worn deep in rugged stone. Behind the town, beyond evergreen forests and rising hills, the white splendor of Mount Hood is visible.

While holding a pastorate here, Frederic Homer Balch (1861-91) wrote *Genevieve: A Tale of Oregon* (published in 1932) and finished *The Bridge of the Gods* (1890). Hood River has also been the home of George W. Cronyn (1888-   ), author of historical novels, and Anthony Euwer (1877-   ), Oregon poet, who has described the region in *Rhymes of Our Valley*. The late Billy Sunday, evangelist, was a resident of the area for many years.

The old ADAMS HOUSE, home of the late Dr. E. L. Adams, one of the town's founders, is at the western edge of town. A fountain modeled after one of the lesser ones in the gardens of the Palace of Versailles, and reproductions of French statuary are on the grounds.

Except for a few trails ELIOT PARK, within the gorge of Indian Creek, is as primitive as it was before the coming of white men, and is one of the most beautiful of Oregon's many wilderness tracts.

The APPLE GROWERS ASSOCIATION CANNERY (*open to visitors*) is in operation from late August, when the canning of Bartlett pears begins, until late December, when the canning of low-grade apples is completed. The commercial activity of the town centers about the immense fruit-growing industry of the valley of the south. The Apple Growers Association, organized in 1914, is a producers' co-operative marketing organization with a large membership. It has sent the Hood River apple, noted for its crispness and flavor, to the markets of the world.

The HOOD RIVER DISTILLERIES (*open to visitors*) manufacture cull fruits into brandy.

The COLUMBIA GORGE HOTEL, **162.6 m.** (R), is a large structure of striking lines, built in 1921-22 by Simon Benson, pioneer lumberman. Just below the hotel the picturesque WAW-GUIN-GUIN FALLS drop over a sheer cliff to the river below. Nearby is the CRAG RATS CLUBHOUSE, owned by a mountain-climbing organization having a membership limited to those who have climbed at least three major snow peaks; members must climb at least one major snow peak annually to remain in good standing.

At **165.7 m.** is MITCHELL TUNNEL (*watch for traffic signals*), bored through a solid cliff overhanging the river. In its 385-foot length are hewn five large arched windows overlooking the Columbia. The great projecting rock through which the bore was made was known among the Indians as the Little Storm King, while the sky-sweeping mountain above was called the Great Storm King.

The village of VIENTO (Sp., *wind*), **168.6 m.**, is fittingly named, for the wind blows constantly and often violently through the gorge. Old-fashioned touring cars have sometimes lost their tops during the winter gales that sweep with terrific force over the highway.

VIENTO STATE PARK, **168.7 m.** (R), is an attractive wooded area that is popular as a picnic ground; through it runs scenic Viento Creek.

At **170 m.** Starvation Creek empties into the Columbia. Here is STARVATION CREEK STATE PARK. At this point the highway crosses a deep fill, where in 1884 a train was marooned for two weeks in 30-foot snowdrifts. The winter storms are frequently accompanied by silver thaws of peculiar beauty in the Columbia Gorge. Crags, boulders, trees, and telephone and power lines are then ice-coated in fantastic forms.

The current of LINDSAY CREEK, **171.2 m.**, pours down from the cliffs.

SHELL ROCK MOUNTAIN, **172.4 m.** (2,068 alt.), is opposite WIND MOUNTAIN, which is in Washington. Geologists believe that these were formerly a single mountain and the Columbia gradually cut a channel through it. Indian legend is that the Great Spirit set the whirlwinds blowing in constant fury about Wind Mountains as a punishment to those who, breaking the taboo, had taught the white men how to snare salmon.

US 30 passes through a continuous park for several miles.

CASCADE LOCKS, **181.1 m.** (120 alt., 1,000 pop.). Here in 1896 the Federal Government built a lock-canal around the unnavigable rapids of the Cascades, which figured dramatically in the history and legends of the Columbia. These cataracts, with their fall of almost 40 feet, now under 32 feet of water, were of comparatively recent geologic origin. They were caused by great masses of rock and earth that slipped from the heights of Table Mountain. The fishing Indians of the coast came to this place to visit and barter with the hunting Indians of the interior. The resident tribes laid toll upon their neighbors and harassed all travelers, though the strict discipline of Dr. John McLoughlin maintained unmolested passage for his traders and trappers. Lewis and Clark had equipment stolen from them near here. The free-booters joined the war on the whites but were subdued by a detachment of troops under the leadership of young Lt. Philip H. Sheridan.

The graceful bateau, paddled by French-Canadian *voyageurs* or by Indians, and the swift canoe were the only means of transportation here for several decades after the discovery of the Columbia. Although the fur brigades often rode the crest of churning spring floods, it was usually necessary to unload the boats at this point and carry the heavy bales of fur overland to the calm water below. The first wagon trains had much difficulty here. Some came down the river on home-made rafts that carried their dismantled wagons; the wagons were landed and reassembled for the portage at the Cascades, but the rafts were let down to the lower level with ropes. Samuel K. Barlow, a leader of the 1845 migration, determined to try a route that cut south of Mt. Hood to avoid the Columbia Gorge. The company experienced serious difficulties before the members were rescued. Not long afterward the route Barlow had conceived was opened and named for him.

The first made road on the Oregon side of the river was completed in 1856. Less than six miles in length, it ran from the Cascades to the site of Bonneville, passing over a point of rocks at the base of which the portage railroad was later built. The ox-teams labored by steep grades to an elevation of 425 feet to get past this point. Later, toll roads were opened for the passage of cattle and for the pack trains to the interior, but not until 1872 did the legislature make an appropriation to build a road through the great gorge. From this crooked and narrow trail the present highway was developed.

The growth of steamboat transportation necessitated more adequate transfer facilities here. The first portage railway was a crude affair with wooden rails and with cars operated by mule power. Later strap-iron rails were laid and small steam locomotives supplied power. The first of these, called the *Oregon Pony*, is on exhibition at the plaza grounds of the Union Station in Portland. These tram lines were outmoded when the Oregon Railroad and Navigation Company line was built.

The entrance (R) to the BRIDGE OF THE GODS is at **181.6 m.**; it is a cantilever toll bridge (*cars, 50¢; good for return within three hours*) that occupies a place where, according to Indian legend, a natural bridge at one time arched the river. This bridge, they say, was cast into the river when Tyhee Sahale, the Supreme Being, became angry with his two sons, who had quarreled over the beautiful Loo-wit, guardian of a sacred flame on the bridge. The two sons and the girl, crushed in the destruction of the bridge, whose debris created the Cascades, were resurrected as Mount Hood, Mount Adams, and Mount St. Helens. The legend of the natural bridge was used by Frederic Homer Balch in his romance, *The Bridge of the Gods*.

At **183 m.** (R) a marker points to the Washington shore, where a REPRODUCTION OF FORT RAINES commemorates the battle of Bradford Island; in March, 1856, two or three hundred Indians unsuccessfully attempted to take the small military post.

EAGLE CREEK PARK, **184 m.** (L), one of Oregon's finest recreational areas and picnic grounds, was constructed and is maintained by the U. S. Forest Service. On the banks of plunging Eagle Creek are rustic kitchens and tables and extensive parking facilities.

At BONNEVILLE, **185.4 m.** (50 alt., 800 pop.) is a large STATE FISH HATCHERY for the artificial propagation of Royal Chinook, Sockeye, and other salmon. An average of 14 million Chinook and Sockeye salmon fingerlings are released each year to make their way to the sea. The salmon mature in the ocean, but return to fresh water, usually at four years of age, to spawn, in most cases at the headwaters of the stream in which they were hatched. Both the male and female die after spawning.

The waters of Tanner Creek have been diverted to flow through the hatchery for use in the 45 ponds. When the fingerlings are released, they go through the creek to the Columbia, down which they make their way to the ocean. Before the small salmon are released, a certain number are marked by clipping part of the fins with manicuring scissors; the practice has enabled hatchery officials to determine that a large percentage of salmon released here return to the hatchery. From the storage pond 40 or 50 salmon at a time are transferred into what are called taking ponds, the male and female being separated. When the eggs of the female are ripe for taking, she is put on a wooden platform and hit on the head with a short length of iron pipe, which stuns her. Cleaner eggs are obtained by cutting the tail of the fish to let the blood. The eggs are taken through an incision in the belly and placed in a galvanized bucket. The average number of eggs to a female Chinook salmon is 4,700 though 11,000 have been obtained. The milt is then stripped from a male salmon held over the eggs. The fertilized eggs are allowed to remain in buckets of water and milt for a short time, and then are placed in wire baskets and set in troughs of cold running water, where they hatch out in 50 to 70 days, the length of time depending entirely upon the temperature of the water.

The salmon emerge from the eggs tail first, the egg sac remaining attached to the belly of the little fish and providing it with food for a period of four to five weeks. The little fish are then placed in the open ponds to develop. Their feed consists of the ground parent salmon, which has been preserved in cold storage, ground to a paste with smelt, salmon eggs, and condemned canned salmon.

More than 90 percent of the eggs taken at the hatchery are hatched and returned to the Columbia at fingerling size, able to care for themselves, whereas in the natural process of spawning the percentage that reaches fingerling size is very low, owing to the natural enemies of the salmon.

Bonneville was named for Capt. Benjamin Bonneville, whose exploits were narrated by Irving. He became the first commander of Fort Vancouver after the settlement of the Oregon boundary question.

Nearby is BONNEVILLE DAM, whose construction was begun by the Federal Government in 1933 and completed in February, 1938. The dam, designed by Army engineers, is a concrete barrier between the Oregon and Washington shores, 1,250 feet in length, its middle section resting on Bradford Island, an old Indian burial ground. The structure, 180 feet wide at the base and 170 feet high from the lowest foundation, impounds the waters of the Columbia River to an average depth of 30 feet for 44 miles upstream to a point four miles above The Dalles, and has submerged many of the river's beauty spots and historic sites.

The main features are a single-lift lock, 76 feet wide and 500 feet long, near the Oregon shore; a hydroelectric power plant with two complete generators, each of 43,200 kilowatts capacity; a gate-controlled spillway 900 feet long intended to pass the maximum flood of record without raising the previously attained flood elevation at or above the Cascades; and fishways designed to permit salmon to ascend the river to their spawning grounds. The navigation lock is (1938) the highest single lift passage in the world for ocean-going vessels, which must be raised 66 feet. With the deepening of the Columbia River between Vancouver, Wash., and the dam to 27 feet, the river will be navigable by sea-going craft for 176 miles inland. The final cost of the project, after installation of its hydroelectric units with a capacity of more than 500,000 horsepower, will be more than $70,000,000.

The dam offers an economic blood transfusion to an area of approximately 200,000 square miles between the Cascades and the Rockies. It means water transportation and cheap electric power in this vast region that has suffered from lack of both.

The JOHN B. YEON STATE PARK, **187.4 m.**, was named in honor of an early highway builder. It overlooks the Columbia Gorge, where the river has carved fantastic cliff walls, and sculptured rocks that rise 2,000 feet above the valley floor.

At **188 m.** the highway crosses McCord Creek.

Left **0.5 m.** from the eastern end of the bridge on a trail along the falls in the perpendicular walls by the stream to a grotto where a fossilized tree protrudes from under a deep layer of basalt and conglomerate.

At the eastern end of the McCord Creek bridge is a large stump that is believed to have matured long before the Cascade Range was thrown up.

At the village of WARRENDALE, **188.8 m.**, (14 pop.) are the North American Fox Farms. When litters exceed the average of from three to five, the little foxes here are frequently nursed by house cats.

HORSETAIL FALLS, **192.1 m.**, slant down a 208-foot wall of columnar basalt, forming the design that gave the falls their name. The stream drops so close to the highway that it constantly tosses showers of spray across the pavement. East of the falls ST. PETERS DOME, a 2,000-foot monolithic column, towers against the sky.

ONEONTA GORGE, **192.3 m.**, is a deep, irregular gash with high perpendicular walls between which flows a sparkling creek. Mosses, flowers, and ferns cling to the walls, and fossilized trees, caught by an ancient lava flow, are now entombed in its sides.

Left from the highway on a trail leading to ONEONTA FALLS at the shadowed head of the gorge. The stream has worn away the rock, forming the ravine.

MULTNOMAH FALLS (L), **194.5 m.**, are the most noted of all falls along the Columbia. The waters drop 620-feet into a maple- and alder-fringed basin. In summer the mist sprays the willow and the nodding fern, but in the frosty air of winter it congeals in fantastic forms, glittering with a cold brilliance, and hangs in magic festoons from the crenelated wall.

Left from Multnomah Falls on a foot trail that leads across a bridge spanning the short stretch of creek between the upper and lower falls. The trail continues to LARCH MOUNTAIN, **6.5 m.** (4,095 alt.). The ascent is gradual. Visible here is a vast expanse of mountain ranges.

WAHKEENA (Ind., *most beautiful*) FALLS, **195.1 m.**, named for the daughter of a Yakima chieftain, are particularly delightful. The waters hurl themselves from a precipice 242 feet in height, then riot in alternate falls and cascades. Wahkeena Creek Springs pour from a woodland basin a mile and a half above the cliff over which the waters plunge.

MIST FALLS, **195.3 m.**, were mentioned by Lewis and Clark. In their 1,200-foot drop the nebulous waters are often dissipated by the wind to float away in mist, no water reaching the basin below.

COOPEY FALLS, **197.4 m.**, drop 117 feet. According to an Indian legend, this was the site of a battle of giants.

BRIDAL VEIL, **197.5 m.** (40 alt., 204 pop.), is a lumber-mill town tucked in a recess below the highway. Since most of the waters are confined in a lumber flume, Bridal Veil Falls rumble scantily over the cliff, and flow under the bridge spanning Bridal Veil Creek. This beautiful mountain stream is the only one along the Columbia that has been harnessed for commercial use.

Directly across the river are the CAPE HORN PALISADES, a series of cliffs rising perpendicularly from the river to a height of more than 400 feet.

Sharp rocks, known as the PILLARS OF HERCULES or SPEEL-YE'S CHILDREN, the latter name commemorating the feats of the Indian coyote-gods, rise (R) beyond FOREST HILL.

In the depths of the 11-acre park of SHEPPERD'S DELL, **199.3 m.**, a 140-foot waterfall appears to gush from solid rock. A white arch of concrete spans a chasm 150 feet wide and 140 feet deep. Nearby the parapeted highway rounds a dome-shaped rock, known as BISHOP'S CAP or MUSHROOM ROCK.

LATOURELLE FALLS, **200.5 m.**, take a sheer drop of 224 feet into a sparkling pool at the base of an overhanging cliff. LATOURELLE BRIDGE, which commands an excellent view of the shining waters pouring from the vertical wall, lifts its three 80-foot arches 100 feet above the stream.

The GUY W. TALBOT PARK, **200.6 m.**, 125 acres of wooded land with many picnic nooks and vantage points, overlooks the Columbia River.

Winding along the forested mountain side and looping in sharp curves as it climbs, the highway reaches CROWN POINT, **202.8 m.**,

725 feet above the river on an overhanging rocky promontory, from
which is a view considered the most spectacular along the highway.
In the ascent, the highway makes a wide curve, in the center of which
is the VISTA HOUSE, designed to command views up and down the
Columbia. This impressive octagonal stone structure, designed in the
English Tudor style modified to conform to the character and topography of the landscape, was built at a cost of $100,000. The foundation
about the base of the house is laid in Italian style, no mortar having
been used. Masons from Italy did the work at this point and elsewhere
along the highway. The wind-swept height, once known as Thor's
Crown, commands a dramatic view of the river east and west for many
miles. The massive wall rises sheer and high above the Columbia
River, and, chiseled into the wall or suspended from it, the highway
spirals to the summit.

The SAMUEL HILL MONUMENT, **204.1 m.,** is a 50-ton granite
boulder dedicated to the man who was chiefly responsible for the building of the Columbia River Highway. A parking space (R) affords a
view of the river, the mountains of Washington, and Crown Point.

CORBETT, **205.4 m.,** set in rolling hills, is at the eastern end of a
cultivated area. The road cuts between the cliffs and the SANDY
RIVER, **209.9 m.** The steep walls (R), of volcanic pudding-stone, are
watered by numerous freshets in spring and embroidered with bright
flowers and ferns in summer. This stream, flowing from the glaciers
on the southern slope of Mount Hood, was discovered by Lt. William
Broughton on October 30, 1792, and named Barings River for an
English family. The bluffs near one of the river's two mouths now bear
the name of the discoverer. Lewis and Clark passed this point on
November 3, 1805, and in their *Journals* record the immense quantities
of sand thrown out. They compared the stream with the Platte River,
noted its two mouths, and called it Quicksand River, a name that appeared in maps and accounts for about 50 years. The river is noted
locally for its annual run of smelt (eulachan), which arrive in millions each February or March to spawn. These fish, eaten and praised
by epicures among the early explorers, are so oily that, dried, they
were burned to provide illumination; hence the name "candle fish."
When the small, silvery-white fish appear, the word goes out that "the
smelt are running Sandy." Cars soon block the highway for miles, while
hundreds of people, with sieves, nets, buckets, sacks, or birdcages, snare
the fish (*special license required; 50¢*). Shops become overstocked
with smelt. Truck gardeners along the Columbia and many residents of
Portland formerly used them for fertilizer until prohibited by law.

In early days overland travelers were at first not particularly impressed by this part of the country. Their long journeys, begun along
the Missouri in late April or early May, usually brought them to Oregon after the rainy season had begun. Traveling and sleeping without

SCALPED HUNTER (1869)

THE COLUMBIA GORGE

shelter, sometimes for weeks they had no opportunities to dry their clothes. It was always a matter of wonder to them that their health continued to be good. One trader, after many days of travel in continuous rain, wrote ruefully in his diary that as he fell asleep on the soggy ground he was reminded of his beloved grandmother's admonition that he must never permit himself to sleep between damp sheets.

Between truck gardens and dairy farms, US 30 traverses the rolling lands of the widening Columbia Valley, and past orchards, bulb farms, and suburban homes. The highway crosses the Willamette River.

PORTLAND, **228.2 m.** (32 alt., 301,815 pop.) (*see OREGON GUIDE*).

Railroad Station. Union Station, SW. 6th Ave. and Johnson St., for Union Pacific R.R., Southern Pacific R.R., Northern Pacific Ry., Great Northern Ry., and Spokane, Portland, and Seattle Ry.

Accommodations. Hotels and rooming houses of a wide price range; well-equipped trailer camps along main highways near city; many furnished apartments rented by the week.

Points of Interest. St. Charles Hotel, Esmond Hotel. *U.S.S. Oregon,* Oregon Historical Society Museum, University of Portland, Sanctuary of Our Sorrowful Mother, and others.

Right from Portland on US 99, which crosses the Columbia River to VANCOUVER, Wash., **7.8 m.** (115 alt., 15,786 pop.), oldest place of permanent white habitation west of the Rockies and north of California. Mills, docks, grain elevators, and canneries flank the riverside, from which streets stretch back into the business section between modern brick and terra-cotta structures intermingled with severely plain or crudely ornate early structures.

Factories now stand at the point where, in November 1792, Capt. George Vancouver's lieutenant, William Broughton, landed from the *Chatham.* When, in 1824, Governor George Simpson and Chief Factor John McLoughlin decided to transfer the Hudson's Bay post from Fort George to this place (*see WHY A TRAIL TO OREGON?*), they were determining the seat of the government for all the land west of the Rockies between the boundaries of California and Alaska. The Chief Factor was the administrator of the feudal powers vested in his company, the economic overlord, and the diplomatic representative of his government in the region. He also became the host of all visitors to the area, the physician-in-chief to whites and natives, the judge and jury in trials for crime, and the manager of the only wholesale and retail store in a vast wilderness. From Fort Vancouver, as the settlement was called in early days, he established trading posts in many spots, including Alaska, the Sandwich Islands, and California; and he began agricultural development of the country around his capital and in the Willamette Valley. Had he chosen to refuse supplies, credit, and protection from Indians to the missionaries and settlers coming to the area in the days before the United States had developed great interest in the territory, he would doubtless have stopped the movement to Oregon because those returning to the States would have circulated unfavorable reports of the opportunities available there. Without settlers beyond the Rockies it is possible that the United States would not have been able to establish its claim to the country.

Fort Vancouver had a stout palisade of 20-foot fir posts enclosing an area of 750 by 500 feet, in which were 40 wooden buildings and a stone powder magazine. Workshops, storehouses, and dwellings ranged around the central trading court; and opposite the main entrance of double-ribbed and riveted gates stood the executives' dwelling—with two 18-pounders mounted before it. A schoolhouse and a chapel were less frequented than were the dining hall and Bachelors' Hall, to which the men repaired after their meals. The latter resembled a baronial hall of feudal days, the walls being covered with weapons and trophies.

In 1826 the Chief Factor opened a sawmill and installed a forge. Within a few years he had 700 head of cattle nearby.

In 1833 the Hudson's Bay Company established the first circulating library on the Pacific Coast, shipping books and papers, among them the London *Times*, from England to Vancouver. John Ball, who arrived with Nathaniel Wyeth in 1832, was pressed into service by the Chief Factor to open the first school.

While the Chief Factor assisted people from the United States to settle south of the Columbia River, knowing that Great Britain had already decided that this country would undoubtedly be lost when the territorial dispute was settled, he strictly adhered to his company's orders to prevent settlement north of the river.

The first man from the United States to attempt to settle on the present townsite was Henry Williamson, of Indiana, who hacked out a clearing early in 1845. On March 20, McLoughlin wrote to his superior, "We found a shack built four logs high in the forest west of the fort. I ordered the men to pull the place down and destroy the fence surrounding it." Williamson, however, rebuilt his cabin and filed the claim at Oregon City.

The next settlers arrived on Christmas Day, 1845; they were Amos and Esther Short, with their eight children. Williamson asserted they tried to jump his claim. The Hudson's Bay Company also rebuffed them and refused supplies. In the following year, by the treaty of 1846, the United States won control of what is now Washington as well as Oregon; in this same year McLoughlin was forced to resign his post.

When, in 1848, a military post was established here, Williamson platted the townsite and named it Vancouver City. New settlers were arriving down the Oregon Trail and the census of 1850 listed 95 houses in the newly organized Clark County, of which Vancouver was made the seat. Two schools were opened and a ferry franchise was granted for river service. A newly appointed county agent, R. H. Lansdale, replatted the townsite, ignoring the earlier lines that started from a great cottonwood on the riverbank, called the Witness Tree. Lansdale not only kindled private boundary disputes but also infringed on the military reserve. With the Hudson's Bay Company, now merely a foreign business concern, and the missionaries as claimants against the War Department, six parties were involved in the controversy; but the Army and the Shorts persevered in occupation. Patriots changed the town's name to Columbia City.

The town flourished, being on the route of much immigrant travel, having a garrison for protection during the period of Indian warfare, and possessing a site at the junction of the Willamette where produce could be transferred to sea-going vessels.

In 1852 the gay Bonneville returned to the Columbia Valley, now as a lieutenant-colonel in command of a post in the area from which he had been politely dismissed twenty years before. Several men who were later prominent in the Civil War served here early in their careers.

The gold rushes to Idaho and eastern Washington contributed to the town's prosperity. Local men engaged in river transportation made fantastic profits; the little *Tenino* cleared $18,000 for her owner on a single trip.

The middle 60's saw many fetes and lavish entertainments, and a rise of cultural interest. For the Saint Patrick's Day ball of 1866 at the Alta House, tickets cost $5, including supper. In 1867 an amateur dramatic society played *Robert Macaire*, a melodrama, and later *Toodles*, a comedy. A traveling troupe appeared in 1869, playing *Nan the Good For Nothing* and *A Kiss in the Dark*.

The growth of the town slackened after the gold fever had abated, but with the construction of a railroad from Kalama to Tacoma (1872-73) and its eventual extension southward, Vancouver reinforced its position as shipping center for a large agricultural area.

The bronze PIONEER MOTHER, Esther Short Park, 8th Street between Columbia and Esther Streets, designed by Avard Fairbanks, presents a woman, flintlock in hand, with three children clinging to her skirts. A plaque on the obverse side of the monument shows a woman peering anxiously from a covered wagon while her husband walks beside the wagon watchfully directing his oxen. Esther Short, for whom the park was named, had a hard journey over the plains, bearing a child on the way. When employees of the Hudson's Bay Company appeared to raze the Short cabin at Vancouver and drive the family away, she slapped the leader in the face so forcibly that he was knocked down, and fled.

The COVINGTON HOUSE (*open 11-4, 2nd and 4th Tues. each month*), southwest corner 39th and Main Streets, built about 1845, is a restoration of the oldest house in the State. Built by Richard Covington of roughly squared logs and clapboard siding, with a high, sloped roof, it reveals the influence of the Hudson's Bay Company structures in its mortise and tenon joints. Known for its entertainment, Covington's home was a social center for young officers and trading company officials during the 1850's.

VANCOUVER BARRACKS is bounded by 5th Street (Evergreen Highway), 4th Plain Avenue, and E. and W. Reserve Streets. NUMBER TWO BARRACKS, in Officers' Row, is one of the oldest of the 300 buildings on the reservation. Its log walls have been sheathed with siding, but the narrow windows, angular outlines, and peaked roof are characteristic of one of the least graceful periods of American architecture. When young Lt. Ulysses S. Grant was stationed here, he planted potatoes in the nearby lowlands to augment the officers' mess—and his meager income—but spring floods washed his crop away; the current price of potatoes was $45 for 100 pounds.

The FIRST APPLE TREE, E. 7th and T. Streets, west of the polo field, was planted in 1826 by Dr. John McLoughlin. After 1830 the post occupied land between the tree and the river, a quarter of a mile from the water; erosion has washed much of the former area into the river; the site of the factor's mansion and the boundaries of the fort were obliterated long ago.

A dinner guest of McLoughlin's, Capt. Aemilius Simpson, absent-mindedly drew from his pocket several apple seeds that had been given him by a young woman at his farewell dinner in London, with the joking request that they be planted in the wilderness. The factor saw nothing humorous in the request. He soberly insisted on nurturing the seeds into shoots, which matured into the first cultivated fruit trees in the Northwest.

PEARSON ARMY AIRPORT, corner 5th and E. Reserve Sts., has hangars, shops, and administration buildings. Here ended the 63-hour flight across the North Pole made by three Russians who hopped off at Moscow on June 18, 1937, to test the feasibility of air transportation across the top of the world. The Soviet fliers landed at this field because of fog, short of San Francisco, their destination. When asked the reason for their explorations of the Arctic, the spokesman for the trio voiced the feeling that Jefferson had had 150 years before them: "We do not like blank spots on the map."

The GRAVE OF ARTHUR HAINE in the City Cemetery, between 10th and 13th Streets, is marked by a stone of his own design and the epitaph, "Haine Haint." Haine, who died in 1907, left a will saying, "Having lived as an atheist I want to be buried like one—without any monkey business."

Section 14. Portland to Astoria, 104.8 m. US 30.

US 30 runs west from Union St. in PORTLAND, **0 m.**, on St. Helens Road, a part of the Lower Columbia River Highway, and passes through a busy industrial district fronting Portland's lower harbor. Wharves line the Willamette River bank (R), where domestic and foreign vessels are moored. Factories and warehouses occupy the river flats (R), and a high, forested ridge hides from view the Tualatin Valley (L). Gasoline distributing plants (R), with steel tanks behind close-cropped lawns, succeed the factories. There is a virtually unbroken line of steel plants, construction yards, paint factories, and shingle mills.

At **7.2 m.** is the eastern approach to St. John's Bridge, an unusually beautiful structure. This suspension bridge rises 203 feet above the river, thus permitting ocean liners to pass beneath it.

LINNTON, **8.6 m.**, a part of Portland since 1915, retains its individuality. The town was regarded as the possible site of a future metropolis when Peter Burnett settled in the vicinity in 1843. It has become an important commercial center since merging with Portland, though even before the union it was the site of several large mills. Millions of feet of lumber are shipped annually from here.

At **13 m.** is a junction with the Burlington Ferry Road, a plank viaduct leading to a ferry (*free*) crossing Willamette Slough.

Right on this road to the bank, **0.5 m.**, off which is SAUVIES ISLAND (850 pop.), which retains much charm, having quiet country roads, across which swing pasture gates. It has oak groves and several lakes; numerous duck hunters come to this popular recreational area.

Since farming began here the island has had a high reputation for fertility. Bulb culture and truck gardening have become increasingly important in recent years.

The earliest known account of the place was written by Lewis and Clark on November 4, 1805, when they found a village of 200 Indians here. The explorers later called it Wapato Island because of the prevalence of a tuberous marsh plant of that name, the roots of which were used for food by the Indians. The Lewis and Clark party gathered some distance below the village for dinner. "Soon after," Clark recorded, "Several canoes of Indians from the village above came down, dressed for the purpose as I supposed of Paying us a friendly visit, they had scarlet & blue blankets Salor Jackets, overalls, Shirts and hats indepandant of their usial dress; the most of them had either Muskets or pistols and tin flasks to hold their powder, Those fellows we found assumeing and disagreeable, however we Smoked with them and treated them with every attention & friendship.

"dureing the time we were at dinner those fellows Stold my pipe Tomahawk which they were Smoking with, I immediately serched every man and the canoes, but could find nothing of my Tomahawk, while Serching for the Tomahawk one of those Scoundals Stole a cappoe (*coat*) of one of our interperters, which was found Stufed under the root of a tree, near the place they Sat, we became much displeased with those fellows, which they discovered and moved off on their return home to their village."

In 1829 a violent epidemic, possibly typhus brought in by sailors on the *Owyhee* (*see below*), swept through the population, and Dr. McLoughlin moved the survivors to the mainland and burned many of the straw huts of the settlement. The Indians never went back.

In 1834 Capt. Nathaniel J. Wyeth audaciously chose a site for his trading post near the lower end of the island. "This Wappato Island which I have selected for our establishment," he wrote, "consists of woodland and prairie and on it there is considerable deer and those who could spare time to hunt might live well but mortality has carried off to a man its inhabitants and there is nothing to attest that they ever existed except their decaying houses, their graves and their unburied bones of which there are heaps." Wyeth named his settlement Fort William, and set his coopers to work making barrels to carry salmon to Boston. His trading activities met with such firm and persistent opposition from the Hudson's Bay Company that in 1836 he reluctantly abandoned the unprofitable enterprise.

With the Wyeth party was J. K. Townsend, an ornithologist from Philadelphia, who pitched his camp near Fort William, and spent his time collecting birds and snakes, preserving the latter in a keg of spirits. One day he returned to deposit another reptile in the keg and found the spirits gone. A culprit confessed to the dereliction, pleading thirst as an apology.

In 1841 McLoughlin established a dairy here, placing Jean Baptiste Sauvie, a superannuated trapper, in charge. The place has since borne the name of the old dairyman.

Sauvies Island figures prominently in Pacific Northwest literature. Besides its extensive use in Frederic Homer Balch's *The Bridge of the Gods*, it has served as background for Sheba Hargreaves' *Ward of the Redskins*, and appears in *Lightship* by Archie Binns.

At **18.8 m.** the barrier of hills (L) recedes, and the highway enters the Scappoose Plains, a fertile district where potato culture, truck gardening, and dairying are carried on. The Hudson's Bay Company sent men from Vancouver in the late 1820's to raise vegetables and grain. Large dairy barns, with round silos of wood or concrete, and comfortable houses now stand where the trapper-farmers pitched their camps.

SCAPPOOSE (Ind., *gravelly plain*), **21.6 m.** (56 alt., 248 pop.), is an old Indian trading post. Chief Caseno, mentioned in the annals of the Astorians and of the North West Company, had his main village close by. According to Gabriel Franchere, three deserters from the Astorians were captured at this place on November 21, 1811, when their pursuers bribed the Indians with powder and guns that were unfit for use. The brig *Owyhee* from the Sandwich Islands spent the winter of 1828-9 in Scappoose Bay. Disease, spreading from the ship, killed many of the natives. The boat picked up a cargo of salmon and carried it to Boston.

Today Scappoose is a small but prosperous agricultural community. Great underground potato warehouses, their ventilators barely rising above the surface, line the railroad track in the town square, and a large nearby factory pickles cucumbers from the Willamette Slough.

Beautiful MOUNT RAINIER, almost 90 miles to the northeast, is sometimes visible at **23.2 m.** Mount Adams and Mount St. Helens, rising on the far horizon, seem but a few feet apart.

ST. HELENS, **28.9 m.** (98 alt., 3,994 pop.), a river port, is also a market and court town. Its manufacturing plants produce insulating board, pulp and paper, lumber, and dairy products.

St. Helens was laid out in 1847 on the donation land claim of

Capt. H. M. Knighton, who launched the town as an active competitor
of the newly founded village of Portland. He contemptuously referred
to his rival as "Little Stump Town," a title suggested by its denuded
forests. In November, 1850, because of its position near deep water, the
town was advertised as a terminus of the first railroad proposed for
Oregon. The KNIGHTON HOUSE was built in 1847 with lumber brought
around Cape Horn from Bath, Maine. Many of the town's buildings,
including the COLUMBIA COUNTY COURTHOUSE, are built of stone taken
from local quarries.

DEER ISLAND, **34.5 m.**, a little community opposite a river island
of that name, was visited by Lewis and Clark in 1805 and again in
1806. Large herds of sleek cattle graze in the surrounding stump pas-
tures.

The highway passes through a narrow gorge, where the hills (L)
crowd upon the road. The lowlands (R) are sloughs, with growths
of willows and alders.

The highway ascends a rugged promontory; at LITTLE JACK FALLS,
44.3 m. (125 alt.), a cascade (L) tumbles over a precipice almost
100 feet high.

US 30 descends to RAINIER, **47.6 m.** (23 alt., 1,353 pop.), named
for Mount Rainier, which is often visible to the northwest. Rainier
was an important stop in the days of river commerce. The Hudson's
Bay Company boat *Beaver* and the *Lot Whitcomb* of Milwaukee loaded
and discharged freight at its dock.

From the winding curves of RAINIER HILL (671 alt.) there is a
magnificent view of Longview, Wash., and the narrow roadway of the
bridge spanning the river, which is far below. The summit is reached
at **50.9 m.**

Descending, the highway crosses ubiquitous BEAVER CREEK, **51.7 m.**
Within the next 15 miles westward the road spans this stream or its
tributaries a dozen times. The route now runs through cut-over timber
lands along the banks of the creek.

At **62 m.** is a junction with a graveled road.

Right on this road is QUINCY, **1 m.**, center of a drained and diked area of
the Columbia River lowlands; L. here **3 m.** on a dirt road to OAK POINT. The
Winship brothers of Boston, successful in the China trade, attempted to establish a
permanent trading post here in 1810, while Astor was still maturing his plans
for Astoria. Capt. Nathan Winship arrived in the Columbia with their ship, the
Albatross, on May 26, and selected this place, long known as Fanny's Bottom, as
the site for the fortified two-story log post that he built immediately. A June
freshet flooded both fort and garden; later when the Indians grew troublesome,
Winship abandoned the enterprise and returned to Boston.

At **62.4 m.** the low logged-off summits of the Coast Range, 20
miles away, are visible. Denuded of their timber, they form a desolate
ridge against the blue horizon.

CLATSKANIE is at **65.1 m.** (16 alt. 739 pop.). Farmers' co-operative creameries here manufacture dairy products from the milk produced by great herds of cattle on the drained Columbia River lowlands. The raising of vegetables on these lands for canning is a recent and profitable enterprise. Clatskanie (cor. *Tlatskanie*) is named for an early Indian village in the Nehalem Valley. The natives also applied the word to certain streams to indicate the route to the village.

At **74.8 m.** is WESTPORT, one of the many lumbering and fishing towns scattered along the waters of the Columbia.

The highway ascends the Coast Range in a series of hairpin turns to CLATSOP CREST, **80 m.**, overlooking the Columbia River and the country beyond. In the immediate foreground is long, flat PUGET ISLAND, where grain fields and fallow lands weave patterns of green and gray, and sluggish streams form silvery canals. Although the island is close to the Oregon shore, it lies within the State of Washington. It was discovered in 1792 by Lieutenant Broughton of the British Navy, who named it for Lt. Peter Puget.

US 30 twists down to HUNT CREEK, **80.8 m.**, then climbs a spur from which a desolate waste of logged-over land extends in all directions. A high, sharply etched mountain (L), with sides bare of vegetation, shows the results of unrestricted timber cutting. Nearby are green-gray underbrush and silvery branched alders. The route proceeds for many miles through cut-over country. Occasionally a small settlement appears, with rude buildings huddling on tiny patches of cultivated land among the stumps.

Gradually the vegetation of the seacoast is seen. Dogwood, slim alders, and salal bushes—low shrubs with shining olive-green leaves—hug the sandy ground.

At **98.2 m.** US 30 crosses the little JOHN DAY RIVER. Small gardens border its quiet, peaceful course.

On November 7, 1805, Clark wrote, "Ocian in view! O! the joy" in his notes on the "Courses and Distances." His rejoicing was premature, however; the party was merely entering the broad mouth of the Columbia, but buoyed up by their belief that the end of the journey was near, they struggled along through the rain and rough waves out along the northern shore of Gray's Bay (R). On the following day he wrote: "Some rain all day at intervals, we are all wet and disagreeable, as we have been for several days past, and our present Situation a verry disagreeable one in as much, as we have not leavel land Sufficient for an encampment and for our baggage to lie cleare of the tide, the High hills jutting in so close and steep that we cannot retreat back, and the water too salt to be used, added to this the waves are increasing to Such a hight that we cannot move from this place, in this Situation we are compelled to form our camp between the Hite of the Ebb and flood tides, and rase our baggage on logs." On the 9th he wrote: "our camp entirely under water dureing the hight of the tide, every man

as wet as water could make them all the last night and to day all day
as the rain continued all the day, at 4 oClock P M the wind shifted
about to the S.W. and blew with great violence imediately from the
Ocean for about two hours, notwithstanding the disagreeable Situation
of our party all wet and cold (and one which they have experienced
for Several days past) they are chearfull and anxious to See further
into the Ocian, The water of the river being too Salt to use we are
obliged to make use of rain water. Some of the party not accustomed to
Salt water has made too free use of it on them it acts as a pergitive.
At this dismal point we must Spend another night as the wind & waves
are too high to proceed." Sergeant Ordway's comments were much
briefer, but he ended with "Some of the party killed Several ducks in
the course of the day."

At **101 m.** is TONGUE POINT STATE PARK; here is a junction with
a graveled road.

Right on this road to TONGUE POINT LIGHTHOUSE SERVICE BASE, **0.7 m.** Built
on a projection extending into the wide mouth of the Columbia River, this base
is the repair depot for the buoys that guide navigators along the watercourses of
the two States. Tongue Point was so named by Broughton in 1792.

On November 10 the Lewis and Clark party, unable to go far because of the
wind, camped on the northern shore nearly opposite this point. The camp was
made on drift logs that floated at high tide. "nothing to eate but Pounded fish,"
Clark noted. "that night it Rained verry hard. . . . and continues this morning,
the wind has luled and the waves are not high." The party moved on but after
they had gone ten miles the wind rose and they had to camp again on drift logs.
Neighboring Indians appeared with fish. The camp was moved on the 12th to a
slightly less dangerous place and Clark attempted to explore the nearby land on
the 13th: "rained all day moderately. I am wet &C.&C." On the 14th "The rain
&C. which has continued without a longer intermition than 2 hours at a time
for ten days past has destroy'd the robes and rotted nearly one half the fiew
clothes the party has, particularely the leather clothes." Clark was losing his
patience by the 15th; even the pounded fish brought from the falls was becoming
mouldy. This was the eleventh day of rain and "the most disagreeable time I
have experenced confined on the tempiest coast wet, where I can neither git out
to hunt, return to a better situation, or proceed on." But they did manage to
move to a somewhat better camp that day and the men, salvaging boards from
a deserted Indian camp, made rude shelters. The Indians began to give them too
much attention, however. "I told those people . . . that if any one of their nation stole any thing that the Senten'l whome they Saw near our baggage with
his gun would most certainly Shute them, they all promised not to tuch a thing,
and if any of their womin or bad boys took any thing to return it imediately and
chastise them for it. I treated those people with great distance."

The party moved on to a place on the northern shore of Baker Bay, where
they remained for about ten days. From this point Clark went overland to explore,
inviting those who wanted to see more of the "Ocian" to accompany him. Nine
men, including York, still had enough energy to go.

On the 21st, "An old woman & Wife to a Cheif of the Chunnooks came and
made a Camp near ours. She brought with her 6 young Squars (*her daughters
& neices*) I believe for the purpose of Gratifying the passions of the men of our
party and receiving for those indulgiences Such Small [presents] as She (the old
woman) thought proper to accept of.

"Those people appear to View Sensuality as a Necessary evel, and do not

appear to abhor it as a Crime in the unmarried State. The young females are
fond of the attention of our men and appear to meet the sincere approbation of
their friends and connections, for thus obtaining their favours."

Here the explorers had further evidence that English and American sailors
had previously visited the Columbia. The tattooed name, "J. Bowman," was seen
on the arm of a Chinook squaw. "Their legs are also picked with defferent figures," wrote Clark. "all those are considered by the natives of this quarter as
handsom deckerations, and a woman without those deckorations is Considered as
among the lower Class."

Three days later Lewis and Clark held a meeting to decide whether the party
should go back to the falls, remain on the north shore, or cross to the south side
of the river for the winter. The members with one exception voted to move to
the south shore, since game seemed to be more plentiful there, giving them an
opportunity to obtain better food and replenish their stock of clothing. "Janey
(Sacajawea) in favour of a place where there is plenty of pota's." They set up
a temporary camp here on Tongue Point. The rain continued, a steady downpour.
From this place they hunted a suitable site for the permanent camp.

ASTORIA, **104.8 m.** (12 alt., 10,349 pop.), seat of Clatsop County,
occupies a high promontory between the mouth of the Columbia and
Young's Bay. The business district lies on a narrow bench near the
water, with the residential district rising behind it on the headland.
Many of the streets end abruptly against high yellow clay banks where
houses cling so precariously that they seem about to tumble down on
the stores and offices below them. The city's commercial life revolves
about fishing, lumbering, flour milling, and shipping. The shore line
is defined by a row of saw mills, flour mills, tall elevators, and the
masts and smokestacks of the many vessels always crowding the docks.

Beyond, flocks of gulls circle overhead or float on the tide. Their
shrill cries are drowned, when the thick vapors drift in, by the hoarse,
haunting bellow of foghorns. At such times buoy lanterns mark the
river channel, and many red, green, and white lights outline the
fishing nets. By day the water is crowded with small boats, some low
in the water with the weight of their catches, and along the shore in
shallow water horses drag fish seines. The animals strain against the
laden nets, or swim ahead of them when the incoming tide lightens
their labors. During the chief fishing season the horses are often stabled
in barns set on piling in the river, and for months do not set hoof on
dry land.

English and Swedish or English and Finnish are spoken in most
shops of the town, 39 percent of Clatsop County's population being of
Swedish or Finnish descent. There are also a number of Japanese
residents.

The settlement of Astoria began when John Jacob Astor's ship, the
Tonquin, arrived in 1811. (*See WHY A ROAD TO OREGON?*) The
post was built facing north, with the wide estuary, its sandbars and
tumultuous breakers spread out before it, and the promontory of Cape
Disappointment, fifteen miles distant, closing the prospect to the left.
When the expedition arrived the surrounding country was in all the

freshness of spring; the trees were in young leaf, the weather was superb, and everything looked delightful to men just emancipated from a long confinement on shipboard.

Washington Irving wrote: "All hands now set to work cutting down trees, clearing away thickets, and marking out the place for the residence, storehouse, and powder magazine, which were to be built of logs and covered with bark. Others landed the timbers intended for the frame of the coasting vessel, and proceeded to put them together, while others prepared a garden spot, and sowed the seeds of various vegetables.

"The next thought was to give a name to the embryo metropolis; the one that naturally presented itself was that of the projector and supporter of the whole enterprise. It was accordingly named *Astoria.*"

But the War of 1812 changed the picture; the Astorians sold the post to the rival North West Company when they heard that a British sloop was on its way to destroy all American trading posts on the West Coast. When the sloop arrived its captain took formal possession of the territory as an act of war. The North West Company maintained the post as its headquarters in the area until in 1821, when the company was united with the Hudson's Bay Company. In the meantime, in 1818, exclusive British control of the territory ended, with the Oregon country thrown open to joint occupation by Britain and the United States for ten years. In 1824 the Hudson's Bay Company, then owner of the post, determined to move its departmental headquarters to a more suitable spot inland. Astoria was still maintained, however, but merely as a minor post and ship lookout. Thereafter the importance of the place declined rapidly and by 1841 the seat of Astor's would-be capital of the Pacific Coast was merely a half-overgrown clearing holding a shed and single cabin.

Shortly after the departure of the Astorians the Oregon country had its first white female visitor. On April 22, 1814, the North West Company's ship, the *Isaac Todd,* arrived with Donald McTavish, the first Governor of Fort George, and Jane Barnes, an adventurous barmaid who had decided to see the world as a companion to McTavish. Jane changed protectors shortly after her arrival, preferring Alexander Henry, whom she found at the fort. McTavish solaced himself by taking a Chinook wife. Then one day the son of Chief Concomly appeared at the fort, decked out in whale oil and red paint, to ask Jane to be his wife, offering to send a hundred of the valuable sea-otters to her relatives and promising that his other wives should do all the work for her. When she refused his offer he planned to abduct her. Jealousy and wonder over Jane's white skin and London ruffles were becoming intense when both McTavish and Henry were drowned while crossing the Columbia. Jane decided to leave, but, scorning the attentive captain of the *Isaac Todd,* accepted the offer of the captain of the *Columbia,* also in the harbor, to take her home. Jane's later history is obscure but the dusty files of the North West Company show that she later attempted to collect an annuity for her services to the North West Company.

In 1844 immigrants began to arrive in the area and on April 9, 1847, the Astoria post office was established.

Beginning in 1880, Astoria had a brisk growth, but in 1922, when its population had increased to 15,000, fire broke out on its waterfront, and reduced the structures on 32 city blocks to ashes. A reconstruction program was then launched that created a new and modern city.

Astoria is the headquarters of the Columbia River fishing industry. Since the day when, according to Indian legend, the god Talapus created salmon and, with Serpent holding one end of the net, taught the Indians to catch them in spruce-net snares, salmon have been of great economic importance to the lower Columbia. The Hudson's Bay Company engaged to some extent in salmon fishing, but the first commercial cargo to leave the river was taken by the brig *Owyhee* in 1830. Five years later Nathaniel Wyeth's Columbia River Fishing and Trading Company made an unsuccessful attempt to establish the industry, but all activities were of desultory nature until 1868, when the first cannery was built. Others sprang up, and soon salmon was being shipped to many parts of the world. The salmon catch is now the city's chief asset, the annual pack being valued at from three to seven million dollars. Rece ltly the catching of pilchards off the mouth of the Columbia has grown into an industry of major proportions.

The SITE OF FORT ASTORIA is on 15th St., between Duane and Exchange. At the southeast corner of the City Hall is the GRAVE OF DONALD MCTAVISH.

The ASTOR COLUMN, on the summit of Coxcomb Hill (700 alt.), at the end of Coxcomb Rd., is 125 feet high, and bears a spiral frieze depicting the events in the city's history in their historical sequence. Vincent Astor, great-grandson of the founder of Astoria, supplied the funds for its construction. An entrance at its base opens upon a spiral staircase leading to an observation platform a few feet from the top, from which there is a magnificent view of the Pacific Ocean, the Columbia River, and the mountainous wooded region around the city.

The PORT OF ASTORIA TERMINAL is the center of activity on the waterfront. Beginning in 1909, the municipally owned Port of Astoria Corporation has gradually built up extensive properties. Ships from many parts of the world load and discharge cargoes from it and from the smaller wharves along the waterfront.

Nearby are the COLUMBIA RIVER PACKERS ASSOCIATION PLANT, where salmon is canned, and the UNION FISHERMEN'S COOPERATIVE PACKING COMPANY PLANT (*admittance to plants during canning season by permission*).

Left from Astoria on US 101 to the ASTORIA MUNICIPAL AIRPORT, **6.7 m.** (R). Because of its strategic importance as a seaplane base, the Federal Government contributed extensively to its development in 1936.

Left here **1.5 m.** on a graveled road to the SITE OF FORT CLATSOP, the winter encampment of the Lewis and Clark party in 1805-6.

Now overgrown with evergreens, the site is designated by a flagpole set in concrete and is marked by a bronze plaque. The broad stump that served Lewis as a writing desk has decayed. Koboway, the Clatsop chief to whom the fort was given, retired to his lodge leaving the white men's house to fall to ruin. On December 7, 1805, Clark recorded: ". . . after breakfast I delayed about half an hour before York Came up, then proceeded around this Bay which I call (have taken the liberty of calling) Meriwethers Bay the Chrisitan name of Capt. Lewis who no doubt was the 1st. white man who ever Surveyed this Bay [Clark was mistaken about this], we assended a river which falls in on the South Side of this Bay 3 miles to the first point of high land on the West Side, the place Capt. Lewis had viewed and formed in a thick groth of pine about 200 yards from the river, this situation is on a rise about 30 feet higher than the high tides leavel and thickly Covered with lofty pine. This is certainly the most eligable Situation for our purposes of any in its neighbourhood."

On December 8 the whole party gathered at the site selected by Lewis on the Netul River and made camp. Within a short time trees were felled and rude huts erected around an open square. Some of the men were dispatched to the Pacific to make salt from sea water, others were ordered to hunt, and the remainder, working against time and weather, completed the shelters sufficiently to enable the party to move in by Christmas.

On Christmas Day Clark wrote: "at day light this morning we we[re] awoke by the discharge of the fire arm[s] of all our party & a Selute, Shouts and a Song which the whole party joined in under our windows, after which they retired to their rooms were chearfull all the morning. after brackfast we divided our Tobacco which amounted to 12 carrots one half of which we gave to the men of the party who used tobacco, and to those who doe not use it we make a present of a handkerchief, The Indians leave us in the evening all the party Snugly fixed in their huts. I recved a pres[e]nt of Capt L. of a fleece hosrie [hosiery] Shirt Draws and Socks, a p^r Mockersons of white weazils tails of the Indian woman, & some black root of the Indians before their departure. . . . The day proved Showerey wet and disagreeable.

"we would have Spent this day the nativity of Christ in feasting had we anything either to raise our Sperits or even gratify our appetites, our Diner concisted of pore Elk, so much Spoiled that we eate it thro' mear necessity." According to Gass, they were without salt to season even that.

On the 26th the rain continued. Clark says: "we dry our wet articles and have the blankets fleed, The flees are so troublesom that I have slept but little for 2 night past and we have regularly to kill them out of our blankets every day for several past." (Fleas were left by the Indians on each visit.) On the 27th in the *Journals* occurs the entry: "Musquetors troublesom."

On the 29th the natives brought word that a whale had floundered on the shore some distance south, and that their people were collecting fat from it. Although it was planned to start immediately to the place to obtain blubber, severe storms delayed the trip until early in January. At that time Sacajawea made her one recorded plea in her own interests; Clark wrote: "She observed that She had traveled a long way with us to See the great waters, and that now monstrous fish was also to be Seen, She though it verry hard She could not be permitted to See either (She had never yet been to the Ocian)." She was permitted to go with the men, carrying her baby on her back.

Under the leadership of Clark the small party struggled around the headlands to the Tillamook country, 35 miles south of Fort Clatsop. Well-laden with blubber, they returned to the fort. During the late winter and early spring Sacajawea was busy preparing moccasins and suits of buckskin for the explorers.

Clark noted: "With the party of Clatsops who visited us last was a man of much lighter Coloured than the nativs are generaly, he was freckled with long duskey red hair, about 25 years of age, and must Certainly be half white at least, this man appeared to understand more of the English language than the others of his party, but did not Speak a word of English, he possessed all the habits of the indians." In *Adventures on the Columbia* (1832) Ross Cox describes such a man as the son of a sailor who had deserted here from an English ship. He was said to have had the words "Jack Ramsey" tattooed on his arm. "Poor Jack was fond of his father's countrymen," Ross says, "and had the decency to wear trousers whenever he came to the fort [Astoria]. We therefore made a collection of old clothes for his use; sufficient to last him many years." The man was otherwise accounted for by other early visitors; the Indians told them of several parties of white men who had landed on the Oregon coast in the 18th century and of a red-haired sailor who was washed ashore about 1760.

The Clatsops became such frequent visitors at the fort that upon its completion Clark noted ". . . at Sun set we let the nativs know that our Custom will be in future, to Shut the gates at Sun Set at which time all Indians must go out of the fort and not return into it untill next morning after Sunrise at which time the gates will be opened, those of the Warciacum Nation who are very fo[r]ward left the houses with reluctianc." In view of the Indians' differing conceptions of private property, this seems to have been an expedient ruling on the part of the explorers.

By March the leaders believed that the mountain snows would have melted, and the winter quarters could be abandoned. On March 23 Clark reported: "loaded our canoes & at 1 P. M. left Fort Clatsop on our homeward journey. at this place we had wintered and remained from the 7th of Decr. 1805 to this day and have lived as we had any right to expect, and we can say that we were never one day without 3 meals of some kind a day either pore Elk meat or roots. . . ."

Those who write of the Lewis and Clark expedition are apt to stress the discomforts and dangers the party experienced, forgetting that these were the price, fully anticipated and gladly paid, of fulfilling a dream centuries old—that of finding a central route across North America.

Nebraska-Wyoming

ALTERNATE ROUTE

Ogallala, Neb.—Scottsbluff—Fort Laramie, Wyo.—Casper—Muddy Gap—South Pass—Granger, Wyo.; 570. 4 m. US 26, US 87, US 87E, US 287, and unnumbered dirt road.

Between a point seven miles north of Ogallala and Torrington the Union Pacific R.R. parallels the route; Burlington Lines between Northport and Casper; Chicago & North Western Ry. between Orin and Casper.
Graveled roadbed between Ogallala and Bayard; paved between Bayard and Muddy Gap; oiled gravel between Muddy Gap and Hudsons; unimproved dirt road between Hudsons and Granger. Travelers who do not care for rough traveling can turn south on US 287, paved, at Muddy Gap to return to US 30; the route through South Pass is only for the adventurous at present. Hudsons-Farson road will probably be improved in 1939. Inquiry as to weather conditions should be made before following US 87E and US 287, which run through country where blizzards are frequent in winter and spring.
Accommodations limited except in large towns.

US 26 runs northwestward across high tableland into the Wildcat Hills region. Between a point near North Platte, Neb., and Guernsey, Wyo., it follows the north bank of the North Platte River, the route traversed by the Mormon Pioneers, and parallels the Oregon Trail, which was on the south bank. After 1849 the route here was sometimes called the California Trail because of the goal of the major migrations. The Pony Express riders and also the first overland stages went through the valley. Nearly all emigrants bound for central California and Oregon traveled on one riverbank or the other until 1862 and quite a number thereafter. The route was determined by two objectives —Fort Laramie, which offered supplies and protection, and South Pass, the lowest break in the Continental Divide. West of Fort Laramie the trails continued along the North Platte, crossed a low divide to follow the Sweetwater, and left it to reach the pass. The descent from that point to the Green River was easy.

North from US 30 at OGALLALA, 0 m. (see SECTION 3), on US 26, which crosses the North Platte River at 7.7 m. and turns L., following the course of the river.

In the oxcart days few who turned up this valley for the first time failed to experience a quickening of interest. The flat monotonous prairies, not greatly different in appearance from the country many of them had known in the East, were being left behind; the air had an increasing dryness that made their wagon beds and wheels shrink and fall apart; and the bleak, wind-bitten landmarks of the badlands were beginning to make their appearance. The travelers were approaching the foothills of the Rockies, of whose perils and difficulties they had long heard. Members of a generation that had imbibed its ideas of the wilderness from Cooper's Leatherstocking series were bound at this moment to see themselves as fearless Hawkeyes entering the scene of heroic adventure. After 1848, however, those who did not wander from the beaten track and who traveled in the usual tourist season had their romantic dreams of a lonely trek through wilderness rudely shattered. In 1849 and for many years thereafter the overland trails were as lonely as Pennsylvania Avenue on Inauguration Day. Passing Fort Kearney on May 11, 1850, C. W. Smith wrote in his *Journal:* "Nine hundred wagons are reported as having passed this spring." Two days later a member of another train reported three thousand two hundred wagons ahead of his at this point. On May 17 Lorenzo Sawyer noted near the fort: "The opposite bank is lined with emigrant trains on the Council Bluff road." And on May 26 a traveler on the north bank recorded: "The road on our side of the river for miles ahead are lined with teams   from our camp to the Missouri behind us is one continuous line of wagons."

At **2.5 m.** is the junction with State 61.

Right on this improved dirt road to KINGSLEY DAM, **3 m.,** which creates a storage reservoir on the North Platte with a capacity of two million acre-feet of water.

When the Mormon Pioneers camped in this area on May 11, 1847, Appleton Harmon was working on the "machinery for the wagon to tell the distance we travel," Clayton wrote. The dreadfully monotonous process of counting the revolutions of the wagon wheels was nearing an end. That day the Saints, finding no water within half a mile of their camp, resourcefully dug four-foot wells to supply their needs.

On the following day one man found a cured buffalo skin, which was frugally salvaged. The Saints carried very little excess baggage, differing from many later emigrants. In spite of the instructions of Joel Palmer (*see APPENDIX*) and others on the need of carrying adequate supplies of food, nearly every train had many members who thought that they could subsist on game, and therefore filled their wagons with treasured heirlooms and other non-essentials in place of foodstuffs. A few days of travel with the oxen struggling to draw the heavy loads was enough to convince the wiser travelers that their claw-footed tables and mahogany dressers were serious encumbrances. By the time the trains reached this region, where the road was rising steadily, many more pioneer mothers gave reluctant consent when their husbands insisted that finery and Sunday china be thrown away. Diarists of the gold-rush days frequently noted the heaps of discarded goods and mourned because they had no room to carry the valuable articles they could have salvaged.

LEWELLEN, **31.8 m.** (419 pop.), is in a section that ·produces alfalfa, sugar beets, and corn.

Left from Lewellen on a country road that crosses the North Platte River to ASH HOLLOW, **3 m.,** a deep canyon where one route of the Oregon Trail, used chiefly after Fort Sedgwick (*see SECTION 4*) had been established on the South Platte, descended steeply from a plateau to the North Platte. The canyon was so named by Frémont because of "a few scattering ash trees in the dry ravine." The precipitous but now easily passable road through the canyon, bordered by rank, spring-fed vegetation and arching trees, contrasts strikingly with the sweeping yellow wheat fields on the plateau and the sandy banks of the river below. On a knoll close to the river is the SITE OF FORT GRATTAN, a post that was built of sod.

Near the mouth of the hollow is a moist spot where in season wild roses, chokecherries, gooseberries, currants, and ferns cover the ground beneath the tall ash trees. Seven-tenths of a mile from the river are a few small cedars, said to mark the site of a cabin built by trappers in 1846. This cabin was later a general meeting place and unofficial post office. Nearby are a small grove of ash trees and a spring.

Half a mile below the edge of the plateau are the RUINS OF THE JOE CLARY HOUSE; Clary was the first settler here. About midway the road follows ruts of the old trail for a short distance.

At WINDLASS HILL, indicated by a marker, the drivers of covered wagons experienced much difficulty. Early accounts often mention the casualties to men, beasts, and equipment that were common events here. An English traveler who made the trip in 1849 wrote that the descent was so breath-taking that no one spoke for two miles. He reported that riders dismounted to lead their horses, that wagons with wheels locked were steadied with ropes, and that two mules were crushed under a wagon that broke loose. In the 1860's Indians sometimes waited in ambush above the narrow passage.

Ash Hollow and neighboring ravines were popular Indian hunting grounds. It was the scene of a day-long battle between the Pawnee and the Sioux, in which the Pawnee were badly beaten and driven from the North Platte Valley.

By the time the Pioneer Saints reached this point the "roadometer" was operating successfully, but William Clayton was much annoyed to find that Harmon was having it "understood that he invented the machinery . . . which makes me think less of him than I formerly did. . . . What little souls work."

At **33.7 m.** the highway crosses BLUE WATER CREEK, in 1855 the scene of the Battle of Blue Water, also called the Battle of Ash Hollow. Several incidents led up to the battle, notably the killing of Lt. John Lawrence Grattan and his force of 28 men by Sioux (*see below*). Gen. W. S. Harney with more than a thousand men entered the Platte country to subjugate the restless Indians. Most of the Sioux, when ordered to cross to the south side of the Platte River, did so, but one band of Brulé stayed on the north side of the river. It was here at Blue Water Creek that Harney and his men overtook and attacked them.

OSHKOSH, **43.7 m.** (843 pop.), is the seat of Garden County. In 1885 Henry G. Gumaer, Alfred W. Gumaer, Herbert W. Potter, and John Robinson of St. Paul, Neb., established a cattle ranch here. When

CROSSING THE PLAINS

SCOTTSBLUFF

Kirsch

a post office was opened in 1886 the settlement was named for Oshkosh, Wis.

The soil of this district is somewhat sandy. The prairie, rimmed with bluffs on the south and hills on the north, is irrigated and sugar beets are the principal crop.

At **44.2 m.** is the junction with State 27.

Right on this graveled, sandy road (*make local inquiries as to condition*) is the 41,000-acre Federal migratory waterfowl sanctuary, called CRESCENT LAKE RESERVE, **22 m.** Thousands of ducks nest here during the summer. The region includes a number of swamps and lakes.

At BROADWATER, **74.6 m.** (368 pop.), on May 23, 1847, Appleton Harmon wrote in his *Journal:* "I arose in the morning & found it to be a pleasant one verry little air stiring the Sun Shone warm I borrowed Wm. Clatons spy glass & started off to the bluffs after breakfast a bout, ½ past 9 A. M. which was a bout 1 mile distant as I came near the foot off the Bluff I gradually assended until I came to the foot of a Piremid & by going around it I found that I could assend it, by Clambering over the fragments of rocks that had broken off from near the top & ley in a confused mass, half way down the side I succeeded in ascending to its sumit . . . I was here joined by 3 or 4 of the brethering who came to visit the same cenerry . . . we left this & went to another larger & higher some 50 or 60 rods to the East of uss, this we assended from the North side passing huge rocks, that, have been rolled out of their natural place, by the wash off the heavey rains or the convulsive throughs of nature at the crusifixion off our Saveour."

US 26 here turns L. and crosses to the south side of the North Platte, then turns R., still following the river.

BRIDGEPORT, **90.4 m.** (3,653 alt., 1,421 pop.), observes Camp Clarke Days (*four days, first week in Sept.*) annually with a celebration opened by a parade of floats. The oldest settlers are honored; pioneer and Indian relics are on display. There are water contests, athletic events, band concerts, speeches, and a bowery dance.

At Bridgeport is the junction with State 86 (*see SIDE ROUTE C*).

Left from Bridgeport on State 88, a graveled road that passes COURTHOUSE ROCK and JAIL ROCK (R), **5 m.** These old landmarks rise abruptly from a level plain and form the eastern terminus of the Wildcat Hills. Courthouse Rock, according to one account, was named by migrants from St. Louis, who thought it resembled their county building. The top strata of the bluff, worn away on the edges, roughly suggest a classical pediment. Jail Rock nearby, somewhat smaller, is believed to have been named later by cowboys who remembered that a jail is often the structure nearest to a courthouse. The lower parts of the buttes are composed of Brule clay, the upper of Gering sandstone bands alternating with clay. In recent years hundreds of tourists, knives in hand, have emulated the pioneers by carving their names and accumulated wisdom on the faces of the rocks, unaware that this formation weathers quickly. A single heavy storm has been known to change the contours.

Several Indian legends are associated with the vicinity. One concerns a Pawnee hero who was rewarded by the gods with a magic horse for having rescued his grandmother, who had been abandoned by the tribe, in accordance with custom, because of her age. With the aid of this horse he inflicted heavy losses on the traditional enemy, the Sioux, and performed a hunting feat that won him the chief's daughter. Between these exploits he retired to the rocks for communion with his spiritual guides. At one time the Pawnee, forced to retreat down the North Platte Valley before the encroachments of the Sioux, left behind a small rear guard, who were outnumbered and forced to take refuge on top of the bluff. The Sioux encamped at the base, trying to starve out the Pawnee; but the Pawnee lowered themselves one at a time down a crevice in the rock, crept through the sleeping camp, and escaped.

Courthouse Rock was noted by many early explorers and travelers. Parker, the missionary, thought of it as an old castle. James Clyman in his diary of 1844 and Palmer in 1845 described it as an Old World ruin. Bryant estimated that its height was three to five hundred feet and its circumference one mile. On a nearby cliff of the same formation the words "Post Office" had been carved near the top; travelers deposited letters for friends behind them on the trail in boxes hewn in the soft stone base. Gilbert Cole, who passed along the trail in 1852, wrote of the long panorama of rocks, water, and sky in the region and of the cloud shadows on the plain.

BIRDCAGE GAP, **12 m.**, is a break in the Wildcat Range that carried a route of the Oregon Trail in the days when many emigrants followed the South Platte to Julesburg before turning northwest to Fort Laramie. Through it ran the stagecoaches connecting Sidney with the Black Hills. Parts of the trail are still discernible.

At Bridgeport US 26 recrosses the North Platte and follows the north bank.

NORTHPORT, **91.8 m.** (3,688 alt., 150), opposite Bridgeport, was so named because of its position.

At **94 m.** is the SITE OF CAMP CLARKE, as well as the SITE OF THE CAMP CLARKE BRIDGE. In 1876 the first wagon bridge across the North Platte River was built here by Henry T. Clarke of Omaha, to accommodate stages traveling between Sidney and the Black Hills. For a time soldiers guarded both ends of the bridge; a toll of $1 for a team, 50 cents for a person, was charged. The bridge was used until 1900.

At the south end of the bridge were a post office, store, saloon, stage barn, and other buildings destroyed by a prairie fire in 1910.

BAYARD, **107.5 m.** (3,753 alt., 1,559 pop.), was named in 1887 for Bayard, Iowa. The town's chief industry is the manufacture of beet sugar. Local people like to call the area the Valley of the Nile because of its fertility under irrigation. From the town is a wide view of the blue hills of the Wildcat Range on the south side of the river. Standing out distinctly in the center of the valley is Chimney Rock (*see SIDE ROUTE C*), a landmark of the Oregon Trail.

MINATARE (L), **120.4 m.** (3,820 alt., 1,079 pop.), was named for the Minnetaree, a Siouan tribe. Visible from the town is Scott's

Bluff (*see SIDE ROUTE C*), a landmark that rises seven hundred feet above the North Platte River.

At **129.9 m.** is the junction with a graveled road.

Left on this road **1 m.**; R. here on a dirt road running through a farmyard; then on foot. It is necessary to crawl under a barbed-wire fence to reach the GRAVE OF REBECCA WINTERS, **1.5 m.** Rebecca Winters, the mother of Mrs. Augusta Winters Grant, wife of a President of the Mormon Church, was a victim of the cholera epidemic of 1852.

A member of a Mormon train, she was one of many who developed cholera soon after leaving the Missouri; though she did not die of the disease it left her weak and wasted. For five hundred miles she lay on a bundle of quilts in a jolting wagon before succumbing. The Latter-Day Saints have erected a monument over her grave. When the Burlington Route right-of-way was surveyed, the grave was found to be in direct line with the proposed road. The route was changed to leave the grave undisturbed.

SCOTTSBLUFF, **131.9 m.** (4,000 alt., 8,465 pop.), was named for Scott's Bluff (*see SIDE ROUTE C*), which had been named for Hiram Scott, the trapper. The town was laid out in 1899. In the spring of 1905, some satirical person nicknamed it "Venice," because the 10-foot plank sidewalks bordered a foot of water that lay on Main Street and was inhabited by frogs; the citizens finally used sod blocks from two old corrals to raise the street level. The growth of the town has been rapid, the population in 1910 having been only 1,798. Today it is a shipping point for livestock, sugar beets, and grain.

West of Scottsbluff the highway continues along the north bank of the North Platte River, through a hilly country, where in season a patchwork landscape of sugar beets, alfalfa, corn, beans, and wheat is crisscrossed by the irrigation ditches that have made cultivation possible. A successful farmer in this section must of necessity be something of an engineer; he and his workers are seen wading in rubber boots, adjusting dams and water gates, shoveling out ditches, and guiding water into the proper channels.

On the edges of the beet fields are the shacks inhabited from mid-May until October by families of Mexicans, Spanish Americans, and Germans who came to the area from the Volga region between 1900 and 1910. The owners of the beet fields plow, seed, and harrow their land, but contract with migrant workers for the handwork. It is customary in this area for the head of a family to contract to handle as many acres as the size of his household permits; a family with three working members usually cares for about 20 of the average 12-ton-crop acres. Thinning is carried on in late May and early June, hoeing in late July and early August, pulling and topping in October. In 1937 the average payment for a season's work on an acre was $20.50. This wage may be somewhat increased under the terms of the Sugar Control Act of 1937; this act also forbids the labor of children under 14 years of age, though the rule is hard to enforce. During the winter many of the workers live in nearby villages.

Beet-growing is one of the most profitable agricultural activities in Nebraska; the average market price for sugar beets is $6 a ton.

At 134. m. is the junction with a dirt road.

Right on this road to the SCOTTSBLUFF EXPERIMENT FARM (*open to public*), 4 m., maintained by the U. S. Department of Agriculture in co-operation with the University of Nebraska. The farm includes 160 acres of irrigated land and 800 acres of pasture.

It was in this area, on May 29, 1847, that Prest Brigham Young delivered an angry sermon denouncing the Pioneer Saints for their light-heartedness. He felt that they were too much enjoying the expedition whose solemn purpose was to find the Promised Land. On Saturday, May 22, Clayton had written: "The evening was spent very joyfully by most of the brethren, it being very pleasant and moonlight. A number danced till the bugle sounded for bed time at nine o'clock. A mock trial was also prosecuted in the case of the camp vs. James Davenpot for blockading the highway and turning ladies out of their course. . . . We have had many such trials in the camp which are amusing enough and tend among other things to pass away the time cheerfully." But on the following Friday night he wrote that "Elder Kimball came to the next wagon where some of the boys were playing cards. He told them his views and disapprobation of their spending time gaming and dancing and mock trying, etc., and especially profane language uttered by some." It was on the following morning that Young gave his rebuke. In the course of it, according to Clayton, he said, "I have let the brethren dance and fiddle and act the nigger night after night to see what they will do, and what extremes they will go to, if suffered to go as far as they would. . . . The brethren say they want a little exercise to pass away time in the evenings, but if you can't tire yourselves bad enough with a day's journey without dancing every night, carry your guns on your shoulders and walk, carry your wood to camp instead of lounging and lying asleep in your wagons, increasing the load until your teams are tired to death and ready to drop to earth. . . . Suppose the angels were witnessing the hoe down the other evening, and listening to the haw haws the other evening, would they not be ashamed of it."

Young's irritation was perhaps excessive but it was understandable. In settled places he encouraged recreation and himself took part in formal dances. Here, however, he was nearing the most difficult and dangerous part of the journey and responsibility for the success of the home-finding expedition rested heavily on him.

At MITCHELL, 141.7 m. (3,945 alt., 2,058 pop.), are the SCOTTS BLUFF COUNTY FAIR GROUNDS.

HENRY, 155.2 m. (167 pop.), originally built in Wyoming, was moved into Nebraska because the inhabitants wanted the advantage of a difference in railroad freight rates.

At **155.5 m.** US 26 crosses the Wyoming Line. Nearby is the SITE OF AN ASTORIAN CAMP; here Robert Stuart and the men he led camped for several months in the winter of 1812, on their journey from Astoria to St. Louis.

Near the Wyoming Line is the SITE OF THE FIRST RED CLOUD AGENCY. The establishment of Red Cloud Reservation marked the end of the warfare carried on by Red Cloud, chief of the Ogallala Sioux, against the whites. In 1875 the agency was moved to another site.

In Wyoming the highway continues through the North Platte Valley, following a prehistoric Indian trail as well as the route of the returning Astorians in 1812-1813, of Captain Bonneville in 1832, and of innumerable migrants in later years.

When the Mormon Pioneers reached this point their minds were still filled with Young's sermon and the promises they had made for better conduct. Clayton said he "never noticed the brethren so still and sober on a Sunday."

TORRINGTON, Wyo., **163.4 m.** (4,098 alt., 1,811 pop.), named for Torrington in England, is the seat of Goshen County, which has no bonded indebtedness; royalties from oil, iron, coal, and other minerals reduce taxes and help to maintain public schools. Lying chiefly on the north side of the Platte River, Torrington is the trade center of an area producing sugar beets, potatoes, alfalfa, and seed crops. The annual Goshen County Fair is held here (*usually second week in September*).

At **167.4 m.** is the junction with a dirt road.

Left on this winding road **2 m.** to the ranch of the Lincoln Land Company, on which is the SITE OF THE ROCK RANCH BATTLE. One old building on the ranch was formerly a trading post; in it are a hundred holes, locally called port holes, that have been blocked up. Guns were thrust through these during attacks. It is said that in the early 1850's a party of emigrants, who had slaves with them, stopped at the post to rest. During the day they were attacked by Sioux. Some of the Negroes were killed and were buried under the floor.

At LINGLE, **173.3 m.** (4,150 alt., 415 pop.), situated about a mile north of the Platte River, is a HYDROELECTRIC POWER PLANT of the North Platte Federal Reclamation Project.

At **175.3 m.** (L), across the river from US 26, is the SITE OF THE GRATTAN INCIDENT of August 18, 1854. Accounts of what happened here vary. According to the most reliable version, a party of Mormons bound for Utah was passing an encampment of Sioux at this place; a lame cow at the rear of the caravan wandered into the Indian camp. For some reason the migrants did not go after her but proceeded to Fort Laramie, where they reported the incident. The fort was temporarily in command of Lt. John Lawrence Grattan, a recent West Point graduate, who lacked frontier experience. Grattan came to the camp with an interpreter and 28 other men and learned that the cow had been killed and eaten; he demanded that the Indians surrender those who had killed the animal. When the Indians refused, Grattan rashly ordered his men to fire into the tepee of the chief offender. The Indians returned the fire; Grattan and five soldiers fell immediately, and others were overtaken and killed. Though Grattan's superior officers deeply regretted the affair, both because of the deaths of the soldiers and the enmity aroused among the Indians, they had to admit that Grattan had conducted himself unwisely and that the Indians had acted under extreme provocation.

For some time afterward, Fort Laramie was almost in a state of siege.

At **176.3 m.** (L), across the river from US 26, is the SITE OF FORT BERNARD, a trading post built in 1849 that consisted of one crude log structure. According to Ware's *Emigrant Guide to California,* this post had "accommodations far inferior to those of an ordinary stable."

FORT LARAMIE, **183.6 m.** (4,250 alt., 245 pop.), bears the name of the nearby fort, which took its name from the river. The river was named for Jacques La Ramée, an early trapper (*see SECTION 5*).

Left from the town of Fort Laramie on a marked dirt road that is carried across the North Platte on a three-span bridge.

OLD FORT LARAMIE, **2 m.**, on 180 acres, has been acquired by the State of Wyoming and is to be made a National Monument. A number of early buildings remain, including the blacksmith shop and supply house, the commissary, and soldiers' and officers' quarters.

This place, on the North Platte near the mouth of the Laramie River, was one of the most important points on the road to Oregon and California. The first buildings were erected about a mile upstream. It was settled in 1834 as a fur-trading post, Fort William, by Robert Campbell and William Sublette and named for the latter. A year later the post passed into the hands of Fitzpatrick, Sublette, and Bridger and shortly afterward became a post of the American Fur Company, under which it was called Fort John. By 1839 the settlement had grown and was surrounded by a rectangular stockade 15 feet high, with lookout towers on two opposite corners. About 1846 the American Fur Company built a new post a mile upstream and called it Fort Laramie, which almost from the beginning had been the popular name of the place. The old post was demolished soon afterward. Three years later the American Fur Company sold its property here to the U. S. Government and Fort Laramie became a military post.

From 1834 until 1862, when part of the westbound traffic began to move farther south, the post was the real jumping-off-place for almost everyone on his way to the mountains, to the Columbia, and to Utah and California. Until after the Mormons reached Utah this was the last point short of the Hudson's Bay territory where it was always possible to buy supplies. (Though Jim Bridger established a post in the Green River Valley about 1843, he was often away from home when travelers most wanted his aid.) At Fort Laramie travelers could always find traders and Indians with the latest news on conditions of the route and the attitude of the Indians. After the Federal Government set up a military establishment here during the gold rush, the fort was the scene of even greater activity. The commandant, in addition to keeping an eye on the Indians, had to act as nursemaid for reckless and improvident pioneers. Some arrived at this point, which was less than half way along the trail, without supplies or the possibility of buying them. Others lacked most of the equipment necessary for the difficult travel westward.

In 1851 the stage line operated by John Hockaday and William Liggett began to carry mail, express, and sometimes passengers to western posts. Horses were changed here. After the overland line was put in operation Fort Laramie was a regular stage station. In 1860 and 1861 one of the most exciting regular events was the arrival and departure of the Pony Express riders; this was one of the relay points where riders would wait with saddled horses for the transfer of the mail from the East and the West.

From the beginning the post was a rendezvous for Indians as well as whites; they came here to steal—when they dared, to beg, to trade, to watch the white men, to parley, and to share the local excitement. Indian children and dogs played about the stockades and squaws stood about wide-eyed and watchful. Sometimes there would be more than a hundred lodges on the nearby land. Gamblers, traders, hunters, prospectors, and journalists were always about after the great migration had begun.

Hunting parties of pleasure seekers also outfitted here. The most spectacular expedition of this sort to leave the post was that of Sir George Gore, who traveled in truly imposing state with Jim Bridger as his guide.

A number of important treaties with the Indians were signed at or near Fort Laramie. Not all were successful. The treaty of 1851 was considered the eventual source of the hostilities that terrorized the northern plains for a score of years (*see SIDE ROUTE C*).

When the Indians were making their last attempt to drive away the invaders, they drove off stock, pillaged emigrant wagons, and killed ranchmen and traders, keeping those at Fort Laramie constantly on the alert for attack. Although the years 1862-65 were the "bloody years" on the Great Plains, the years of greatest danger here were between 1867-77. In 1867 Congress created a peace commission with a view to obtaining safety for travelers along the trans-continental railways and the overland routes. In 1868 this commission succeeded in negotiating the Sioux Treaty, by which the country north of the North Platte River and east of the summit of the Big Horn Mountains was recognized as belonging solely to the Indians. This treaty was later broken by white men who pushed into the Indian country in their eagerness to reach the Black Hills gold fields.

On June 2, 1847, Appleton Harmon, the Pioneer Saint, here wrote in his diary: "we went in to the Fort & was kindly & genteelly receivd by Mister Bordeaux the maniger or master of the Fort he invited us in to a room upstairs which look verry mutch like a bar room of an eastern hotel it was ornamented with several drawings Portraits &c a long desk a settee & some chairs constituted the principle furniture of the room it wass neat & comfortable Mr Bordeaux, answered the meney questions that was asked by us a bout the country the Natives &c he sed the seasons ware ginerally dry that thare had been no rain for 2 years until within a few days he said that the Soux would not disturb the emegrants but the crows ware verry annoysome that they came & robed them of 25 horses about 10 days ago they crept along under the bank of Larrieme fork until within 80 rods of the fort in the day time then rushed out between the fort & the horses & drove them of in Spite of the guards, (for there ware 2 a herdding them at the time) and had themsafe before one forse could reach the spot from the fort, The remainder of their horses ware guarded by 4 men all the time and put in the Fort at night, they had just sent off 600 packs of robes to fort Pier on the missouri river the distance nearly 300 miles, they said that some traders ware thare yesterday that said that 6 days drive ahead that the Snow was midled deep 10 days ago & that it would be dificult to find feed for our teams he said that thare ware buffalo 2 days drive ahead & some grisseley Bairs that he expected some oregon emegrants soon he said that the next fort of trading post we came to was fort Bridgeer the other side of the mountains."

Emigrants were less of a novelty here and troops were in command in 1853 when James Farmer, another Mormon emigrant, arrived. "we then entered Fort Laramie consisting of a few wooden houses and about 67 soldiers stationed here it lies in the hollow high Bluffs all around they have 6 pieces of cannon and all seem very happy there are stores here where we can purchase anything we need but very high flour 15 dollars a sack."

Here are the RUINS OF THE ENLISTED MEN'S BARRACKS, which were three hundred feet in length and built of cement, or grout; the limestone was quarried from nearby hills by the troops. The walls are more than 20 inches thick. The dance hall on the second floor was a rendezvous for cowboys and soldiers and the scene of many celebrations. It was particularly gay in the days when cattle from Texas were being driven past the fort on their way to the plains of Wyoming and Montana for fattening before being shipped to market.

The GUARD HOUSE, built in 1849-59 of stone, has a double-barred window. The dungeon is in good condition. Directly north, on the edge of the parade ground, is the SITE OF FORT WILLIAM.

The SUTLER'S STORE, constructed of adobe, is probably the oldest building in Wyoming. Jim Bridger lived here when serving the post as a scout. Here in 1868 Red Cloud signed the Sioux Treaty, and here in 1872 one of the Janis brothers was killed during a Christmas Day brawl. This store was not only the trade center for people living hundreds of miles around, especially from 1856 to 1872, but also contained banking facilities.

OLD BEDLAM, the officers' club, was built by the Government in 1851 at a cost of $70,000. The fact that all lumber for its construction was hauled by oxen from Fort Leavenworth, Kans., largely accounts for its cost. It was to Old Bedlam in 1866 that "Portugee" Phillips brought news of the disaster at Fort Phil Kearney in which Capt. W. J. Fetterman and 80 men were killed. Phillips' ride was made in subzero weather, through blizzards and with hostile Indians on every side.

On the south bank of the North Platte River, in the tongue of land about three-fourths of a mile above its junction with the Laramie, is the SITE OF FORT PLATTE (*see above*). In *Rocky Mountain Life*, Rufus B. Sage, the journalist who visited this spot about 1841, related a typical story of the period. "The night of our arrival at Fort Platte was the signal for a grand jollification to all hands, (with two or three exceptions) who soon got most *gloriously drunk*, and such an illustration of the beauties of harmony as was then perpetrated, would have rivalled Bedlam itself, or even the famous council chamber beyond the Styx.

"Yelling, screeching, firing, shouting, fighting, swearing, drinking, and such like *interesting* performances, were kept up without intermission,—and woe to the poor fellow who looked for repose that night—he might as well have thought of sleeping with a thousand cannon bellowing at his ears.

"The scene was prolonged till near sundown the next day, and several made their egress from this beastly carousal, minus shirts and coats,—with swollen eyes, bloody noses, and empty pockets,—the latter circumstance will be easily understood upon the mere mention of the fact, that liquor, in this country, is sold for four dollars per pint.

"The day following was ushered in by the enactment of another scene of comico-tragical character.

"The Indians encamped in the vicinity, being extremely solicitous to imitate the example of their illustrious predecessors, soon as the first tints of morning began to paint the east, commenced their demands for firewater; and, ere the sun had told an hour of his course, they were pretty well advanced in the state of how came ye so, and seemed to exercise their musical powers in wonderful rivalry with their white brethren.

"Men, women, and children were seen running from lodge to lodge with vessels of liquor, inviting their friends and relatives to drink; while whooping, singing, drunkenness, and trading for fresh supplies to administer to the demands of intoxication, had evidently become the order of the day. Soon, individuals were noticed passing from one to another, with mouths full of the coveted fire-water, drawing the lips of favored friends in close contact, as if to kiss, and ejecting the contents of their own into the eager mouths of others,—thus affording the delighted recipients tests of their fervent esteem in the heat and strength of the strange draught.

"At this stage of the game the American Fur Company, as is charged, commenced dealing out to them, gratuitously, strong drugged liquor, for the double purpose of preventing a sale of the article by its competitor in trade, and of creating sickness, or inciting contention among the Indians, while under the influence of sudden intoxication,—hoping thereby to induce the latter to charge its ill effects upon an opposite source, and thus, by destroying the credit of its rival, monopolize for itself the whole trade.

"It is hard to predict with certainty, what would have been the result of this reckless policy, had it been continued through the day. Already its effects became apparent, and small knots of drunken Indians were seen in various directions, quarrelling, preparing to fight, or fighting,—while others lay stretched upon the ground in helpless impotency, or staggered from place to place with all the revolting attendencies of intoxication.

"The *dram-a*, however, was here brought to a temporary close by an incident which made a strange contrast in its immediate results.

"One of the head chiefs of the Brule village, in riding at full speed from Fort John to Fort Platte, being a little too drunk to navigate, plunged headlong from his horse and *broke his neck* when within a few rods of his destination. Then was a touching display of confusion and excitement. Men and squaws commenced bawling like children;—the whites were bad, very bad, said they, in their brief to give Susu-ceicha the fire-water that caused his death. But the height of their censure was directed against the American Fur Company, as its liquor had done the deed. . . ."

Near Fort Laramie the Mormon Trail crossed to the south bank of the North Platte and united with the Oregon Trail.

GUERNSEY, **196.5 m.** (4,361 alt., 656 pop.), bears the name of a ranchman, Charles A. Guernsey. The town, beautifully situated just below the mouth of the picturesque Platte River Canyon, is a trade center and supply base for the iron mines and limestone quarries nearby. The surrounding region has yielded abundant traces of prehistoric man; archeological excavations have uncovered implements of war and agriculture used by the primitive inhabitants. Embedded in the concrete of an OREGON TRAIL MARKER here, which bears the official Oregon Trail bronze plaque, are many relics that were found on the old trails, including ox and mule shoes, bullets, wagon irons, and guns.

The small HIGH SCHOOL MUSEUM (*free*), housed in the basement, contains Indian and pioneer relics, geological specimens, and artifacts from the Spanish Diggings. Among the relics is a small Mason and Hamlin melodeon brought to Fort Laramie by ox team; it is still in good condition.

1. Left from Guernsey on a dirt road to REGISTER CLIFF, **3.3 m.**, a chalk bluff that was a popular autograph album of early travelers. Of the thousands of names daubed and cut here, about seven hundred are still legible. One is dated 1842. The cliff was first called Sand Point. The wide, grassy meadow at its base was often used as the first campsite west of Fort Laramie. Traders named Ward and Guerrier operated a post here for a time; Ward moved away in 1856, in 1857

becoming the post trader at Fort Laramie, and in the same year Guerrier was killed when a keg of powder exploded.

A number of people who died on the trail were buried at the base of Register Cliff.

2. Right from Guernsey on an oiled highway that leads to HARTVILLE, **6 m.** (4,900 alt., 189 pop.). The area often held a populous Indian camp long before the coming of white settlers and, until the past decade, traces of the camp could be found throughout the canyon in which the town lies. Rings of flat rocks outlined the positions of the tepees and lodges. Scrapers, arrowheads, and stone axes were formerly found in abundance, as well as grinders with which the red and brilliant yellow clays were prepared for purposes of personal adornment.

Hartville became a settlement as the result of a copper strike that brought hundreds of prospectors and miners from the Black Hills. As the center of a copper district, the town became a wild spot, with saloons, dance halls, and gambling houses running full swing at all hours. Cowboys from nearby ranches added their noise to that of the miners. There was much gunplay and little law. In the old cemetery near town lie a number of men who "died with their boots on"; the early funeral services were usually conducted by a bartender. After the copper boom the town was not entirely abandoned; a store, a saloon, and a lodging house were kept in operation to serve the ranchers. In 1899-1900, when eastern capital arrived to develop the iron deposits at the nearby Sunrise and Chicago mines, the old mining camp life revived. Tents and dugouts housed a large part of the population, as there was neither time nor material for the construction of buildings. Later, construction gangs from the Burlington Route, which was then being extended from Nebraska to connect with the Colorado & Southern R.R. running north from Cheyenne, added their wages to the stream of money that flowed into the camp from the pockets of miners and settlers. With the completion of the railroad and the centralization of mining operations in the Sunrise mine, the floating population of Hartville vanished. The town, while modern, has retained much of its frontier appearance.

Northwest of Hartville is SLADE (SAWMILL) CANYON, named for Jack Slade, the stage line division superintendent (*see SECTION 4*). There is a story that Slade turned bandit after he had to leave the stage service and that this was a rendezvous for his gang. But this hardly accords with Slade's character as vouched for by those who best knew him. After Slade had asked the advice of officers at Fort Laramie (*see SECTION 4*) as to what action he should take against the threatening Jules Reni and had privately been told that he had better kill him, he sent four men ahead to the stage station where Jules was reported to be. Slade followed on the box of the stage and at the station killed Jules, who had already been captured. He then returned to the fort, told his story, and was exonerated; according to the frontier code he had done the only possible thing. The most reliable reporters of the incident said that the oft-repeated story that Slade pinned Beni to a shed by the ears before killing him and later used one of the ears as a watch charm, was pure folklore.

Another exploit connected with Slade took place not far from this canyon. In the spring of 1861 an American and a Mexican, who were riding the stage as U. S. Mail service employees, had a quarrel that resulted in the death of the American. Slade, who had to maintain law and order along his division, at once prepared to run the Mexican out of the country. The killer had taken himself to the Sarah ranch at the head of Guernsey Lake. Slade sent word to Sarah to turn the Mexican out but Sarah retorted that he offered accommodations to travelers and that he would not turn away anyone who paid his bill. Several nights later a coachload of Slade's men arrived at the ranch; in the fight that followed, Sarah, his wife, an Indian staying at the house, and an old Frenchman were killed. One guest named Winters made his escape and ran the 25 miles to Fort Laramie. Immediate reparation was demanded, but without avail; no effort whatever was made to apprehend the murderers. Sarah's family included four children, whose ages ranged from a few months to 12 years. The eldest girl, with the baby on her back, and another sister had climbed out of a rear window and escaped. A few weeks later their bodies were found on the prairie. The boy, who became separated from his sisters, was found by a stage driver who took him to the stage station. He was eventually adopted by Slade and went with the Slades when they left the area.

In time Slade began to drink to excess and when under the influence of liquor was insanely violent. He eventually went to live near Virginia City, Mont., and after one of his outbreaks in 1864 was hanged by vigilantes.

At SUNRISE, **7 m.** (4,900 alt., 360 pop.), are the Sunrise Mines. In 1900 C. A. Guernsey obtained options on the mining claims in this vicinity and sold them to a Colorado company. The GLORY HOLE, or pit of the Sunrise Mines, is so large and deep at present that both the Colorado and Wyoming Capitols could be housed in it with room to spare, while the Washington Monument could be placed on the lowest level and would rise only a few feet above its rim. Men at work on the far side of the pit resemble pygmy cave-dwellers; ladders and ore cars cling to sheer walls. Ore from the mines is shipped to smelters at Pueblo, Colo. Early explorations indicated that quarrying operations had been carried on in this pit by the Indians, the material probably having been used by them for paint.

At **197 m.** is the junction with a dirt road.

Left on this road to WARM SPRINGS, **2.5 m.**, also known as the Emigrant's Laundry Tub, which was on the Oregon Trail. This large spring has an abundant flow at a temperature of 70 degrees throughout the year, and remains unfrozen during the coldest weather.

A major problem of trail travelers—at least the tidier members of the trains— was that of keeping their clothes clean and in order. On the plains clothes usually had to be washed with cold water because there was relatively little if any wood near the camp sites and buffalo chips did not make a very hot fire. Most of the migrants failed to realize in advance what kind of clothing would be suitable for the overland journey and how hard travel would be on their garments. This was particularly true of the women. By the time the trains reached the mountains the members were often clothed in rags or in highly unsuitable garments. One traveler told of seeing women in beribboned party dresses heavily coated with dust and grime. Few people took enough shoes with them and many had to travel the last miles with their feet wrapped in rags.

Frémont camped by this spring in 1842. Nearby is an old limekiln, which was probably used in the 1870's or 1880's in the purification of the water.

At **198.5 m.** is the junction with a dirt road.

Left on this road a short distance to COLD SPRING, an early landmark. On the hill above the spring are rifle pits, believed to have been thrown up by a band of whites when protecting themselves against Indians.

US 26 runs almost due west towards LARAMIE PEAK (alt. 10,274), which rises sheer in the distance.

At **210.5 m.** is the junction with US 87; R. here on US 87, which follows the North Platte.

The SITE OF THE HORSESHOE STAGE STATION, **231 m.**, is on Horseshoe Creek, near which was timber and good pasturage. In 1868 an attack was made on the place by Ogallala and Miniconjou led by Chief Crazy Horse.

The place was occupied by Marion Thornburg, William Warrell, and John R. Smith. On the morning of March 19 their dogs were so uneasy that two of the men went out to investigate. They found 60 or 70 Indians lurking nearby and hastily returned to the house, which was surrounded by a stout stockade. Shortly afterwards the Indians came into the open, and the white men fired on them, killing two and wounding two. Though the band was large, the men felt reasonably safe behind the stockade because they had plenty of food and ammunition and the well was within the enclosure. The Indians, however, burned the stockade and the stables. Toward evening the aborigines retired but shortly afterward returned. About midnight the Indians set fire to the house and the whites retreated to a cellar under the kitchen; there they began hastily to dig a tunnel. While the Indians whooped and howled about what they believed to be a funeral pyre, the besieged men made their escape. They hurried to Twin Springs where two men were living; these joined them on a retreat to Fort Laramie after having cached provisions under the floor of their shack and set the house on fire. On the following day they met a trapper, who joined the party. Shortly afterward, near Little Cottonwood Creek, the Indians discovered them; the whites hid for a time in a wooded ravine but when they attempted to steal away from it two of them were killed and a third, wounded and on the point of being captured, killed himself. The remaining men defended themselves as best they could and finally managed to effect a truce by offering the Indians the articles cached under the Twin Springs ruins; the Indians, according to their code, had avenged the death of those killed in the initial attack and were willing to withdraw.

GLENDO, **233.7 m.** (4,718 alt., 201 pop.), is a trade center for ranches.

BRIDGER'S CROSSING, **246.6 m.**, was used by some migrants on the trail. A ferry is said to have once been operated here by Jim Bridger for a short time.

At **247.6 m.** is the junction (R) with US 20, which unites with US 87 westward, whence the highway runs through badlands dotted with unusual sandstone formations.

DOUGLAS, **260.9 m.** (4,815 alt., 1,917 pop.), the seat of Converse County, is the trade center of a livestock-raising and farming area. There are oil wells in the vicinity. Large shade trees line the straight streets.

During the 1870's and 1880's Fort Fetterman, about eight miles northwest, was the supply point for the stockmen of the country and a small settlement grew up near it. When in 1886 it was announced that the Fremont, Elkhorn & Missouri Valley Ry. would extend its lines westward from Chadron, Neb., foresighted people began to settle not far from the confluence of Antelope Creek and the North Platte River. Before long the ranchmen, hearing of the larger stocks of merchandise in the new tent town, began to come here to do their trading.

The first church services in Tent Town were held in May, 1886, in a saloon, by two theological students. The altar consisted of a card table. The bar nearby was partly hidden by a new wagon cover and only a few bottles remained in sight.

Tent Town soon had three streets and a newspaper, *Bill Barlow's Budget*. The editor of the paper, Morris Clark Barrow, who wrote under the pseudonym "Bill Barlow," gained much attention for his philosophic and humorous writings. For two years Barrow was city editor of the Laramie *Boomerang* under Bill Nye.

About June 1, 1886, it was announced that a railway station and townsite would be established some 10 miles east of Fetterman on a sagebrush flat, on the opposite side of the river. Shortly afterwards, when the Pioneer Townsite Company had laid out the new town of Douglas, Tent Town was put on wheels and in three days was moved here.

On August 29 the first passenger train arrived, loaded with people, and the sale of lots was started. For the next 60 days there was continuous pounding of hammers from daylight until dark. Five brick buildings and many shacks were built. Construction crews mingled with soldiers and cowboys and for a time the new town had a turbulent life. During the first year of its existence there were 25 saloons, but before long the number decreased to six.

Livestock men were attracted to the region because of the abundance of water and the good pasturage. One of the oldest cattle brands in the State, the SO, was in use nearby in 1870. In the 1880's many big outfits ran cattle into the area from Texas and the range was soon very much overstocked. When the March storms of 1887 came on cattle died by the thousands.

Although several large cattle and sheep outfits grazed in the vicinity, the lands were gradually homesteaded, and fences forced the cattle kings to move their herds and flocks to more remote places. The slowness with which the land was claimed was owing to the fact that the land office for the area was in Cheyenne, about 200 miles away by wagon road.

The STATE FAIR GROUNDS, on the bank of the Platte River at the west end of Center St., occupy several acres. The buildings include racing stables, grandstands, poultry houses, exhibition halls, a 4-H club building, and the Old Timers' Log Cabin. The Old Timers' Cabin, built of logs in 1926, with funds gathered by popular subscription, houses many relics of the frontier days and is the headquarters of the Wyoming Pioneer Association.

At **263.4 m.** is the junction with a graded road.

Right on this road to the SITE OF FORT FETTERMAN, **7 m.,** about a quarter mile from the right bank of La Prele Creek on a small plateau. The fort was established July 19, 1867, and named in honor of Capt. William J. Fetterman, who was killed by Indians near Fort Phil Kearney on Dec. 21, 1866.

After the garrisoning of Fetterman, a number of Arapaho of the Black Coal and Little Wolf bands and Cheyenne of the Dull Knife groups traded here, but they ceased their visits late in 1876 and 1877.

On March 1, 1876, Gen. George Crook left Fort Fetterman with 10 companies of cavalry, two companies of infantry, and 10 pack trains, for the purpose of forcing the Indians to stay on the reservations; during the following summer conflicts were frequent. In November of that year Gen. Ronald S. McKenzie led a large force from the Powder River territory, where they encountered Dull Knife's band of Cheyenne. In the battle that followed, 173 lodges and all of the Indians' ammunition and supplies were destroyed.

At **283.7 m.** (1) is the GRAVE OF A. H. UNTHANK, who died July 2, 1850, while on his way to the Oregon country. It is a more substantial marker than was usually put over the grave of an emigrant.

During the summer months plants and flowers of many kinds cover the prairies here with color. In this section of the State Indian paintbrush, the Wyoming State flower, grows along the mountain streams and on the plains. The wild iris, fireweed, blue violet, mountain phlox, sweet pea, scarlet bugler, forget-me-not, rose gentian, checker bloom, sand lily, prairie larkspur, and others are on the foothills and the higher plateaus. The dandelion, soapweed, round and bayonet cacti, nodding wild onion, white loco, showy milkweed, and pussy willows are native to the plains. The common sagebrush, as well as the prickly pear, is abundant in the arid foothills.

GLENROCK, **288.5 m.** (4,900 alt., 819 pop.), has good accommodations. The refineries of the Continental Oil Company are west of the town. A 30-acre park, with seats, benches and tables, ovens, swings and other conveniences, is just north of the tourist camps on the eastern outskirts. The town is the trade and social center of a large area and has facilities unusual in a place with such a small population.

The Upper Platte Indian Agency, established here near Deer Creek Station, a telegraph outpost, formed the nucleus of the town. As further settlement took place the site was called Mercedes. Later William Nuttall found coal and developed mines nearby and the settlement was renamed in his honor. Glenrock came to life with the building of the railroad in 1886 and 1887.

Left from Glenrock a dim trail leads to MORMON CANYON, **5 m.,** on Deer Creek. A party of Mormons came here in 1853 to grow. foodstuffs for migrating Saints. They remained for several years. Traces of irrigation ditches and the ruins of buildings are visible.

As the Mormon Pioneers creaked slowly along through this area they found the route more difficult but enjoyed the new scenes and plentiful meals of game. William Clayton was taking pleasure in the operation of his "roadometer" and guarded it with care. Other migrants visited the Mormons to examine it, but the Saints maintained a reserve toward them based on past experience with "gentiles." At intervals Clayton erected signboards with mileages and directions for the benefit of the Saints who were to follow the pathfinders. Clayton and others constantly consulted the report of Frémont, which was their guidebook, and checked their observations against his. Later the Mormons prepared their own guidebook for the use of their travelers.

Near La Bonte Creek they had met some friendly trappers who told the Pioneers of the difficulty of the Upper Platte Crossing. Appleton Harmon wrote of this meeting: "they gave us the privilege of a boat that they had on the North fork of the platte a bout 5 days drive a head to do our ferrying in several waggons ware sent a head sutch as before those emegrants that are jest a head of us all so to kell some buffalo for they say they are plenty on the river."

PARKERTON, **292.5** (5,000 alt., 367 pop.), is in the heart of the Big Muddy oil fields. Oil was first developed in this basin in 1915. Maximum production was reached in 1919 when the field yielded about 8,000 barrels a day, from about 200 wells. In 1936 daily production averaged about 1,500 barrels.

At the railroad station here is the GRAVE OF ADA MAGILL, aged 6 years, who died July 3, 1864. The child was a member of a wagon train bound for Oregon.

EVANSVILLE (R), **309.4 m.** (5,103 alt., 174 pop.), is chiefly a collection of White Eagle and Texas Oil Company refineries.

CASPER, **312.4 m.** (5,103 alt., 16,619 pop.) (*see WYOMING GUIDE*), the second largest city in Wyoming, was named for Fort Casper.

In 1885 the Chicago & North Western Ry., then operating from Omaha to Chadron, Neb., announced plans to extend its line to this place, where settlement had already begun. Business was being carried on in tents and crudely constructed shacks but there were nearly a hundred residents when the first passenger train arrived on June 15, 1888.

Soon after the establishment of the new town a rumor spread that gold had been discovered in Casper Mountain; businessmen, laborers, cowboys, and many others dropped their work, bought picks and shovels, and started for the hills. For a time there was intense local excitement, and then it died as suddenly as it had arisen.

In the fall of 1888 drilling for oil was begun in the Salt Creek field. The first oil refinery in the State was erected here in 1895. It was a number of years later, however, that the real oil boom began. North of the city are the Teapot Dome oil fields.

It was not uncommon at night during the oil boom times to see 2,500 people milling up and down unpaved Center Street, since there was no other place to go. Street fights were common and were enjoyed by the crowds. The Bucket-of-Blood Saloon was the hangout of drillers, construction workers, and roustabouts at the rigs, and a fight could be witnessed there at almost any time.

In the city is a PIONEER MONUMENT, erected in 1911. It is an obelisk, 40 feet in height, of Indiana limestone.

On June 11, 1847, the Pioneer Saints reached a point near the site of this town. They decided to camp because two companies of Missourians were but half a mile ahead of them and Missourians had been among their bitterest enemies in the east. Harmon reported: "we got up our teams at a bout 2 AM. and after confabulating for a half hour a bout whether to cross the river here or to go a bout 4 *ms* a head whare our brethering that had gone to git possesion of the ferry who as we under Stood by Br Chesley who came back & met us was buiseyly engaged in ferreing 2 of the small bands of the oregon emegrants 25 waggons in all for which they received a bout 33 dollars in remuneration they took the loading acrost in the Leeather Skift & drawed the waggons through the river by means of a rope fastend to the end of the tonge & thus drawing them through they rec in payment flour at $250 per hhd Bacon at 6 cts per lb &c we traveled 4 ms & camped in a ½ circle on the bank of a river ½ a mile east of the place whare they ware aferrying, our H unters had killed 3 buffalo which was verry fat a black bair 2 or 3 cubs & several antilope."

Left from Casper on a graveled road that runs westward between the junction of US 87 and US 87E to Upper Platte Crossing, **2.5 m.** Thrifty Brigham Young was delighted with the amount of business being carried on near here by the Saints who had gone ahead to pre-empt the boats left by the trappers; the men had added to their ferrying facilities by building two rafts. The main body of the Pioneers arrived at this point on Saturday and lingered several days. Young had intended to take the whole party forward with him; but as bodies of emigrants willing to pay for ferriage continued to arrive and word came that a large train, possibly of Saints, was advancing along the Platte, he felt it wise to allow some of the brethren to remain behind and continue business, which was paid for chiefly with grain. The Saints had only a limited amount of foodstuffs and the season was too far advanced to make it possible to raise crops that season, when they finally decided on a place of settlement. Elder Woodruff wrote: "It looked as much of a miracle to me to see our flour and meal bags replenished in the Black Hills as it did to have the children of Israel fed with manna in the wilderness."

Appleton Harmon was one of nine men selected to remain and help run the ferry. Young left strict instructions, which the brethren agreed to follow, as to how they should conduct and protect themselves. As reported in Harmon's phonetic spelling, Brigham Young instructed: "be a greed in all your operations act ing in concrt keeping to gether continually and not Scatter to hunt &c and at your leasure moments put you up a comfortable room that will afford your selves & horses protection a gainst the Indians should a war party pass this way, but first of all See that your boats is properly Secured by fastining raw hides over the tops of the ca noos or some better process compleete the landings, and be care fol of the lives & property of all you labor for remembering that you are responsible for all accidents through your carelessness or negligence and that you retain not that which belongeth to the Traveler

SETTLERS (1864)

ALONG THE TRAIL

"For one waggon familey &c you will charge $1.50 cts payment in flour & provisions at State Prices or $3.00 in cash but you had better take young stock at a fair valuation in Stead of cash & a team if you shall want the same to remove

"Should general Emegration cease before our breathering arive Cash your effects & re turn to laramie and wait their arival, and come on with them to the place of location, and we promise you that the Superintendant of the ferry Shall never lack wisdom or knowledge to devise & council you in righteousness and for your best good, if you will all ways bee a greed and in all humilety watch & pray with out ceasing

"When our Emegration Companies arive if the river is not fordable ferry them and let them who are able pay a reasonable sum the council of their camp will decide who are able to pay

"Let a Strict a count becept of everry mans labor also of all waggons & teams ferried and of all receipts & ex penditures allowing each man acording to his labour and justice, and if eney one feels a greeved let heim not murmer but be patient until you come up and let the council decide, and the way not to bee a greeved is for everry man to love his brother as him self

"By order and in behalf of the council we remain your Brothering in Christ

Brigham Young President"

Among those left behind were Luke Johnson, who was an amateur doctor and dentist, and Davenport, the blacksmith; Young had seen the heavy demand for the services of these craftsmen and determined to use them to augment the Mormon community funds. After the main body of Pioneers started westward those who remained behind decided to move the ferrying equipment a short distance eastward to what seemed a better position. They discovered that three other men, who had come in advance of an Oregon-bound train, had also started a ferrying business, but the equipment of the rivals was primitive and the men lacked skill, so, by a judicious lowering of the established rates—considered a justifiable departure from Young's instructions—the Saints soon achieved a monopoly. Two Saints who were sent back to Deer Creek (Glenrock) for some "stone coal" erected a signboard there:

"Notice

"To the ferry 28 *ms* the ferry good & safe maned by experienced men black Smithing horse & ox Shoing done all so a wheel right

Thomas Grover,"

On Sunday, July 27, 1847, Harmon wrote: "a Company of 11 wagons drove up Mr Cox foreman we ferryed them for $16.00 in cash & done $3.75 worth of blacksmithing for them Capt Brown arived with his Battalion a bout 8 A. M. Capt Saunders company arived a bout 2 P. M. and refused to pay us 75cts a waggon for ferrying them & so they went up the river a bout 2 ms & Swam the river & got a raft that was left thare by Some of the former Companies & commenced operations Some Jobs of Smithing Commenced for Capt Browns Company 7 of Capt Saunders Co got Sick of raft ing & returned to us & we ferryed them for 75cts a wagon the morning of the 28th"

But "Capt" Saunders' attempt to take his company across without expense was unsuccessful. On July 30 Harmon reported: "Capt Brown & his Detachment Started asall So Amasa Lyman we ferryed Capt Saunders Co or the remainder of it who had refused to give us 75 cts a waggon they havein worked 2 days & got 2 waggons a crost only, & then returned to us & wated until we ferryed 90 waggons that ware a head of them & they paid us $1.00 a waggon for the 12 waggons remaining we then ferryed Capt Higgins Co of 23 waggons for $23.00 in cash allso Capt McClays Co of 23 waggons & Capt Taylors Co of 12 waggons & Capt Patter Sons Co of 16 waggons & done $6.50 worth of black Smithing this day we have ferryed 73 waggons & made 2 extra trips 2 of the trips Namely, Pugmyer & East man Stade here on a furlow."

By July 1 Harmon wrote that the "brethering" were "all verry tiard and wanted rest," but Oregon emigrants continued to arrive in large numbers. On July 3 they had an eastbound visitor who bore a letter from "prest" Young. Harmon recorded it as follows:

"June 29, 1847 Little Sandy

"Mr. Thomas Grover and Company

"we introduce to your notice Mr. James Bridger who we expect ed to have seen at his fort he is now on his way to Fort Laramie we wish you to cross him& his 2 men on our a count BY he was agoing to Laramie & expected to return to his fort in time to Pilot the Pioneers through to Salt Lake he said that he could take us to a place that would Suit us, thare ware 4 of our Soldiers form Browns detachment came back with Mr Bridger on a furlow & was agoing to the States."

The throngs of customers continued to arrive and on July 8 Harmon noted: "thare was done $6.40cts worth of black Smithing & Some other jobs commenced Luke Johnson got $3.00 for cleaning teeth & Doctoring which was put into the jineral pile."

On July 16 the Saints witnessed a social event: "Stil remained here gitting work done near evening a young man by the name of Jacob Cooper was married to Kittean Huckelbee by ex Squire Tullis of said Company from the State of Indianna."

The brethren accumulated a considerable number of cattle by their labors; in caring for them they were "assisted by Yerick a faithful watch dog and 3 or 4 other assistant dogs."

When the tourist season was over the Mormon ferrymen went on to Fort Bridger for the winter, as Young had told them to do, and in the spring Harmon returned to Winter Quarters to help his family on the overland journey.

When Lorenzo Sawyer reached this place, in 1850, Mormons were still carrying on the ferry business, but by this time they were willing to accept cash payments. The charge was $4 a wagon and $.25 for each head of cattle. The Mormons had made additions to the equipment; a pulley and ropes drew some wagons across the stream. Because of the time needed to take large numbers across the river, various traders came here at intervals to do business while the travelers awaited their turns. In June, 1850, when Kit Carson was here with a herd of horses and mules for sale, the banks of the river were so covered with travelers that people had to register and wait their turns for ferriage; sometimes it would be nearly a week before they could obtain service and foresighted companies approaching this place sent horsemen ahead to make reservations for them. The well-to-do also offered higher pay for quick service.

In 1859 Louis Ganard built a thousand-foot bridge of cedar logs on cribs filled with stone. The structure, which cost about $60,000, was called Platte Bridge. Indians found the spot favorable for raiding wagon trains and in July, 1859, a few droops were stationed here, but they were withdrawn in the following April. More troops were sent in May, 1862, but a formal post was not established until 1863. One of the early telegraph stations was here; the Indians repeatedly broke the wires and burned the poles in the area.

In the summer of 1865 some three thousand Sioux, Cheyenne, and Arapaho assembled under cover on the hills north of the river in the neighborhood of the bridge, planning to attack it. On the morning of July 25 a small Government wagon train, consisting of 14 teams, 5 wagons, and 10 soldiers of the Eleventh Kansas Cavalry, started for this place from Sweetwater Station (*see below*), where they had taken supplies for troops. They camped at Willow Spring. During the night 21-year-old Lt. Caspar W. Collins, who had gone to Fort Laramie to obtain horses for his men, arrived here on his way to Sweetwater Station, where he was then stationed. Collins learned that a large party of Indians had appeared in the afternoon and had driven off a number of horses from the Government herd. A detachment from the garrison, pursuing the Indians, had killed High-Backed Wolf, a chief.

Word came that the wagon train encamped at Willow Spring was in great danger. The commander of the troops here ordered Lieutenant Collins to proceed with 25 men to relieve and escort the train to Platte Bridge. When the group advanced across the bridge they were immediately attacked by Indians. Collins and four of his men lost their lives. The wagon train that Collins and his detachment had attempted to escort to the fort was later practically annihilated (*see below*).

In November, 1865, the post at Platte Bridge was named FORT CASPER in honor of Lt. Caspar Collins. A clerical error resulted in the spelling, "Casper." The post and the bridge have been reconstructed.

Left from Casper on US 87E, which runs southwest through a stretch of rolling prairie and semidesert country along the North Platte River.

At **321.7 m.** is BESSEMER BEND, a pleasant valley at the west end of the Casper Mountain foothills and along the east bank of the North Platte River. The ranches in this valley are protected from the winds that usually sweep down over the country, and a large spring on the west side of the river furnishes water for use in irrigation.

In 1812 Robert Stuart and his six companions, on their return trip from Astoria to St. Louis, erected a cabin in this bend near where Poison Spider Creek flows into the river.

On December 10, Stuart wrote: "Relying with confidence on the snugness of our retreat which from its isolated situation we supposed sufficiently concealed to elude even the prying investigation of Indian spies, we were astonished and confounded at hearing the savage yelp early this morning in the vicinity of our Hut—Seizing our arms we rushed out when twenty three Arapohays made their appearance and after the first surprise was over (*on either side*) they advanced in a friendly manner, telling us they were on a war excursion against the Absarokas who had (*some time ago*) stole a great many of their Horses, taken some of their women prisoners & were then on a River six days march to the Northward where they were going in hopes of obtaining revenge. . . ."

The following day Stuart added: "The behaviour of the Indians was far more regular and decent than we had any reason to expect from a War party; they threw up two breastworks of Logs where the whole excepting Cheif and his Deputy betook themselves to rest tolerably early; these two we permitted to sleep in our hut, and one of us remained awake alternately all night—They all ate voraciously and departed peaceably about 10 A.M. carrying with them a great proportion of our best meat in which we willingly acquiesced—They begged a good deal for ammunition but a peremptory refusal soon convinced them that all demands of that nature were unavailing and they laughingly relinquished their entreaties. . . ."

Fearing that the Indians might return in a different mood, the party packed and left the hut on December 13, moving eastward to camp in the vicinity of the site of modern Torrington (*see above*).

Nearby is the SITE OF BESSEMER, a town established in the summer of 1888 and called by its enthusiastic citizens the "Queen City of the West." The site was surveyed, 49 blocks were platted, and grounds were reserved "upon which to erect the future capitol buildings of Wyoming." For a time a stage ran twice daily between Casper and Bessemer. In 1889, when Natrona was separated from Carbon County, Bessemer was a rival of Casper for the county seat. It is said that at least three times as many votes were cast as there were men, women, and children in Bessemer; Casper electors were said also to have exercised their franchise more than once that day. Only the Bessemer vote was thrown out, however, and Casper became the seat of Natrona County. Two years later the county took over the bridge at Bessemer because of unpaid taxes. The town soon disappeared.

Southwestward the highway runs through BESSEMER CANYON, also called Jackson Canyon, for William H. Jackson, who served as photographer in Dr. F. V. Hayden's first Geological Survey party in this area. The route skirts the eastern bank of the Platte River for two miles. From the western end of the canyon the PEDRO MOUNTAINS, with GARFIELD PEAK of the Rattlesnake Range beyond, are visible (R).

At **322.7 m.** is the junction with a road.

Right on this dirt road to THE GOOSE EGG RANCH, **2.5 m.**, whose large stone house was built in 1880. The lumber, hardware, and other material were hauled by freight teams from Cheyenne, a distance of 225 miles. This was the scene of an incident described in Owen Wister's *The Virginian;* two cowboys decided to play a joke on their friends who were attending a dance here, and secretly exchanged the clothing and blankets on the sleeping infants of the dancers. The parents did not discover the mistake until early morning when they had driven many miles on their homeward journeys.

The dirt road runs through the supposed RED BUTTES BATTLEFIELD, **4 m.** In this battle which occurred July 26, 1865, 21 out of 24 men were killed. The men, under the command of Sgt. Amos J. Custart, left Sweetwater Station on July 25 (*see above*), after having been warned that Indians were gathering in the neighborhood. Nonetheless, Custart refused to make a forced march to the Platte Bridge and went into camp for the night near Willow Spring. In the meantime Collins was being started from Platte Bridge Station to escort the wagons to safety. Custart's company was attacked by warriors of five tribes: Cheyenne, Sioux, Arapaho, Blackfeet, and Comanche. Three of the whites escaped by running to the river. The others sought the shelter of the wagons, which were quickly corralled. The Indians rolled logs in front of themselves as breastworks, gradually overwhelmed the soldiers, and mutilated their bodies beyond recognition.

At **324.7 m.** are the RED BUTTES (R). There is a sharp contrast between the fertile Platte River Valley and the alkali and sand country to the west. A sign here says that the Battle of Red Buttes was fought here on July 26, 1865, but the actual site of the battle (*see above*) is some four miles from the buttes.

FREMONT'S ISLAND, **338.7 m.**, on the west bank of the North Platte River, is the site of a camp of Lt. John C. Fremont when on his first trip to the Far West in 1842.

ALCOVA, **342.9 m.** (6,000 alt.), is in a beautiful valley encircled by rock-ribbed hills. The townsite was purchased in 1891 by an eastern syndicate; a score or more hot springs flowed at that time from the solid rock walls of the nearby canyon and the promoters of the town attempted to popularize the place as a health resort. Despite the efforts of the company, the settlement remained small for more than 40 years. In 1933 new life was injected into the town as a result of the Congressional appropriation for an irrigation project.

1. Left from Alcova on a graveled road to the major site of the CASPER-ALCOVA IRRIGATION AND POWER DEVELOPMENT, **1 m.** A total of $22,-700,000 was originally earmarked for this project by the Public Works Administration, but the amount was later reduced to $7,000,000. The project includes the Seminoe Dam, the Alcova Diversion Dam, and the Casper main canal. It has two units, containing 35,000 acres and 31,000 acres apiece.

2. Left from Alcova on a trail to the Grand Canyon of the Platte in which are the FIERY NARROWS, **7 m.,** so named by Robert Stuart and his party, who were here on October 31, 1812. The name of the canyon has been changed a number of times; it is now commonly called Pathfinder Canyon. On the northern rim, 500 feet above the turbulent waters of the river, are the REMAINS OF A CABIN, whose roof is a ledge projecting 16 or 18 feet. The sides, chimney, and fireplace are built of flat rocks. A hole in the front wall, evidently a doorway, was probably covered with cowhides in winter. A high window in the eastern wall commands a wide view. It is said that in the early days half a dozen cattle rustlers used this cabin as a hide-out.

3. Left from Alcova on a rough, lonely trail to MONUMENT CREEK, **18 m.,** and a spot marked with a slab of rough Pennsylvania granite. S. Morris Waln of Haverford, Pa., and C. H. Strong of New York City went West early in the spring of 1888 on a hunting and prospecting trip. They had a wagon, a team of mules, and two saddle ponies; a man named O'Brien had been hired in Denver to act as cook, guide, and teamster. Near Rock Creek, Wyo., they found game in abundance and remained in that vicinity two days. Half a month later the bodies of two men were discovered here by cowboys riding the range. Various clues, including a letter that had been torn up and scattered near a campfire, established the identities of the murdered men as Waln and Strong. O'Brien, the murderer, was trailed to Aspen, Colo., where he had disposed of the mules and other property stolen from the travelers. From Aspen he went to Colorado Springs, and there stole some horses. He was later captured, tried and convicted of horse stealing, and sentenced to 14 years in the penitentiary. He was never tried for the Wyoming murders.

West of Alcova US 87E runs through open country where antelope are frequently seen; it leaves the North Platte banks.

At **348.9 m.** is the junction with a graveled road.

Left on this road to the PATHFINDER DAM, **6 m.,** completed in 1919 at an approximate cost of $1,200,000. The dam is 95 feet wide and 218 feet high. At the base are tunnels and a culvert through which three huge columns of water rush forth in a foaming spray. The Pathfinder Reservoir spreads over 22,700 acres. Large diversion tunnels, cut through solid granite, are on both sides of the river.

At **355.9 m.** is the junction with a dirt road.

Right on this road to the SITE OF BOTHWELL, **2 m.** During the summer of 1889 the town had a store, a blacksmith shop, a newspaper called the *Sweetwater Chief*, a post office, and a saloon owned by Jim Averell. But the owner suspended publication of the newspaper for lack of news and support, the storekeeper moved away, the blacksmith shop was closed, and the settlers drifted away. Two graves remain—those of Jim Averell and his consort, Ella Watson. Ella, known as Cattle Kate, ran a hog ranch near Averell's saloon and store. Averell's place was a hang-out for rustlers, though cowboys also came there for a night's carousal; before they left the place Averell usually had all their money and Cattle Kate had the promise of her brand on from one to half a dozen calves. In a few months Kate's fenced-in pasture held a herd of questionable origin. Cattle owners of the neighborhood decided that drastic measures must be adopted. Accordingly, a group of cowmen took Averell and the woman to Spring Creek gulch, some five miles from Averell's place, and hanged them from the limbs of a scrub pine. The deputy sheriff, who later found the bodies, brought them back here for burial. In time six men accused of the lynching were arrested but the case was dismissed.

At **366.9 m.** the highway is across the river from the SITE OF SWEETWATER STATION at the Sweetwater Crossing. The highway here runs close to the Oregon Trail. James Abbey found the Sweetwater "a small stream of clear water, twenty yards wide, with a very swift current. The country is quite barren and grass very short; no wood, even for culinary purposes, our substitute for which is wild sage and buffalo chips. Near this point are several small lakes, the water of which has evaporated, leaving deposits or incrustations of carbonate of soda. They resemble ponds of frozen water. Several trains of emigrants have here supplied themselves with saleratus for culinary purposes. . . ."

Sweetwater Station was a military post established by the Government for the protection of travelers on the trail. Fights with the Indians were frequent in this vicinity. On April 3, 1863, Indians, presumably Cheyenne, attacked the station, but were driven off after they had severely wounded one soldier.

In 1849 Appleton Harmon, sent from Salt Lake City to take up his work again at the ferry, wrote of an incident in this area:

"While passing from Independance Rock to Willow Springs a party of Crow Indians came up with us and traveled along with us. as we ware passing large herds of Buffalo & antilope we though to avail our Selves of a Supply of the former, and acordingly commenced our pursuit, the indians Joined in the chace and one of the expert ones Seemed to take the lead Charged upon a herd and run them until the fattest ones began to lag behind then selected his choice, & prohibited enyone to fire at it until he give the Signal they chaced the Cow to the road and to the verry place whare we ware to camp then gave the Signal when a Shower of arrows & musketry was pourd into the fatieuged animal which brought her to the ground we drove up our waggons and camped for the night, dressed the Buffalo and kept a dilegent watch through the night for fear of treacherey and next day proceeded on accompanied by the Indian party who ware Swaped for theirs some times gitting 2 & 3 for one . . . we stoped at the Willow Springs for our noon halt whare we finished our trades and after our refreshment Started on and Br. M. D. Hambleton haveing taried a fiew maments in trying to make a nother trade. as we ware perhaps 3 or 4 hundred yards distant and just passed over a little hill one Indian catched his horse the others pulled him off and gave him in exchange a quiver Bow & 3 arrows and exclamed in Broken English Swap Swap, acompaning the expresion with a sighn Signifying the Same they then mounted their horses and drove off their prize in a South wester ly direction direction over the Sand hills at the light of Speed and by the time Br. Hambleton came up with us and had told his Story the red skims ware out of Sight and probablly 2 miles distant."

In April, 1850, a General Conference of the Church of Jesus Christ of Latter-Day Saints meeting at Salt Lake City appointed Harmon an elder of the Church and drafted him for a period of missionary work in England. Shortly afterward he set out for "the States" with other missionaries and resumed the writing of a daily journal. On this overland journey he met many of the victims of the gold rush fever; some were near South Pass in May, having come from the Missouri in an incredibly short time—39 days.

On May 17 he wrote: "This morning we found the river risen conciderable but forthunately we ware acrost it but the golddiggers had it yet to cross, it put them to conciderable trouble, meney of them got their goods wet and one waggon capsised, and Blankets, Kettles, Pans, Bottles, Buckets, and lumber could be seen floating off down the river, Several men jumped in to save all they could and right waggon while others followed down the stream to save the floating articles as they would come near to the shore in passing a bend in the river and Sometimes wadeing in up to their middles to catch a passing article. in this way they Saved most of their goods altho their sugar flour and Salt would be a total loss."

On May 21 "we met a hardy Scotch man with his all upon a wheel barrow going to the gold mines, he had traveled in this way one thousand miles and felt encouraged with the prospects before him and fully believed that he could make the journey in that way. and said he could travel as fast as eney of the horses or mule teams—that he never lost eney Sleep for fear of a Stampeed or of his hosses being Stole by the Indians."

By June 3, 1850, Harmon, now a seasoned overland traveler, had become exasperated by the foolhardy manner in which the men rushing to the mines had equipped and were conducting themselves.

"We met a continual Stream of Emegration for the mines runing meney of them half prepaird frantick mad Crasey or distracted, because a Latter-day Saint. had in California oncaped Some of the Shineing Ore, and exposed it in all its tempting excitement to a frantick world who with eager spetites Swallowed down everey favourable tale of a few forthunate ones whose Stories lost nothing by being often told until they had increased the desire for gold in to a dreadful malady, known as the (yellow) Gold fever which during this year 1850 is carreying off an agregate of 40000 Souls via. an overland route to California and like the Colerey it did not give them eney to mutch warning to prepair for their long Journey of two thousand miles a cross extensive plains deserts streams and ruged mountains, and they in their hurey had started none to well prepaird. and it was not uncomon to see a man that his horse had died or been stolen by the Indians, with a rifle and pack on his back, with Scarce a weeks provisions, following in the wild prevelent excitement faceing the ruged path, that I had just passed over a part of, then on over ruged ways, Crosing the Sirenavada Mts. their paths ware yet 1200 miles long yet."

INDEPENDENCE ROCK, 367.2 m. (L), a landmark on the Oregon Trail covering an area of more than 53 acres, resembles a huge prehistoric animal sprawling on the arid plain. Almost every one who traveled through South Pass camped near the formation—and before 1850 most of them found enough energy to climb it and paint their names in black, red, or yellow on its face. By that year several Mormons "with stone-cutting tools were located on the spot and did a profitable business in cutting names on the rock at a charge of from one to five dollars, according to the location," as an emigrant, Theodore Potter, reported. Potter, who displayed the usual hostility of the period toward the Saints, added bitterly that after the Mormons had "made a nice fortune from the emigrants by cutting their names for a fancy price, and when they had passed on erasing their names and cutting others in their places." It is apparent that Potter had hoped to immortalize his name here, because he ended the story with "So transient is our fame."

When Wyeth went by in 1834 the custom of autographing this rock was already well established; a member of his party, examining names, found that two Sublettes, Captain Bonneville, Fontanelle, and many others had left their records for posterity on the hard face. Frémont in 1842 innocently left a mark that was later to embarrass him; remembering that many whose names and initials were there had already died, he thought of the formation as a giant gravestone and left a large cross on it, covered with "a black preparation of India-rubber, well calculated to resist the influence of wind and rain." At some later time a group of migrants who were hostile to Roman Catholicism dynamited the rock at this point to destroy what they considered a symbol of that sect. At the time when Frémont was a candidate for the Presidency, the fact that he had placed the cross here was used to inflame feeling against him.

No one knows who first gave the rock its name, but it is assumed that a party of traders did so after celebrating the Fourth of July near it. On July 4, 1862, a group of Masons held a lodge meeting on top of the rock and the State lodge in 1920 commemorated the event with a plaque that was cemented to the face. Since then a number of other commemorative plates have been added. On July 4, 1930, the rock was formally dedicated to the memory of the pioneers of the West in the course of the Covered-Wagon Centennial sponsored by the Oregon Trail Memorial Association.

It was in this area that westbound travelers neared the most difficult stage of their journeys. The oxen and cattle were beginning to show the strain of the overland haul and anxious householders spent their evenings anointing sore hoofs with grease and gunpowder, or other home remedies, and padding the yokes that were making ugly sores on the necks of the oxen. Many articles that had seemed indispensable at earlier stages of the journeys—when fine furniture and like vanities were discarded—were here recklessly thrown away in the hope of lightening the loads. In the 1850's and 1860's the area around Independence Rock and westward was strewn with anvils, bellows, plows, bar iron, stoves, kegs, axes, and even extra wheels and axletrees.

US 87E bears southwest from Independence Rock, crossing flat sage-covered country along the Sweetwater to DEVIL'S GATE, **373 m.**, a cleft in the granite mountain. The river turns abruptly west and passes through the chasm.

Many of the Mormon Pioneers attempted to explore the gate; the group that included Brigham Young reported gayly on their return that the devil would not let them pass. The brethren with whom Clayton visited the gap fired off a rifle and rolled pieces of rock into the crevasses in order to hear thundering reverberations. The walls of the gorge are of gray granite. A streak of black granite running from the bottom to the top of the southern ridge at first sight appears to be a roadway. Neither the appearance of the gorge nor any other evidence indicates that the opening was cut by erosion. It seems rather to have been formed by some convulsion of nature. The chasm, 330 feet deep, is only 30 feet wide at the bottom. Capt. Hiram M. Chittenden, who with a corps of engineers made an investigation of the gorge in 1901-02 with a view to constructing a dam, pronounced the gate "one of the most notable features of its kind in the world."

During the days when the Indians were actively opposing the white advance, they frequently lay in ambush not far from this place. Troops were sent here at intervals in the 1860's to provide protection.

In the early 1860's four women, members of a train camped at this point, climbed to the top of the ridge above the gorge. One of them, 18 years old, venturing too close to the edge, fell and was killed. She was buried in the gorge and her grave board was inscribed with this epitaph:

"Here lies the body of Caroline Todd
Whose soul has lately gone to God;

Ere redemption was too late,
She was redeemed at Devil's Gate."

At **375.3 m.** is a monument erected in memory of the Mormon handcart party marooned here in 1856. This company (*see SECTION 3*), containing 576 European converts, was the last to start. It was late in the year when they reached central Wyoming, and they met storms and blizzards. One by one they gave up, and groups were strung along the route for about a hundred miles. When Brigham Young was apprised of their plight he dispatched 20 wagons loaded with provisions. Members of the rescue party were shocked by the condition of those who were still alive and by the number that had died of cold and hunger. More than a hundred died near here in nine days; they were buried in a trench two miles above the gate.

In telling of his journey past this place in 1843, Frémont dictated to bright-eyed Jessie: "Here passes the road to Oregon; and the broad smooth highway, where the numerous heavy wagons of the emigrants had entirely crushed the artemisia, was a happy exchange to our poor animals."

At MUDDY GAP, **386.5 m.,** is the junction with US 287.

Left here on US 287, following Muddy Creek. At **47 m.,** in RAWLINS, is a junction with US 30 (*see SECTION 7*).

Right from Muddy Gap on US 287, here having a graveled roadbed and following the early overland route for about 34 miles. *(From this point westward there is no paved route uniting the Alternate Route with US 30; those following the Alternate Route west of this point, and particularly those considering travel through South Pass, should make careful inquiries locally concerning conditions of travel. This route is passable only during summer months. Supplies should include a good spare tire, a rope, and food for emergency use. Be sure gas tank is full.)*

US 287 runs northwest approaching the Sweetwater and then westward at the foot of the northern slope of the Green Mountains. Emigrant guidebooks warned travelers of sandy and difficult roads in this area and gave divergent advice as to which bank of the Sweetwater should be followed westward.

At **397.8 m.** is SPLIT ROCK (R), a rocky ridge with a deep cleft. It was a landmark on the overland trail.

At about **408.9 m.** US 287 runs near the SITE OF THREE CROSSINGS, a telegraph and stage station of the 1860's that was on the north bank of the river, near the mouth of Sage Hen Creek.

The highway traverses country that is pungent with the odor of sagebrush. Antelope and sage chickens are plentiful here.

HUDSONS, **431.2 m.**, is chiefly a post office and filling station by the old SWEETWATER BRIDGE, on which US 287 crosses the river. Troops were stationed here at various times to escort the covered-wagon trains.

The *Journal* of William Knox, kept during the overland journey in 1855, contains a typical record of experiences in this area: "it is very Cold Lion one of my oxen came in from the herd with A sore foot the 11 Setterday . . . my ox is very lame we Camped 314½ Miles from the velly I got my ox thron down and dressed his foot with lard and gun Powder I have got two oxen lame out of the four

"the 12 Sunday this morning we renewed our journey sore against my mind on account of it being Sunday I wanted the oxen to rest but I had to submit we traveled about Miles and Camped for the Day

"the 13 Monday one ox left and traveled about 15 Miles

"the 14 Tusday we renewed our journy and Crossed this smal river the 5 time we travled about 22 miles my ox is very lam I feel sorry for him this Day is A very heavy Day Sandy Roads the oxen is giving out My ox feel down

"the 15 Wednesday this morning I got my ox have down and tried to Cut open his foot by working A small Roap back and forward within his Clews untill the Blood came and then power into his foot boiling Tar one ox died this morning Belonging to Bro. Aston there is no feed at this Creek we started very soon this Morning I got A Boy to drive my teem and I drove Lion that is the name of My ox that is lame . . . I did feel like stoping at this place on acount of the feed and the poor ox I started after the wagons with my poor ox some times upon his feet and some times down I got him about 7 Miles past this place and had to leave him where the Road wind round A section of Hills for three Miles I got him about A Mile from the River Bro. Burgas furnished me with one I feel thankful for the same"

At **432.1 m.** is the junction with a dirt road that follows the overland trail (*see below*) through South Pass.

Right (straight ahead) at the junction, continuing on US 287. (*For full description of this route between Hudsons and Fort Washakie, see* WYOMING GUIDE.)

At **31.7 m.** from the junction near Hudsons is the junction with a dirt road that is passable for automobiles during the summer. (*Drive with care.*) This offers the only automobile approach to South Pass at present. Left **24 m.** on this road which passes through ATLANTIC CITY (*limited accommodations*), and SOUTH PASS CITY, **26 m.**, now merely a store and gasoline station. Gold was discovered near here in 1842 by an employee of the American Fur Company, who was killed by Indians shortly afterward. It was 1855, however, before prospectors arrived. Mining was carried on intermittently, with little luck until 1867, when what became the Carissa mine was discovered. South Pass City came into existence almost overnight and it is said to have had a population of about four thousand at one time. Its history is that of many old western mining towns that are now ghosts. In 1869 it won world-wide notoriety when William Bright, a tent-dwelling citizen, became a member of Wyoming's first Territorial Legislature and, moved perhaps by the dearth of "ladies" in the area, introduced and put through the bill that gave women full and unrestricted franchise.

At **35 m.** on the dirt road, close to South Pass, is the junction with the main course of the Alternate Route (*see below*).

US 287 runs northwest beyond the junction with the dirt road to South Pass City. LANDER, **39 m.**, has adequate accommodations (*see WYOMING GUIDE*).

At Lander is the junction (L) with State 287; the route continues on State 287, which runs through the Wind River Reservation.

At **53.6 m.** is a junction with a graveled road.

Left **1 m.** on this road to WIND RIVER, the original settlement on the reservation. Here is an old blockhouse with portholes, used by the settlers and soldiers as a fortification.

The road continues to the old WIND RIVER CEMETERY, **3.2 m.**, which contains what is probably the GRAVE OF SACAJAWEA, the Boat Pusher, often mistranslated Bird Woman; the woman buried here died on April 4, 1884. There has been much controversy about the death of the woman who guided and aided the Lewis and Clark expedition on its trip to and from the Pacific Coast in 1804-5. On the basis of a single entry in a post record that the "wife of Charbonneau" had died, it has been contended that the Shoshone woman died when a young woman. Painstaking research by two people, one representing the Federal Government, has amassed a record of incidents and evidence, not yet refuted, to prove that Sacajawea eventually left her half-breed husband, married a Comanche, left the Comanche reservation after his death, and rejoined her fellow-tribesmen about 1843. A few stories are told of her later years. One concerns her efforts to reconcile her relatives to the white invaders, whom she had aided in their first penetration of her homeland. Another tells of her constant repetition of the story of the "big fish" she saw on the Pacific Coast (*see SECTION 14*) and of her auditors' scornful "Liar!" There are also tales of her wanderlust, which moved Slade, the stage-line division agent, to give her a pass enabling her to visit the West Coast again.

FORT WASHAKIE, **54.6 m.** (5,570 alt., 30 pop.), is the U. S. Indian Bureau Agency for the Wind River (Shoshone) Indian Reservation.

Left from US 287 on the dirt road (*impassable for automobiles, 1938*) branching near Hudsons (*see page 191 at 432 m.*). The road follows the Sweetwater and also the broad course of the old trail to South Pass. The rise to this pass is gentle but the scenery has a grandeur that is typical of the area along the Continental Divide.

At **442.7 m.** (R) is the SITE OF ST. MARY'S TELEGRAPH STATION, also called Rocky Ridge.

During the brief existence of the Pony Express the riders used South Pass. It was one of the pleasures of migrants to watch the swift passage of "The Mail." The riders loved to put on impressive bursts of speed as they passed the plodding trains, but they were grateful for the protection afforded by the wagon trains in areas such as this, where there were many hiding places for Indians. Except during July, August, and September, when most of the trains poured over the Divide, the ride took courage. During the Pony Express days the panic of the Indians was mounting. Between reckless slaughter for beef, for pleasure, and for hides to make sleigh and carriage robes, extermination of the buffalo was progressing rapidly. Indian fathers faced the winters without adequate supplies of meat—their chief foodstuff—for their families; slow, dreadful starvation seemed the fate of all the tribesmen. While they did not dare attack well-organized trains, lone riders were objects of their vengeance.

The road forks Rock Creek at **449.7 m.** A short distance upstream near this creek is the CAMPSITE OF WILLIE'S COMPANY of the Mormon handcart migration of 1856. This was one of the brigades that started westward late in the season and reached the mountains after winter had begun; the first severe storm overtook them near the Upper Platte Crossing. The hardier struggled on. Help was rushed to the immigrants from Salt Lake City (*see above*) but many succumbed. Most of the survivors were carried or escorted to Salt Lake City but a few men were left behind at Devil's Gate to guard the property that had to be abandoned on the road.

When Appleton Harmon returned to Wyoming with his family in 1848 on their way to Salt Lake City, he wrote feelingly of his hunting experiences along the Sweetwater: "when the camp was leying Still, I went with 5 or 6 others after tramping untill the Sun began to approach toward the western Horizen we discovered the object of our Search namely a band of Buffalo, we then Cast lots which 2 of us Should go and commence an assult. it fell on my Self and Ira Spaulding. after Crawling for Conciderable distance we keeping a Small bunch of grees-wood between us and the Buffalo we Suceeded in giting with in rifle Shot we then commenced our attact both rifle Shots took affect the wounded anamal ran a fiew yards and Stoped and we had to wait for him to die not dareing to approach him while he had life for he was rather a ferotious loking and acting Sort of anamal. we then dressed the buffalo took each of us a back load and Started for our Camp and the Sun went behind one of the grey granate range of the Sweet watter *Mts.* and son its gilding rays upon the Snow coverd peak gradually disappeards and the red Sky of the west turned grey like other parts of the Horison and the little Stars grew bright and twinkled in the distance. the moon cold and pale we watched as it began to Sink behaind those ruged peaks that a Short time preveous had Concealec the King of day from our view, while we ware taking what proved to be a circuitous route. as we passed a long the Hard beaten trails of the Buffalo the Smell of the fresh meat caused the wolves to howl and follow our track. we after Clambering over one or 2 raged Cliffs and long! long! walk at last came in Sight of our Camp fires and after 2 hours smart walking came tired to our camp about 2 O'clock in the morning. and I had 40 lbs of good Beef for my day and nights work."

BURNT RANCH, **464.7 m.**, a stage and telegraph station of the early days, was twice burned by Indians. Here was the eastern end of the Lander Road, the only part of the road to Oregon that was improved by the Federal Government. It was a cut-off to Fort Hall and crossed the Divide through a gap north of South Pass and 500 feet higher. It was built between 1857 and 1859 and named for Col. F. W. Lander, the engineer in charge of its construction. Lander reported that 9,000 emigrants used it in 1859, the first year it was open. It was planned in part because of the feud in progress between the Federal Government and the Mormons in order to take travelers north out of the Mormon Territory, but the dispute was ended by 1858; and Brigham Young provided most of the laborers required to build the road. After the first few years it fell into disuse, much former Oregon Trail traffic shifting to the Cherokee Trail when the older route was blocked by hostile Indians.

SOUTH PASS, 474.7 m. (7,550 alt.), during the first half of the nineteenth century was used by the vast majority of those traveling between the Missouri and the Columbia Basin. Some historians believe that the first white men to use the pass were the eastbound Astorians, but others dispute the matter. If Robert Stuart and his party happened to find this passage over the Continental Divide, no one in the following decade realized the fact; credit for the discovery is generally given to an Ashley party led in 1824 by Smith and Fitzpatrick. The pass is not impressive; the approach is so gradual that Frémont likened it to the slope of Capitol Hill in Washington. Travelers eager to celebrate as they passed from the Atlantic to the Pacific slope were often puzzled to know at what point the transition was actually made. Joel Palmer in the list of mileages at the rear of his guide-journal (*see APPEN-DIX*), in noting the Divide, departed from dry statistics long enough to note "Here Hail Oregon."

Captain Bonneville, in 1832, was the first to take wagons over it.

Frémont wrote of 'the pass: "We left our encampment with the rising sun. As we rose from the bed of the creek, the snow line of the mountains stretched grandly before us, the white peaks glittering in the sun. . . . The ascent has been so gradual, that, with all the intimate knowledge possessed by Carson, who had made this country his home for seventeen years, we were obliged to watch very closely to find the place at which we had reached the culminating point. . . ."

Lorenzo Sawyer said: "Most emigrants have a very erroneous idea of the South Pass, and their inquiries about it are often amusing enough. They suppose it to be a narrow defile in the Rocky Mountains, walled in by perpendicular rocks hundreds of feet high. The passage of this point is somehow regarded important, which causes a great rush to get through the 'pass.' The fact is they are in the South Pass all the way up the Sweet Water. The 'pass' is a valley some twenty miles wide, with the Sweet Water mountains on one side, and Rattlesnake mountains and the Wind River range on the other. . . . The summits of the whole range are buried in deep snows, which extend far down their sides."

In the pass is a monument commemorating the religious service held here by Dr. Marcus Whitman on July 4, 1836. With Dr. Whitman was a colleague, the Rev. H. H. Spalding; the wives of the two men were the first white women to reach this part of the Oregon Trail. It is reported that here Dr. Whitman knelt to pray with a Bible in one hand and an American flag in the other.

Near the pass are two springs named, by romantic early travelers, Atlantic and Pacific. It was a routine boast made by each migrant that he had drunk a rare brew, waters of the Atlantic mixed with those of the Pacific.

PACIFIC SPRINGS, **479.9 m.**, is by the site of a stage station of the same name. This place was a favorite camp site.

The old trail closely follows Pacific Creek through a long stretch of sagebrush-covered country to the CROSSING OF THE LITTLE SANDY, **506.9 m.** In Ware's *Emigrant's Guide to California* it was advised:

"When you cross the Dry, or Little Sandy, instead of turning to the left and following the river, strike out across to the Big Sandy, twelve miles. If you get to the river along through the day, camp 'till near night. From the Big Sandy to Green River, a distance of thirty-five miles, there is not a drop of water. By starting from the Sandy at the cool of the day, you can get across easily by morning. Cattle can travel as far again by night as they can during the day, from the fact that the air is cool, and consequently they do not need water."

Near South Pass the Mormon Pioneers met eight traders on their way back from Oregon; one of them, named Harris, decided to return to Fort Bridger with the Saints. Harris had six different copies of the Oregon newspaper, the first issue dated February 11, 1847, and also a copy of the *California Star*. The brethren examined them eagerly, but Clayton noted with disappointment that they found "little interesting news." As they descended from the pass the trader did a lively business, selling skins and buckskin pants, jackets, and shirts; Clayton thought Harris asked very high prices for his goods, and the brothers, though good swappers themselves, found it "difficult to obtain even a fair trade." Brigham Young later discouraged the greenhorn vanity that demanded expensive buckskin garments.

A far more important meeting took place near the Crossing of the Sandy. Here the Saints met Jim Bridger, the scout, whom they had planned to consult at his post about the advisability of settling near the Great Salt Lake. Brigham Young had read various reports of this region, last of all Frémont's—which was much more encouraging than most of the others. He had also read of the possibilities of cultivation by irrigation and remembered the fertility of the irrigated Nile Valley. In tentatively selecting the Salt Lake region as a place of settlement, he had been governed first by the fact that the area was then a part of Mexico and as such not subject to the United States Government. His second reason was even more practical: the so-called desert region, he said, was not a get-rich-quick land and therefore would not attract many immigrants; those people, Saints included, who were willing to homestead in a region demanding hard work would make a body of more than ordinarily desirable citizens.

Bridger was on his way to Fort Laramie, but obligingly offered to camp with the Saints for the evening and tell them what he knew. Bridger knew the West better than any other man, but his rambling manner of answering questions and giving information annoyed the methodical Clayton. Bridger did not advise the Saints to settle around the Great Salt Lake, though he admitted that there was rich land around the northern end; at one minute he was discouraging the homeseekers by stories of the region's aridity and of the mean character of the Indians, and in the next telling them that there was a region about a hundred miles southeast of the lake that was the promised land, if such a thing existed. He also said that the Utah mountains held great mineral wealth, including gold and silver. Brigham Young had heard enough; he determined to go forward and judge the region for himself. Bridger promised to return and guide the Saints to desirable spots (*see above*) and continued his journey with a note from Young providing him free passage on the Mormon-operated Platte ferry. By the time he returned the Saints had already settled.

While the majority of the emigrants for many years went southwest from this point to Fort Bridger, others made short cuts, turning west over routes followed by the fur traders, the chief of which was known as Sublette's Cut-off. It was not popular, however, because there was a 50-mile stretch between the Big Sandy and Green Rivers that was without water. The cut-off crossed Green River near Names Hill.

At FARSON, **513.7 m.** (6,580 alt.), is the junction with US 187 (*see SIDE ROUTE A*), a paved road that branches north from US 30.

West of US 187 a dirt road in poor condition continues along the general route of early overland travelers. It roughly follows the course of the Sandy to its junction with GREEN RIVER, **544.4 m.** There was no special ford where the majority of the emigrants crossed this branch of the Colorado, though in later years a ferry was established at the mouth of the Sandy. The banks of Green River were soft and the lumbering passage of a few wagons was enough to turn them into a morass.

At **570.4 m.**, at the northern end of GRANGER, is the junction with US 30N (*see SECTION 7*).

Wyoming

SIDE ROUTE A

Rock Springs—Pinedale—Jackson; 178.2 m. US 187.

Route paved between Rock Springs and Sublette's Flat; oiled gravel between
Sublette's Flat and "The Rim"; remainder paved except for a five-mile graveled
stretch. During winter months the highway between the junction with US 89
and Jackson is closed because of snow. Accommodations limited except in Pinedale and Jackson.

North from Rock Springs, **0 m.** (*see SECTION 7*), on US 187,
which traverses rolling plains.

PILOT BUTTE (L), **4.5 m.**, a formation along Bitter Creek that
was a landmark for those traveling on the Overland Trail, now serves
the same purpose for airplane pilots.

THE WELLS, **25 m.**, a ranch on high prairies where sage hens and
antelopes are numerous, has large corrals and sheep-shearing pens.

EDEN, **37 m.** (6,590 alt.), where cabins, supplies, and a telephone
are available, is the center of a 28,000-acre irrigation project. In a
pleasant little valley much scientific work is carried on by the STATE
AGRICULTURAL EXPERIMENT STATION. Horace Greeley spent the night
of August 16, 1859, in a very primitive log cabin here.

In the neighborhood of FARSON, **41.6 m.** (6,580 alt.), emigrants
who came through South Pass crossed the Big Sandy. Here the dirt
road that roughly follows the old trail crosses US 187. (*See ALTER-
NATE ROUTE.*) James Abbey, in his *A Trip Across the Plains* (1850),
wrote of his journey in this region: "The mirage has deceived us several times today. While worn with travel and thirsting for water, there
might be seen, sometimes to the right, sometimes to the left, and then
in front, representations of large rivers, lakes and streams of pure
water; but as we would advance in the direction whence they would
appear, they would recede or fade away, leaving nothing to view but
the barren desert and the blighted hopes of the weary traveler . . ."

At **42.1 m.** (L) is the SITE OF THE BIG SANDY STAGE STATION,
destroyed in 1862 when the Indians made an organized attack on every
stage station between Big Sandy and Thirty-two-Mile Creek.

HAYSTACK BUTTE (R), **51 m.**, is visible for many miles as the
highway traverses a long stretch of open country.

SUBLETTE'S FLAT (L), a favorite camping place of the early-day
trappers, extends along the highway for some miles. On the flat is Sublette's Spring.

PINEDALE, **100.1 m.** (7,175 alt., 219 pop.), the seat of Sublette

County, is a modern trade center in a ranching area and an outfitting point for automobile and pack trips to the surrounding recreational region of lakes, forests, and mountains. The earliest white settlers entered Green River Valley in 1878 and 1879, to occupy the natural meadows of the lower Green River and the Piney Creeks. They were attracted to the region because it afforded pasturage for herds even during the most severe winters.

Stock-raising is still the leading industry in the vicinity; sheep, cattle, and horses—both draft and saddle—are bred.

At **111.3 m.** is the junction with US 89, which has an oiled gravel roadbed.

Left on US 89 is DANIEL, **2 m.** (7,192 alt., 30 pop.), on Green River; it is a supply point for the surrounding valley.

1. Right from Daniel **4 m.** on a dirt road in fair condition to the SITE OF FORT BONNEVILLE, established in August 1832, by Capt. B. L. E. Bonneville, who had journeyed to this spot with 110 men, 28 mule-drawn wagons, horses, oxen, provisions, ammunition, and merchandise. The fort was promptly dubbed "Fort Nonsense" because of its situation in hostile Indian country.

Bonneville's cavalcade was the first of its kind to reach the Rockies. According to Irving in his *Adventures of Captain Bonneville*, "the unusual sight of a train of wagons caused quite a sensation among these savages; who thronged about the caravan, examining everything minutely, and asking a thousand questions; exhibiting a degree of excitability, and a lively curiosity, totally opposite to that apathy with which their race is so often reproached. . . .

"Some of the (Indian) scouts, who were ranging the country at a distance from the main body, had discovered the party of Captain Bonneville. They had dogged it for a time in secret, astonished at the long train of wagons and oxen, and especially struck with the sight of a cow and calf, quietly following the caravan; supposing them to be some kind of tame buffalo. Having satisfied their curiosity, they carried back to their chief intelligence of all that they had seen. He had, in consequence, diverged from his pursuit of vengeance, to behold the wonders described to him. 'Now that we have met you,' said he to Captain Bonneville, 'and have seen these marvels with our own eyes, our hearts are glad.' In fact, nothing could exceed the curiosity evinced by these people as to the objects before them. Wagons had never been seen by them before, and they examined them with the greatest minuteness; but the calf was the peculiar object of their admiration. They watched it with intense interest as it licked the hands accustomed to feed it, and were struck with the mild expression of its countenance, and its perfect docility.

"After much sage consultation, they at length determined that it must be the 'great medicine' of the white party; an appellation given by the Indians to anything of supernatural and mysterious power, that is guarded as a talisman. They were completely thrown out in their conjecture, however, by an offer of the white men to exchange the calf for a horse; their estimation of the great medicine sank in an instant, and they declined the bargain."

Ostensibly, Bonneville came into the territory as a fur trader; when Irving rewrote and elaborated on the notes of the expedition, which he had bought from Bonneville, he accepted the officer's version of his reason for going west. Other writers have done the same without question, and many have made scathing remarks about Bonneville's lack of success as a trader and the amount of time he wasted on social diversions, drinking with British and French trappers, and paying court to Indian women.

At the time Bonneville went west various people were trying to spur the U. S. Government into imperialistic activity in Oregon. Although many reports had been made to the Federal Government by traders who had visited the Columbia Basin by sea and land, there had been no careful, official report on the region since Lewis and Clark had visited it. If the United States were to attempt to end by force the treaty on the joint occupancy of Oregon with Great Britain, if citizens of the United States were to be encouraged to settle in the territory, it was necessary for the Government to know exactly what the British were doing in Oregon and to have maps of the intricate terrain.

Publicly, Bonneville received leave from the Army to try his hand at trading; but a Bonneville letter dated July 18, 1831, and recently discovered in files of the War Department, says: "I have now completed arrangements to enable me to collect information . . . promised in my letter to you dated at Washington City the 21st of May last." The letter was written to Maj. Gen. Alexander McComb, General-in-Chief of the U. S. Army (1828-41). Bonneville wrote to him two years later: "I would not have presumed this much were I not aware how desirous you are of collecting certain information respecting this country . . . I have constantly kept a journal . . . The information I have already obtained authorizes me to say this much; that if the government ever intend taking possession of Oregon, the sooner it shall be done, the better."

Bonneville supplied the War Department with maps; he also estimated the strength of the British at Vancouver and Walla Walla, as well as the military force he believed would be necessary to seize Oregon; and made suggestions as to where military posts should be erected along the road to Oregon. Much has been made of the fact that Bonneville's name was dropped from the Army rolls in May 1834, his leave having extended only to October 1833; but military records show that Bonneville received $1,600 for pay, subsistence, and servants between October 1832 and September 1834.

The Continental Divide was, in this region, the more or less accepted boundary of the territory acquired by the Louisiana Purchase, and South Pass provided the main route of travel through it. A post at this point, on the western slope of the Divide and close to the transcontinental trail, provided ample opportunities to see who was going where. The fort was a solid though rudely built affair, but Bonneville soon abandoned it.

Near this spot in 1835 Dr. Marcus Whitman, who had come west with the Rev. Samuel Parker in company with fur traders, met a Nez Perce chief, who "expressed great satisfaction at seeing us and said he was very simple and ignorant about the worship of the Almighty. That ever since he had heard of the worship of the whites he had been unhappy. He said he had heard something about the worship of God from the traders but he did not understand it; it had only reached his ears; he desired to be taught so that it might sink deep into his inward parts." This convinced Whitman that he need not go farther before reporting to the American Board of Missions that there was a field ripe for missionary harvest. He immediately started back east while Parker went into Oregon to scout for mission sites.

Before Whitman started back he performed a number of medical services, including at least one operation. In 1832 Jim Bridger had been wounded in the back by an arrow whose head had remained for three years in his flesh. Whitman extracted it. The operation was difficult "because the arrow head was hooked at the point by striking a large bone, and a cartilaginous substance had grown around it. The doctor pursued the operation with great self-possession and perseverance; and his patient manifested equal firmness. The Indians looked on meanwhile with countenances indicating wonder, and in their own peculiar manner expressed great astonishment when it was extracted."

2. Left from Daniel **1 m.** on a dirt road to the site known as LA PRAIRIE DE LA MESSE. When Flathead Indians went to St. Louis to ask for some of the white medicine men for their tribe, they had Roman Catholic priests in mind. But the Catholics had no missionaries available for several years. Finally, in 1840, Father Pierre J. DeSmet was sent out. Traveling with an annual expedition of the American Fur Company, he reached this place and on July 5 celebrated

mass before a motley, yet respectful, crowd of Indians, white men, fur traders, hunters, and trappers. The altar, erected on a small mound, was decorated with bows and arrows and garlands of wild flowers. The spot was afterwards pointed out by the Indians as the Prairie of the Mass. Father DeSmet was the founder of missions in the Bitter Root Valley and at Coeur d'Alene, and was in and out of the Northwest for many years.

In 1925 the Knights of Columbus of Wyoming placed a monument—a STONE ALTAR—on this spot. Mass is now celebrated here annually.

US 187 continues north from the junction with US 89.

At **133 m.** US 187 leaves the Green River Valley region and enters the WYOMING NATIONAL FOREST at "The Rim" (7,921 alt.). The forest lies in a great horseshoe around the headwaters of Green River and is largely covered with lodgepole pine. More than 230,000 animals, mostly sheep, are grazed on its summer ranges. On the eastern arm of the horseshoe the beautiful peaks of the Wind River Range extend high above timber line; at their base is a little-known region.

The highway passes ranches that cater to tourists. (*Guides and outfits for camping and hunting trips available.*)

At **152 m.** is the entrance to the V-V RANCH, whose acres embrace the spot where the Rev. Samuel Parker preached to the Indians in August 1835. Parker had made the most of every opportunity to visit with the Indians, on the journey overland; the Indians were equally interested in him because the interpreters explained that he was a white medicine man. They were beginning to feel that their own medicine men were not as competent as they should be, since they did not know the magic that provided the whites with technological luxuries. Parker was delighted to find the savages receptive, but much annoyed that he had to communicate with them through interpreters with limited vocabularies.

Of one of his Sabbath services on this journey he wrote: "An Indian whom I attempted to teach last Sabbath, came to me again to-day, and manifested that he wished me to instruct him. I endeavored to communicate to his mind some ideas of God, and sang the hymn, 'Watchman, tell us of the night.' He and those with him, shook hands with me as a token of their satisfaction, and left me. He soon returned, however, bringing others, that they too, might hear what he had heard with so much apparent pleasure, and they again shook hands with me. This was several times repeated. These Indians appear not only friendly to white men, but kind in their intercourse with each other, and in no instance did I witness any quarrels among them. Their minds are uncommonly gifted and noble, their persons are finely formed, and many of them are truly 'nature's grenadiers.' The women are graceful, and their voices are soft and expressive. I was agreeably surprised to see tall young chiefs, well dressed in their own mode, walking arm in arm with their ladies. This is what I had not expected to see among those whom we term 'savages.' It is true that they are heathen, in all the guilt of sin and destitute of the knowledge of God, and the hopes of the gospel, but in politeness and decency, as well as in many other respects, they are very unlike the frontier Indians, who have been corrupted and degraded by their acquaintance with ardent spirits, and wicked white men."

HOBACK CANYON, 165 m., was named for John Hoback, who guided Hunt's party of Astorians over Teton Pass and through this canyon in 1812. The defile is deep, with narrow ledges at the bottom. In many places the road is at the edge of the water. There are evidences throughout of many snow slides. The "Bull-of-the-Woods" is an annual phenomenon; each spring a great slide comes down a steep and winding gulch, crosses the river without touching the ice, rushes up the hillside beyond for several hundred yards, and then returns to the river bed.

Running along the Hoback River the highway skirts a point of rocks north of the river in which there is a large hole resembling a gigantic picture frame, from which is a magnificent view of the lower Hoback River and Valley. A few rods from the hole is a grave commonly believed to be that of John Hoback, who came back into this region as an employee of the Missouri Fur Company. Authorities, however, say that Hoback was killed by Indians on the banks of the Boise River in Idaho, and that this grave holds the bodies of More and Foy, of an 1832 Sublette party, who were killed by Indians when they were proceeding up the canyon ahead of their party.

At 169 m. is the junction with a dirt road.

Left on this road, which parallels the Snake River, into the GRAND CANYON OF THE SNAKE. At 4 m. is COUNT'S HOT SPRING; a crude wooden tub sheltered by a cabin provides an opportunity to bathe. During a flood in the spring of 1927, when the great natural dam across the upper Gros Ventre River gave way and released quantities of water, the Snake River, into which the Gros Ventre flows, rose rapidly and flooded the land far from its banks. When the water receded, several springs, including this one, were found to have changed their positions.

At 178.2 m., at the southern edge of Jackson, is the junction with Wyo. 22 (*see SIDE ROUTE B*).

Idaho-Wyoming

SIDE ROUTE B

Pocatello, Idaho, to Jackson, Wyo.; 160 m. US 91, US 191, Idaho 33, and Wyo. 22.

Most of route paved; remainder graveled. Limited accommodations.

North from POCATELLO, **0 m.** (*see SECTION 8*).

FORT HALL, **12 m.** (4,445 alt., 150 pop.), is the headquarters of the U. S. Indian agency of the FORT HALL RESERVATION, which is occupied by members of the Bannock, Shoshone, and other tribes. The Indians here are engaged in agriculture, and have a reservoir for impounding water to irrigate their lands. They hold annual dances of unusual interest: the Sun Dance about July 24th, followed by the War, Owl, Rabbit, and Grass Dances, each with its own characteristic songs and drumbeats. The Warm Dance, held in late January or early February, is intended to hasten the end of winter. Later there is an Easter Dance accompanied by an egg feast. The Indians on the reservation are excellent artisans; the women engage in many kinds of intricate beadwork upon such articles of clothing as moccasins and vests. These, as well as other products of handicraft, are for sale in Fort Hall stores.

Near the Fort Hall agency, on a road built recently by the Indians, is a lava rock monument commemorating the SITE OF FORT HALL.

On July 14, 1834, Nathaniel J. Wyeth reached the Snake River, and on the following day selected this spot for the establishment of a trading post. He had contracted to transport three thousand dollars' worth of merchandise for the Rocky Mountain Fur Company to its Green River rendezvous. At Green River the representative of the company, which was on the point of dissolution, refused to accept the goods. After a short period of indignation Wyeth decided to use them himself, and to establish a post on the upper Snake.

Early in August Wyeth felt that construction was far enough advanced for him to continue to the Columbia. His diary reads: "Having done as much as was requisite for safety to the fort and drank a bale of liquor and named it Fort Hall in honor of the oldest partner of our concern, we left it and with it Mr. Evans in charge of eleven men and fourteen horses and mules and three cows." Wyeth later wrote a letter in which he said that they had "manufactured a magnificent flag from some unbleached sheeting, a little red flannel and a few blue patches; saluted it with damaged powder and wet it in villainous alcohol. . . . After all it makes, I do assure you, a very respectable appearance among the dry and desolate regions of central America. Its bastions stand a terror to the skulking Indians and a beacon of safety to the

202

fugitive hunter. It is manned by 12 men and has constantly loaded in the bastions 100 guns and rifles. These bastions command both inside and outside of the fort."

In 1838, after Wyeth had given up his attempt to compete with the Hudson's Bay Company, he sold the post to that company, which enlarged it.

Fort Hall became the most important trading post in the Snake River Valley. It was the only inhabited place between Fort Bridger, Wyo., and Fort Boise, Idaho. Here the immigrants on the Oregon Trail made preparations for the last stage of their journeys to the mouth of the Columbia River or to California. Members of wagon trains coming out of the lonely deserts and valleys eastward could see from afar its cool whitewashed walls and its red flag lettered "H.B.C."; old trappers said the letters stood for "Here Before Christ." The post became the rendezvous of Indians, Spaniards, and French Canadians, priests, doctors, and missionaries, as well as hordes of nondescript adventurers of all kinds. Some came to rest, some to trade, some to celebrate on liquor distilled from wild honey, and some to heal wounds made by Indian arrows. The fortified trading center covered half an acre of ground and was surrounded by a wall 5 feet high and 19 inches thick. Within the stockade were dwellings, stores, and barns, all overshadowed by a two-story blockhouse or bastion. Standing on a sagebrush-covered plain between warring Indian tribes, it was in constant danger of attack.

After the Whitman party had arrived at the fort in 1836 with the two-wheeled cart they later managed to take as far as Fort Boise, no vehicle reached Fort Hall for four years. In 1840 one wagon was brought in by Joel P. Walker, and two others by missionaries. Warned that it was not possible to take them farther, these emigrants continued their journeys with pack horses. It was not until after 1843 that carts were used regularly west of this point.

Fort Hall was somewhat east of the point where a trail to California left the Oregon Trail. At the post emigrants anxiously collected news and gossip concerning the routes ahead of them and many changed their minds as to where they wanted to go within a few hours of their arrival at the post. If they met people who told of Indian attacks and difficulties on the California route, which crossed northern Nevada, they were apt to decide to turn toward Oregon. On the other hand, a single discouraging report on the difficulty of going down the Columbia River Valley would start some of them on their way to California. In the days when California was under foreign sovereignty, people from the United States who had settled in that area sent propagandists to Fort Hall and other key points to induce immigrants to join them and strengthen their numbers.

Palmer relates in his *Journal of Travels over the Rocky Mountains, 1845-46:* "While we remained in this place [Fort Hall], great efforts were made to induce the emigrants [bound for Oregon] to pursue the

route to California. The most extravagant tales were related respecting
the dangers that awaited a trip to Oregon, and of the difficulties and
trials to be surmounted. The perils of the way were so magnified as to
make us suppose the journey to Oregon almost impossible. For instance,
the two crossings of Snake river, and the crossing of the Columbia, and
other smaller streams were represented as being attended with great
danger; also that no company heretofore attempting the passage of
these streams, succeeded, but with the loss of men, from the violence
and rapidity of the current; as also that they had never succeeded in
getting more than fifteen or twenty head of cattle into the Willamette
valley. In addition to the above, it was asserted that three or four tribes
of Indians, in the middle region, had combined for the purpose of preventing our passage through their country, and should we attempt it,
we would be compelled to contend with these hostile tribes. In case we
escaped destruction at the hands of the savages, that a more fearful
enemy, that of famine, would attend our march; as the distance was
so great that winter would overtake us before making the passage of
the Cascade Mountains.

"On the other hand, as an inducement to pursue the California route,
we were informed of the shortness of the route, when compared with
that to Oregon; as also of many other superior advantages it possessed.

"These tales, told and rehearsed, were likely to produce the effect
of turning the tide of emigration thither. Mr. Greenwood, an old mountaineer, well stocked with falsehoods, had been dispatched from California to pilot the emigrants through; and assisted by a young man
by the name of McDougal, from Indiana, so far succeeded as to induce
thirty-five or thirty-six wagons to take that trail."

The fort was abandoned in 1855 but continued to serve as a trail
resting place until a flood demolished it in 1863. For many years its
site was forgotten. A well, formerly in the center of the stockaded
area, and triangular rifle pits, now bedded in grass, are all that remain.

BLACKFOOT, **25 m.** (4,505 alt., 3,199 pop.), was named for the
Blackfoot Indians.

US 91 here closely follows the course of the Snake River, running
through Idaho's potato-growing area, the center of which is SHELLEY,
42 m. (4,624 alt., 1,447 pop.). From the highway can be seen the
mountain range that spills westward from the Wyoming Line (R) and
the fertile valley that reaches away to the volcanic lava plains (L).

IDAHO FALLS, **52 m.** (4,709 alt., 9,429 pop.), third city in size
in the State, has a large municipally owned hydroelectric plant; its
electric power rate is one of the lowest in the Northwest, and, because
of revenues from public utility operation, its city tax rate is about a
third of the average in Idaho. The town has one of the few potato-flour
mills in the world.

The TAYLOR TOLL BRIDGE at Idaho Falls, of which only the stone abutments remain, was built across Snake River in 1866-7. The timbers were hauled from Beaver Canyon, 80 miles north, and the iron was obtained from old freight wagons and from a wrecked steamboat on the Missouri River. The stage station and post office here were formerly called Eagle Rock because a great stone out in the river was for many years the nesting place of an eagle.

US 191 leads northwest from Idaho Falls. Soon after REXBURG, **81 m.** (4,861 alt., 3,048 pop.), was founded in 1883 under instructions from the Mormon Church, mills and a school were established; five years later a college was opened. Typical Mormon planning is seen in the breadth of the town's streets.

At **86 m.** is the junction with Idaho 33.

Straight ahead **7 m.** on US 191 is ST. ANTHONY (4,958 alt., 2,778 pop.), named for St. Anthony Falls in Minnesota. The town is the center of the seed-pea industry in eastern Idaho.

Left **7 m.** from St. Anthony on an unimproved road that leads to the SITE OF FORT HENRY, near the point where the village of Egin now stands. This broad flat valley was first explored by Andrew Henry of the Missouri Fur Company. In the fall of 1810 Henry moved across the Continental Divide and established this post on the north fork of the Snake River, known ever since that time as Henry's Fork. The trading post consisted of several cabins and a dugout. After Henry and his band had trapped here and traded with the Shoshone for a brief period they abandoned the place. While the group had not been molested by Indians, there was little game, and the men had been forced to kill their horses for food during the severe winter.

In October, 1811, the fort was used by the Astorians under the leadership of Wilson Price Hunt. It was here that Hunt, yielding to the desires of most of his party, made the mistake of agreeing to attempt the remainder of the journey by water. Fort Henry was occupied long enough for the Astorians to build 15 cottonwood canoes in which to venture down La Maudite Rivière Enragée (Fr., *the accursed mad river*), as the Snake was named by Hunt's *voyageurs* after they had come to grief upon its falls and cascades (*see SECTION 9*).

For nearly a century the exact site of the old fort was unknown, but in 1927 a rock was unearthed that bore the inscription: "Al the cook but nothing to cook." This stone and two others inscribed "Gov't Camp, 1811" and "Fort Henry 1811 by Captain Hunt" are now in Rexburg.

Right from US 191 on Idaho 33; fishing is good along the entire length of this road.

Near DRIGGS, **127 m.**, seat of Teton County, is the largest bed of coal known to exist in the State. This town was named for Don C. Driggs (1867-1933), its founder.

TETON BASIN, **130 m.**, formerly called Pierre's Hole, is one of the most famous points of rendezvous in the history of the American fur trade. Partners and chief traders of the fur companies came here annually to meet the trappers who brought in the beaver skins collected during the perilous winter expeditions; the trappers were paid off, or drew supplies for further expeditions, and were encouraged to drink and gamble themselves into debt to the companies. The carousels, with their gun and fist fights, were notorious. Often groups from rival companies met at the same time in the valley, which is 30 miles long and 15 wide—"under the Three Tetons," as the records of the Rocky Mountain Fur Company described it. Nez Perces, Flatheads, and other Indians pitched their lodges nearby to trade, steal, and share the excitement. The Indian girls also looked forward to the rendezvous, hoping to have the luck of acquiring white or half-breed husbands. Most of the trappers made such matches, sooner or later, because the Indian women were the only ones able to share the wilderness life.

In 1835 the Rev. Samuel Parker wrote: "A few days after our arrival at the place of rendezvous, and when all the mountain men had assembled, another day of indulgence was granted to them, in which all restraint was laid aside. These days are the climax of the hunter's happiness. I will relate an occurrence which took place near evening, as a specimen of mountain life. A hunter, who goes technically by the name of the great bully of the mountains, mounted his horse with a loaded rifle, and challenged any Frenchman, American, Spaniard, or Dutchman, to fight him in single combat. Kit Carson, an American, told him if he wished to die, he would accept the challenge. Shunar defied him. C. [Kit Carson] mounted his horse, and with a loaded pistol, rushed into close contact, and both almost at the same instant fired. C's ball entered S's hand, came out of the wrist and passed through the arm above the elbow. Shunar's ball passed over the head of Carson; and while he went for another pistol, Shunar begged that his life might be spared. Such scenes, sometimes from passion, and sometimes for amusement, make the pastime of their wild and wandering life. They appear to have sought for a place where, as they would say, human nature is not oppressed by the tyranny of religion, and pleasure is not awed by the frown of virtue. . . . They disdain the common-place phrases of profanity which prevail among the impious vulgar in civilized countries, and have many set phrases, which they appear to have manufactured among themselves, and which, in their imprecations, they bring into almost every sentence, and on all occasions. By varying the tones of their voices, they make them expressive of joy, hope, grief, and anger. In their broils among themselves, which do not happen every day, they would not be ungenerous. They would see 'fair play,' and would 'spare the last eye'; and would not tolerate murder, unless drunkenness or great provocation could be pleaded in extenuation.

"Their demoralizing influence with the Indians has been lamentable, and they have practiced impositions upon them, in all the ways that sinful propensities dictate. It is said they have sold them packs of cards at high prices, calling them the Bible; and have told them, if they should refuse to give white men wives, God would be angry with them and punish them eternally; and on almost any occasion when their wishes have been resisted, they have threatened them with the wrath of God. If these things are true in many instances, yet from personal observation, I should believe, their more common mode of accomplishing their wishes has been by flattery and presents; for the most of them squander away their wages in ornaments for their women and children. . . ."

Those who came to the fur rendezvous were of many types; in addition to the partners and agents of the fur companies, there were *voyageurs* and "mountaineers." The first were French-Canadian boatmen who had served in the Canadian fur trade where the business was carried on along the shores of the innumerable lakes and rivers. In the United States they were employed in transporting the furs and supplies on the rivers between the rendezvous and headquarters. The second were either employees of the fur trading companies or independent trappers; they usually pursued their hazardous vocations alone or in small companies. They were, according to Irving in *Adventures of Captain Bonneville*, "hardy, lithe, vigorous, and active; extravagant in word, and thought, and deed; heedless of hardship; daring of danger; prodigal of the present, and thoughtless of the future. . . . There is, perhaps, no class of men on the face of the earth . . . who lead a life of more continued exertion, peril, and excitement, and who are more enamored of their occupations, than the free trappers of the West. No toil, no danger, no privations can turn the trapper from his pursuit. His passionate excitement at times resembles a mania. In vain may the most vigilant and cruel savages beset his path; in vain may rocks and precipices, and wintry torrents oppose his progress; let but a single track of a beaver meet his eye, and he forgets all dangers and defies all difficulties. At times, he may be seen with his traps on his shoulder, buffeting his way across rapid streams, amid floating blocks of ice; at other times, he is to be found with his traps swung on his back climbing the most rugged mountains, scaling or descending the most frightful precipices, searching, by routes inaccessible to the horse, and never before trodden by white man, for springs and lakes unknown to his comrades, and where he may meet with his favorite game. Such is the mountaineer, the hardy trapper of the West; and such, as we have slightly sketched it, is the wild, Robin Hood kind of life, with all its strange and motley populace, now existing in full vigor among the Rocky Mountains."

In 1832 occurred the Battle of Pierre's Hole. The annual rendezvous had begun to break up. There were various accounts of the battle; the one most often quoted is in Irving's *Adventures of Captain Bonneville*. It is pure melodrama. The careful reporter, the Rev. Samuel Parker, wrote in his *Journal*: ". . . I was shown the place where the men of the fur companies, at the time of their rendezvous two years before, had a battle with the Blackfeet Indians. Of the Blackfeet party there were about sixty men, and more than the same number of women and children; of the white men in the valley, there were some few hundred who could be called into action. From the information given me, it appeared that these Indians were on their way through this valley, and unexpectedly met about forty hunters and trappers going out from rendezvous to the south-west on their fall and winter hunt. These Indians manifested an unwillingness to fight, and presented tokens of peace; but they were not reciprocated. Those who came forward to stipulate terms of peace were fired upon and killed. When the Indians saw their danger, they fled to the cotton-wood trees and willows which were scattered along the stream of water, and, taking advantage of some fallen trees, constructed as good defense as time and circumstances would permit. They were poorly provided with guns, and were still more destitute of ammunition. The trappers keeping out of the reach of their arrows, and being well armed with the best of rifles, made the contest unequal; and it became still more unequal, when, by an express sent to rendezvous, they were reinforced by veterans in mountain life. The hunters keeping at a safe distance, in the course of a few hours killed several of the Indians, and almost all their horses, which, in their situation, could not be protected, while they themselves suffered but small loss. Those killed, on both sides, have been differently stated, but considering the numbers engaged, and the length of time the skirmishing continued, it could not have been a bloody battle; and not much to the honor of civilized Americans. The excuse made for forcing the Blackfeet into battle is, that if they had come upon a small part of the trappers, they would have butchered them and seized upon the plunder. If heathen Blackfeet would have done so, civilized white men should not. . . .

"When night approached, the hunters retired to their encampment at the place of rendezvous, and the Indians made their escape. Thus the famous battle of Pierre's Hole began and ended. . . ."

Parker added in a footnote: "Since my return, I have seen an account of this battle [i.e., Irving's], written by a graphic hand, in all the fascinating style of romance, representing the Indians as having entrenched themselves in a swamp, so densely wooded as to be almost impenetrable; and there they kept the trappers at bay, until they were reinforced from rendezvous. When the Blackfeet saw the whole valley alive with horsemen, rushing to the field of action, they withdrew into the dark tangled wood. When the leaders of the several hunting parties came into the field, they urged their men to enter the swamp, but they hung back in awe of the dismal horrors of the place, regarding it impenetrable and full of danger. But the leaders would not be turned from their purpose—made their wills—appointed their executors— grasped their rifles, and urged their way through the woods. A brisk fire was opened, and the Blackfeet were completely overmatched, but would not leave their fort, nor offer to surrender. The numerous veteran mountaineers, well equipped, did not storm the breastwork, even when the Blackfeet had spent their powder and balls, but only kept up the bloody battle by occasional firing during the day. The Blackfeet in the night effected their retreat; and the brave mountaineers assembled their forces in the morning, and entered the fort *without opposition.*

"With those who have seen the field of battle, the glowing description, drawn out in long detail, loses its interest; for although I saw it, yet I did not see dense woods, nor a swamp of any magnitude any where near."

Arrows and spear points, and occasionally stone axes and tomahawks, are still found on the battlefield.

Pierre's Hole continued to be one of the notorious spots of the West long after the fur trade had disappeared from the area because of the depletion in the number of beavers and the displacement of beaver hats by silk ones. It saw many battles during the cattle days. But it has settled down to a polite old age with dog racing and a winter ski carnival to attract visitors.

Idaho 33 crosses the Wyoming Line at **141 m.;** beyond this point the highway is Wyo. 22.

The route leads through TETON PASS (8,429 alt.), which offers one of the most spectacular views in the West. JACKSON, **160 m.** (6,209 alt., 538 pop.), seat of Teton County, is the chief outfitting center for big-game hunts and trail trips in the TETON NATIONAL FOREST, whose headquarters is here.

The town is the center of JACKSON HOLE, a beautiful and fertile mountain valley of approximately four hundred square miles. It was named in honor of David Jackson, an associate of Jedediah Smith and Captain Sublette. Traversed by the Snake River and crossed by numerous streams that flow into the Snake, the valley is formed by the Wind River Mountains on the east, the Gros Ventre Mountains on the south, and the Teton Range on the west. Yellowstone National Park is on the north. Rugged, snow-capped peaks are mirrored in the several crystal-clear lakes of the valley.

Long before its discovery by white men, Jackson Hole was the hunting and trapping ground of roving bands of Indians and may have been the home of a prehistoric race. Recently what appears to have been the site of a prehistoric village with stone foundations has been discovered.

Here for many years the fur trader held rendezvous with the Indian and swapped baubles, merchandise, and whiskey for valuable furs; here the Indians fought and failed to halt the whites as they pushed westward; here the cowman made his own law and rid the country of the outlaw, the cattle rustler, and the horse thief; and here today come thousands of visitors in search of recreation.

John Colter, a member of the Lewis and Clark expedition, is said to have been the first white man to visit what is now Jackson Hole. As the party was on its way down the Missouri he met traders who asked him to go back with them to the mountains and he promptly asked to be discharged from the exploring group whose work was nearly completed. Colter came south through the Big Horn Basin, crossed Union Pass, and went up Hoback Canyon into Jackson Hole in 1807. Then he climbed Teton Pass, passed through Pierre's Hole and, returning to Wyoming, discovered the wonders of Yellowstone National Park.

The Astorians, Jim Bridger, William Sublette, Captain Bonneville, and many other traders of note passed through the valley. In the possession of Al Austin of Jackson is a flintlock rifle that was found near the Hoback River. It bears marks indicating that it was manufactured in London, England, in 1776. This may have been dropped by the Astorians or by some Canadian trapper.

The first white settlers arrived about 1883, but the valley remained isolated for some years owing to the lack of roads. Some ranches in Jackson Hole are vast estates of thousands of acres. There are other thousands of acres of virgin lands.

Several ranches in the valley specialize in purebred cattle. The cattle and horses are branded in the spring and fall round-ups. Owing chiefly to the isolation of the country, Jackson Hole is the home of many wild animals, including a large elk herd. There are also bear, deer, moose, and mountain sheep. Against the picturesque background many famous "Western" motion pictures have been filmed, notably *The Covered Wagon* and *The Big Trail*.

In 1890 John D. Sargent brought a sailboat of clinker design to the valley. It was carried in by four men on the old Conant Trail, over which Owen Wister's Virginian followed the cattle thief Trampas. The boat was used to carry supplies from the southern end of Jackson Lake, where the road ended, to the Marymere Ranch, later known as the May Lou Lodge. Jackson Lake was earlier known as Lake Biddle, in honor of Nicholas Biddle, the editor of the *Lewis and Clark Journals*, published in 1814.

At Jackson is the junction with US 187 (*see Side Route A*).

Nebraska

SIDE ROUTE C

Bridgeport—Chimney Rock—Scott's Bluff—Horse Creek Treaty Ground; 55.1 m. Neb. 86.

Graveled roadbed; limited accommodations except in Gering.

West from BRIDGEPORT, **0 m.** (*see ALTERNATE ROUTE*), on Neb. 86, which crosses the North Platte and then turns R. along its south bank, roughly following the course of the Oregon Trail.

CHIMNEY ROCK, **16 m.** (4,242 alt.), rising abruptly from the valley floor, is an eroded formation with a bare, conical base of reddish sandstone covering about 40 acres. From the center rises a narrow shaft about 150 feet high. The pinnacle is weathering away more or less rapidly. Though it does not particularly resemble a chimney, it has borne the name since Joshua Pilcher gave it in 1827. The Indians called it the Tepee.

Most western explorers and travelers described the formation. The eastbound Astorians passed it in 1813, as did Lt. John C. Frémont in 1842; he thought it looked like a factory chimney. The Rev. Samuel Parker, who climbed to the base of the column, objected to calling it a chimney and recommended Beacon Hill. Members of his party amused themselves by shooting away small projections at the top of the spire, pieces of which they carried away with them as souvenirs. Bonneville was content with "shaft" or "column" as descriptive terms, and estimated the height at 525 feet. Least impressed of all was the diarist of the Birmingham Emigrating Company, whom it reminded of a potato hole (the mound over a vegetable cache and its identifying stake).

A natural amphitheater at the base of the rock has for many years been used for the presentation of a pageant, *The Gift of God* (*adm. free*), performed on four successive nights about the middle of June. In this pageant, composed by the Rev. Louis Kaub, the life of Christ is portrayed by 125 actors to music provided by a hidden choir. The only man-made parts of the setting are a stone front to the cave stable and three white crosses on a knoll. Many spectators camp overnight on the patrolled grounds and most of them bring basket meals.

At **20.8 m.** is McGREW (128 pop.).

Left from McGrew on a country road to TABLE ROCK, **11.5 m.** South of this point are STEAMBOAT ROCK, TWIN SISTERS, and SMOKESTACK ROCK, all landmarks named by early travelers.

GERING, **34 m.** (3,902 alt., 2,531 pop.), seat of Scotts Bluff County, was named for Martin Gering, a Civil War veteran and banker who was a member of the group formed in 1887 to plat the town. The town's chief industrial plant is the Great Western Sugar Company's refinery.

The people here, like those of other western Nebraska towns, have interests more akin to Wyoming and Colorado than to Nebraska; the larger Colorado newspapers have more circulation in the region than have those of Omaha or Lincoln.

A two-day celebration known as Oregon Trail Days is held here annually during the week in which July 17 falls. This date was chosen because the group of trappers led by William Sublette, the first man to take wagons across the plains, camped near the site of the town on July 17, 1830. Among the features of the celebration are the display of pioneer relics, Sioux dances and songs, a public wedding, and a parade with floats commemorating historical events and advertising local industries.

Left from Gering on State 29, a graveled road, to the junction with a dirt road, **2 m.;** R. here to ROUBIDOU PASS, **8 m.,** used by wagon trains before Mitchell Pass was cleared.

The pass is named for a French fur trader, Basil Roubidou, who at one time contracted smallpox and was abandoned by his comrades; he was rescued by a Sioux medicine man, who nursed him back to health. In 1848 he established at the western end of the pass a trading post that was destroyed about 1852 by the Arapaho. A stone marker indicates the spot where the post's blacksmith shop stood. Southwest of Roubidou Pass is SIGNAL BUTTE, which is entirely separated from the main range and almost perpendicular on each side.

Northwest of Signal Butte, on the bank of a dry creek, is a quarry excavated by a field party from the University of Nebraska Museum. Here were found the bones of 30 or 40 bison of a species now extinct. Some Indian artifacts unearthed with the bones indicate a culture earlier than that of the Plains Indians.

A short distance north of Signal Butte is Kiowa Creek, where a battle was fought in 1865 between the Sioux and the Kiowa.

On State 29 at **7 m.** is HELVAS CANYON, a minor gap in the Wildcat Hills, near which a trading post and blacksmith shop were established in 1849, probably by the American Fur Company.

At **10 m.** the highway crosses STAGE HILL, so called because the stage-coaches between Kimball and Gering passed over it. On the hill is the WILDCAT STATE GAME PRESERVE (*shelters, picnicking facilities, trails*), an 840-acre tract of extremely rugged country. The ravines and higher slopes are wooded with pine, and the canyon floors are overgrown with cottonwood, oak, boxelder, willow, chokecherry, and buffalo berry. Wild flowers dot the open spaces in season; the most common are the wild rose, cream-colored yucca, and brush morning glory.

SCOTTS BLUFF NATIONAL MONUMENT, **36.7 m.** (*camping and picnicking facilities*), a tract of 3,240 acres just south of the North Platte River, was acquired by the National Park Service in December, 1919.

SCOTT'S BLUFF (4,662 alt.), which rises 750 feet above the plain, was always a point of major interest to early overland travelers, many of whom, in order to do local sightseeing, camped near its base. The name is also applied to the nearby group of bluffs. The lower two-thirds of the bluff is a flesh-colored clay similar to that in the badlands along the river; the top third is sandstone.

The ravines, the northwestern slope, and the summit bear a light growth of juniper and pine. A hard stratum of volcanic ash, just above the talus slope on the west face of the bluff, was formerly covered with names and dates. The inscriptions have almost entirely flaked off.

In *The Adventures of Captain Bonneville,* Irving told the origin of the name:

"A number of years since, a party were descending the upper part of the river in canoes, when their frail barks were overturned and all their powder spoiled. Their rifles being thus rendered useless, they were unable to procure food by hunting and had to depend upon roots and wild fruits for subsistence. After suffering extremely from hunger, they arrived at Laramie's Fork. . . . Here one of the party, by the name of Scott, was taken ill; and his companions came to a halt, until he should recover health and strength sufficient to proceed . . . they discovered a fresh trail of white men, who had evidently but recently preceded them. What was to be done? By a forced march they might overtake this party, and thus be able to reach the settlements in safety. Should they linger they might all perish of famine and exhaustion. Scott, however, was incapable of moving; they were too feeble to aid him forward. . . . They determined, therefore, to abandon him to his fate. Accordingly, under pretence of seeking food, and such simples as might be efficacious in his malady, they deserted him and hastened forward upon the trail. They succeeded in overtaking the party of which they were in quest, but concealed their faithless desertion of Scott, alleging that he had died of disease.

"On the ensuing summer, these very individuals visiting these parts in company with others, came suddenly upon the bleached bones and grinning skull of a human skeleton, which by certain signs they recognized for the remains of Scott. This was sixty long miles from the place where they had abandoned him; and it appeared that the wretched man had crawled that immense distance before death put an end to his miseries."

The ORECON TRAIL MUSEUM (*free*), at the base of the bluff, is constructed of brick painted a buff-cream; it is modern in style and is without windows. In it are about 150 maps and water colors, and three dioramas. A large collection of historical relics, fossils, and artifacts has also been accumulated through loans and donations.

Right from the museum on Summit Road, built at a cost of nearly half a million dollars. The view from the top is fantastic but beautiful. Not far from this road, at the foot of the bluff on the eastern side, is (R) HIRAM SCOTT SPRING. Scott's body was supposedly found here.

MITCHELL PASS, **37 m.,** divides the bluff in half. Before 1852 travelers used the Roubidou Pass (*see above*). This route was impassable until it was cleared, probably by soldiers from Fort Laramie, Wyo. Mitchell Pass was traversed by Pony Express riders, by the first stages, and by emigrant trains; the first transcontinental telegraph line ran through it.

A military post, first called Camp Schuman and later Fort Mitchell, was established near here in 1864 for the protection of travelers.

HORSE CREEK TREATY GROUNDS, 55.1 m., is near Horse Creek, which flows into the North Platte River. The creek was so named because in 1824 Thomas Fitzpatrick was robbed of his horses here by Indians. The largest assembly of Indians in American history gathered here with Government representatives in September, 1851, when the Fort Laramie Treaty, covering boundary lines and privileges, was negotiated. Messengers were sent out to the tribesmen a year before the date of the meeting. All the Indian nations of the plains and the foothills, from the Arkansas River to Canada, were told to come to this central place, where there was water for the horses and excellent grazing land. More than 10,000 arrived: Shoshone, Sioux, Cheyenne, Assiniboine, Arapaho, Blackfeet, Arikara, Gros Ventre, Mandan, and Crow. Clusters of tepees made a tent city. A large pavilion was built by the women in the angle between Horse Creek and North Platte River; here the meetings were held, beginning on September 8 when a cannon shot was fired as a signal of the event.

APPENDICES

JEFFERSON'S INSTRUCTIONS TO LEWIS

To Meriwether Lewis, esquire, Captain of the 1st regiment of infantry of the United States of America: Your situation as Secretary of the President of the United States has made you acquainted with the objects of my confidential message of Jan. 18, 1803, to the legislature. you have seen the act they passed, which, tho' expressed in general terms, was meant to sanction those objects, and you are appointed to carry them into execution.

Instruments for ascertaining by celestial observations the geography of the country thro' which you will pass, have already been provided. light articles for barter, & presents among the Indians, arms for your attendants, say for from 10 to 12 men, boats, tents, & other travelling apparatus, with ammunition, medicine, surgical instruments & provisions you will have prepared with such aids as the Secretary at War can yield in his department; & from him also you will recieve authority to engage among our troops, by voluntary agreement, the number of attendants above mentioned, over whom you, as their commanding officer are invested with all the powers the laws give in such a case.

As your movements while within the limits of the U.S. will be better directed by occasional communications, adapted to circumstances as they arise, they will not be noticed here. what follows will respect your proceedings after your departure from the U.S.

Your mission has been communicated to the Ministers here from France, Spain & Great Britain, and through them to their governments: and such assurances given them as to it's objects as we trust will satisfy them. the country of Louisiana having been ceded by Spain to France, the passport you have from the Minister of France, the representative of the present sovereign of the country, will be a protection with all it's subjects: And that from the Minister of England will entitle you to the friendly aid of any traders of that allegiance with whom you may happen to meet.

The object of your mission is to explore the Missouri river, & such principal stream of it, as, by it's course & communication with the waters of the Pacific Ocean, may offer the most direct & practicable water communication across this continent, for the purposes of commerce.

Beginning at the mouth of the Missouri, you will take observations of latitude & longitude, at all remarkable points on the river, & especially at the mouths of rivers, at rapids, at islands & other places & objects distinguished by such natural marks & characters of a durable

215

kind, as that they may with certainty be recognized hereafter. the courses of the river between these points of observation may be supplied by the compass, the log-line & by time, corrected by the observations themselves. the variations of the compass too, in different places, should be noticed.

The interesting points of the portage between the heads of the Missouri & the water offering the best communication with the Pacific Ocean should also be fixed by observation, & the course of that water to the ocean, in the same manner as that of the Missouri.

Your observations are to be taken with great pains & accuracy, to be entered distinctly, & intelligibly for others as well as yourself, to comprehend all the elements necessary, with the aid of the usual tables, to fix the latitude and longitude of the places at which they were taken, & are to be rendered to the war office, for the purpose of having the calculations made concurrently by proper persons within the U.S. several copies of these, as well as your other notes, should be made at leisure times & put into the care of the most trustworthy of your attendants, to guard by multiplying them, against the accidental losses to which they will be exposed. a further guard would be that one of these copies be written on the paper of the birch, as less liable to injury from damp than common paper.

The commerce which may be carried on with the people inhabiting the line you will pursue, renders a knolege of these people important. you will therefore endeavor to make yourself acquainted, as far as a diligent pursuit of your journey shall admit,

with the names of the nations & their numbers;
 The extent & limits of their possessions;
 their relations with other tribes or nations;
 their language, traditions, monuments;
 their ordinary occupations in agriculture, fishing, hunting, war, arts, & the implements for these;
 their food, clothing, & domestic accommodations;
 the diseases prevalent among them, & the remedies they use;
 moral & physical circumstances which distinguish them from the tribes we know;
 peculiarities in their laws, customs & dispositions;
 and articles of commerce they may need or furnish, & to what extent.

And considering the interest which every nation has in extending & strengthening the authority of reason & justice among the people around them, it will be useful to acquire what knolege you can of the state of morality, religion & information among them, as it may better enable those who endeavor to civilize & instruct them, to adapt their measures to the existing notions & practises of those on whom they are to operate.

Other object worthy of notice will be

the soil & face of the country, it's growth & vegetable productions; especially those not of the U.S.

the animals of the country generally, & especially those not known in the U.S.

the remains and accounts of any which may be deemed rare or extinct;

the mineral productions of every kind; but more particularly metals, limestone, pit coal & saltpetre; salines & mineral waters, noting the temperature of the last, & such circumstances as may indicate their character.

Volcanic appearances.

climate as characterized by the thermometer, by the proportion of rainy, cloudy & clear days, by lightening, hail, snow, ice, by the access & recess of frost, by the winds prevailing at different seasons, the dates at which particular plants put forth or lose their flowers, or leaf, times of appearance of particular birds, reptiles or insects.

Altho' your route will be along the channel of the Missouri, yet you will endeavor to inform yourself, by inquiry, of the character & extent of the country watered by it's branches, & especially on it's Southern side. the North river or Rio Bravo which runs into the gulph of Mexico, and the North river, or Rio colorado, which runs into the gulph of California, are understood to be the principal streams heading opposite to the waters of the Missouri, and running Southwardly. whether the dividing grounds between the Missouri & them are mountains or flatlands, what are their distance from the Missouri, the character of the intermediate country, & the people inhabiting it, are worthy of particular enquiry. The Northern waters of the Missouri are less to be enquired after, because they have been ascertained to a considerable degree, and are still in a course of ascertainment by English traders & travellers. but if you can learn anything certain of the most Northern source of the Missisipi, & of it's position relative to the lake of the woods, it will be interesting to us. some account too of the path of the Canadian traders from the Missisipi, at the mouth of the Ouisconsin river, to where it strikes the Missouri and of the soil & rivers in it's course, is desireable.

In all your intercourse with the natives treat them in the most friendly & conciliatory manner which their own conduct will admit; allay all jealousies as to the object of your journey, satisfy them of it's innocence, make them acquainted with the position, extent, character, peaceable & commercial dispositions of the U. S. of our wish to be neighborly, friendly & useful to them, & of our dispositions to a commercial intercourse with them; confer with them on the points most convenient as mutual emporiums, & the articles of most desireable

interchange for them & us. if a few of their influential chiefs, within
practicable distance, wish to visit us, arrange such a visit with them,
and furnish them with authority to call on our officers, on their entering the U. S. to have them conveyed to this place at public expence.
if any of them should wish to have some of their young people brought
up with us, & taught such arts as may be useful to them, we will receive, instruct & take care of them. such a mission, whether of influential chiefs, or of young people, would give some security to your own
party. carry with you some matter of the kine-pox, inform those of
them with whom you may be of its efficacy as a preservative from the
small-pox; and instruct & incourage them in the use of it. this may be
especially done wherever you winter.

As it is impossible for us to foresee in what manner you will be
received by those people, whether with hospitality or hostility, so is it
impossible to prescribe the exact degree of perseverance with which you
are to pursue your journey. we value too much the lives of citizens
to offer them to probably destruction. your numbers will be sufficient
to secure you against the unauthorised opposition of individuals, or of
small parties: but if a superior force, authorised or not authorised, by
a nation, should be arrayed against your further passage, & inflexibly
determined to arrest it, you must decline it's further pursuit, and return.
in the loss of yourselves, we should lose also the information you will
have acquired. by returning safely with that, you may enable us to
renew the essay with better calculated means. to your own discretion
therefore must be left the degree of danger you may risk, & the point
at which you should decline, only saying we wish you to err on the
side of your safety, & bring back your party safe, even if it be with
less information.

As far up the Missouri as the white settlements extend, an intercourse will probably be found to exist between them and the Spanish
posts at St. Louis, opposite Cahokia, or Ste. Genevieve opposite Kaskaskia. from still farther up the river, the traders may furnish a conveyance for letters. beyond that you may perhaps be able to engage
Indians to bring letters for the government to Cahokia or Kaskaskia,
on promising that they shall there receive such special compensation
as you shall have stipulated with them. avail yourself of these means
to communicate to us, at seasonable intervals, a copy of your journal,
notes & observations of every kind, putting into cypher whatever might
do injury if betrayed.

Should you reach the Pacific ocean (One full line scratched out,
indecipherable.—Ed.) inform yourself of the circumstances which may
decide whether the furs of those parts may not be collected as advantageously at the head of the Missouri (convenient as is supposed to
the waters of the Colorado & Oregon or Columbia) as at Nootka sound
or any other point of that coast; & that trade be consequently conducted through the Missouri & U. S. more beneficially than by the

circumnavigation now practised.

On your arrival on that coast endeavor to learn if there be any port within your reach frequented by the sea-vessels of any nation, and to send two of your trusty people back by sea, in such way as shall appear practicable, with a copy of your notes. and should you be of opinion that the return of your party by the way they went will be eminently dangerous, then ship the whole, & return by sea by way of Cape Horn or the Cape of good Hope, as you shall be able. as you will be without money, clothes or provisions, you must endeavor to use the credit of the U. S. to obtain them; for which purpose open letters of credit shall be furnished you authorising you to draw on the Executive of the U. S. or any of its officers in any part of the world, on which drafts can be disposed of, and to apply with our recommendations to the Consuls, agents, merchants or citizens of any nation with which we have intercourse, assuring them in our name that any aids they may furnish you, shall be honorably repaid, and on demand. Our consuls Thomas Howes at Batavia in Java, William Buchanan of the isles of France and Bourbon, & John Elmslie at the Cape of good hope will be able to supply your necessities by draughts on us.

Should you find it safe to return by the way you go, after sending two of your party round by sea, or with your whole party, if no conveyance by sea can be found, do so; making such observations on your return as may serve to supply, correct or confirm those made on your outward journey.

In re-entering the U. S. and reaching a place of safety, discharge any of your attendants who may desire & deserve it, procuring for them immediate paiment of all arrears of pay & cloathing which may have incurred since their departure; & assure them that they shall be recommended to the liberality of the legislature for the grant of a soldier's portion of land each, as proposed in my message to Congress & repair yourself with your papers to the seat of government.

To provide, on the accident of your death, against anarchy, dispersion & the consequent danger to your party, and total failure of the enterprise, you are herby authorised, by any instrument signed & written in your hand, to name the person among them who shall succeed to the command on your decease, & by like instruments to change the nomination from time to time, as further experience of the characters accompanying you shall point out superior fitness: and all the powers & authorities given to yourself are, in the event of your death, transferred to & vested in the successor so named, with further power to him, & his successors in like manner to name each his successor, who, on the death of his predecessor, shall be invested with all the powers & authorities given to yourself.

Given under my hand at the city of Washington, this 20th day of June 1803

Th. Jefferson
Pr. U S. of America

NECESSARY OUTFITS FOR EMIGRANTS TRAVELING
TO OREGON

(From Joel Palmer's *Journal of Travels over the Rocky Mountains,*
1845-1846)

For burthen wagons, light four horse or heavy two horse wagons
are the size commonly used. They should be made of the best material,
well seasoned, and should in all cases have falling tongues. The tire
should not be less than one and three fourth inches wide, but may be
advantageously used three inches; two inches, however, is the most
common width. In fastening on the tire, bolts should be used instead
of nails; it should be at least ⅝ or ¾ inches thick. Hub boxes for the
hubs should be about four inches. The skeins should be well steeled.
The Mormon fashioned wagon bed is the best. They are usually made
straight, with side boards about 16 inches wide, and a projection outward of four inches on each side, and then another side board of ten
or twelve inches; in this last, set the bows for covers, which should
always be double. Boxes for carrying effects should be so constructed
as to correspond in height with the offset in the wagon bed, as this
gives a smooth surface to sleep upon.

Ox teams are more extensively used than any others. Oxen stand the
trip much better, and are not so liable to be stolen by the Indians, and
are much less trouble. Cattle are generally allowed to go at large, when
not hitched to the wagons; whilst horses and mules must always be
staked up at night. Oxen can procure food in many places where horses
cannot, and in much less time. Cattle that have been raised in Illinois
or Missouri, stand the trip better than those raised in Indiana or Ohio;
as they have been accustomed to eating the prairie grass, upon which
they must wholly rely while on the road. Great care should be taken
in selecting cattle; they should be from four to six years old, tight and
heavy made.

For those who fit out but one wagon, it is not safe to start with less
than four yoke of oxen, as they are liable to get lame, have sore necks,
or to stray away. One team thus fitted up may start from Missouri with
twenty-five hundred pounds and as each day's rations make the load
that much lighter, before they reach any rough road, their loading is
much reduced. Persons should recollect that every thing in the outfit
should be as light as the required strength will permit; no useless
trumpery should be taken. The loading should consist of provisions
and apparel, a necessary supply of cooking fixtures, a few tools, etc.
No great speculation can be made in buying cattle and driving them
through to sell; but as the prices of oxen and cows are much higher
in Oregon than in the States, nothing is lost in having a good supply
of them, which will enable the emigrant to wagon through many articles
that are difficult to be obtained in Oregon. Each family should have a

few cows, as the milk can be used the entire route, and they are often convenient to put to the wagon to relieve oxen. They should be so selected that portions of them would come in fresh upon the road. Sheep can also be advantageously driven. American horses and mares always command high prices, and with careful usage can be taken through; but if used to wagons or carriages, their loading should be light. Each family should be provided with a sheet-iron stove, with boiler; a platform can easily be constructed for carrying it at the hind end of the wagon; and as it is frequently quite windy, and there is often a scarcity of wood, the stove is very convenient. Each family should also be provided with a tent, and to it should be attached good strong cords to fasten it down.

The cooking fixtures generally used are of sheet iron; a dutch oven and skillet of cast metal are very essential. Plates, cups, etc., should be of tin ware, as queens-ware is much heavier and liable to break, and consumes much time in packing up. A reflector is sometimes very useful. Families should each have two churns, one for carrying sweet and one for sour milk. They should also have one eight or ten gallon keg for carrying water, one axe, one shovel, two or three augers, one hand saw, and if a farmer he should be provided with one cross-cut saw and a few plough moulds, as it is difficult getting such articles. When I left the country, ploughs cost from twenty-five to forty dollars each. A good supply of ropes for tying up horses and catching cattle, should also be taken. Every person should be well supplied with boots and shoes and in fact with every kind of clothing. It is also well to be supplied with at least one feather bed, and a good assortment of bedding. There are no tame geese in the country, but an abundance of wild ones; yet it is difficult procuring a sufficient quantity of feathers for a bed. The Muscovy is the only tame duck in the country.

Each male person should have at least one rifle gun, and a shot gun is also very useful for wild fowl and small game, of which there is an abundance. The best sized calibre for the mountains is from thirty-two to fifty-six to the pound; but one of from sixty to eighty, or even less, is best when in the lower settlements. The buffalo seldom range beyond the South Pass, and never west of Green river. The larger game are elk, deer, antelope, mountain sheep or bighorn, and bear. The small game are hare, rabbit, grouse, sage hen, pheasant, quail, etc. A good supply of ammunition is essential.

In laying in a supply of provisions for the journey, persons will doubtless be governed, in some degree, by their means; but there are a few essentials that all will require.

For each adult, there should be two hundred pounds of flour, thirty pounds of pilot bread, seventy-five pounds of bacon, ten pounds of rice, five pounds of coffee, two pounds of tea, twenty-five pounds of sugar, half a bushel of dried beans, one bushel of dried fruit, two pounds of saleratus, ten pounds of salt, half a bushel of corn meal; and it is well to have a half bushel of corn, parched and ground; a small keg of vinegar should also be taken. To the above may be added as many good things as the means of the person will enable him to carry; for whatever is good at home is none the less so on the road. The above will be ample for the journey; but should an additional quantity be taken, it can readily be disposed of in the mountains and at good prices, not for cash, but for robes, dressed skins, buckskin pants, moccasins, etc. It is also well for families to be provided with medicines. It is seldom however, that emigrants are sick; but sometimes eating too freely of fresh buffalo meat causes diarrhoea, and unless it be checked soon prostrates the individual, and leaves him a fit subject for disease.

The time usually occupied in making the trip from Missouri to Oregon city is about five months; but with the aid of a person who has traveled the route with an emigrating company the trip can be performed in about four months.

Much injury is done to teams in racing them, endeavoring to pass each other. Emigrants should make an every day business of traveling—resting upon the same ground two nights is not good policy, as the teams are likely to ramble too far. Getting into large companies should be avoided, as they are necessarily compelled to move more tardily. From ten to twenty-five wagons is a sufficient number to travel with safety. The advance and rear companies should not be less than twenty; but between, it may be safe to go with six. The Indians are very annoying on account of their thieving propensities, but if well watched, they would seldom put them into practice. Persons should always avoid rambling far from camp unarmed, or in too small parties; Indians will sometimes seek such opportunities to rob a man of what little effects he has about him; and if he attempts to get away from them with his property, they will sometimes shoot him.

There are several points along the Missouri where emigrants have been in the practice of fitting out. Of these Independence, St. Joseph, and Council Bluffs, are the most noted. For those emigrating from Ohio, Indiana, Illinois and northern Missouri, Iowa and Michigan, I think St. Joseph the best point; as by taking that route the crossing of several streams (which at the early season we travel are sometimes very high) is avoided. Outfits may be had at this point, as readily as at any other along the river. Work cattle can be bought in its vicinity for from twenty-five to thirty dollars per yoke, cows, horses, etc., equally cheap.

Emigrants should endeavor to arrive at St. Joseph early in April, so as to be in readiness to take up the line of march by the middle of April. Companies, however, have often started as late as the tenth of May; but in such cases they seldom arrive in Oregon until after the rainy season commences in the Cascade range of mountains.

Those residing in northern Ohio, Indiana, Illinois, Michigan, etc., who contemplate traveling by land to the place of rendezvous, should start in time to give their teams at least ten days rest. Ox teams, after traveling four or five hundred miles in the states, at that season of the year, would be unfit to perform a journey across the mountains; but doubtless they might be exchanged for others, at or near the rendezvous.

Farmers would do well to take along a good supply of horse gears. Mechanics should take such tools as are easily carried; as there are but few in the country, and those are held at exorbitant prices. Every family should lay in a good supply of school books for their children.

In case of an emergency, flour can be bought at Fort Hall, and Fort Bois, two trading posts of the Hudson's Bay Company, at twenty dollars per hundred; and by forwarding word to Spalding's mission, on the Kooskooskee, they will pack out flour to Fort Bois, at ten dollars per hundred, and to the Grand Round at eight dollars, and will take in exchange dry goods, groceries, etc.; but at Forts Hall and Bois, the company will take nothing in payment but cash or cattle. At Dr. Whitman's station, flour can be bought at five dollars per hundred, corn meal at four dollars, beef at six and seven cents per pound, potatoes, fifty cents a bushel. It is proper to observe that the flour at Spalding's and Whitman's stations will be unbolted. Emigrants however, should be cautious, and lay in a sufficient supply to last them through.

THE UNITED STATES, 1837-1860

1837   Prosperity; panic; recession; depression.
Great activity and excited speculation, first quarter, followed by slackening and depression; many failures; unemployment; complete collapse of cotton market, spring; commodity prices decline; foreign trade restricted.
Money very tight; panic begins, March, in New Orleans; worst in New York, May; general suspension of specie payments; high gold premium; over six hundred bank failures.

1838   Depression; slight revival.
Stagnation gradually yields to improvement and increased activity, summer; commodity prices reach bottom and rise; many failures early in year; further decline in foreign trade.
Money eases; gradual resumption of specie payments by banks begins, May.
Fair wheat crop, lower price; poor cotton yield, high price.
Jason Lee lectures on Oregon.

1839   *Jason Lee sets out for Oregon by sea with 51 settlers.*
Revival; panic; recession.
Continued improvement; revival of land speculation early in year; rapid decline to depression, autumn; many failures; commodity prices collapse after rapid rise; recovery in foreign trade.
Further resumption led by United States Bank, January; money market tightens to panic and bank failures, October; specie payments again suspended, except New England and New York, last quarter.
Excellent wheat harvest, record cotton crop; prices collapse.
War with England over boundary threatened, January.

1840   Depression.
Stagnation; commodity prices decline rapidly; revival of export trade, very small imports, favorable balance.
Continued financial strain, especially in West; slowly easing money market; gold at premium; Sub-Treasury Bill passed; declining security prices.
Large wheat, fair cotton crop; stronger prices.

1841   *In Spring about 500 assemble at Independence, Mo., for trip to California.*
Depression.
Dullness; commodity prices decline; many failures; improved imports and smaller exports cause return to unfavorable balance.
Money easier; attempt to open the Bank of the United States and make resumption general fails, February; many bank failures in West; Sub-Treasury scheme annulled; declining security prices, especially last quarter.
Good wheat, poor cotton crop; higher wheat price, lower cotton.
Tyler, Democrat, becomes President upon death of Harrison.

1842   *In spring White's party of 100 emigrants leaves for Oregon.*
Depression.
Continued dullness; many failures, spring; marked decline in commodity prices, especially last half-year; foreign trade small.
Tight money eases; specie payments resumed in eastern cities, March; bank failures numerous; slower resumption with panics in interior, especially New Orleans, spring; securities reach bottom, February, and rise rapidly, second quarter.

224

Abundant crops, especially cotton; very low prices.
High tariff passed, August; Dorr's rebellion; Seminole War ended.

1843   *In spring about 875 leave the Missouri for the West.*
Depression; revival.
Inactivity gradually yields to improvement, summer, except in South; commodity prices reach low point and improve, autumn; excellent exports, small import trade.
Money easy; active speculation, security prices advancing to July.
Good cereal crops, especially corn; poor cotton yield; very low wheat price.

1844   *In spring 1400-1500 leave the Missouri for Oregon.*
Revival; prosperity.
Continued improvement in manufacturing; prices of manufactured products rise, foodstuffs decline; cotton speculation appears; revived imports, exports dull.
ᵼ Easy money tightens temporarily, February and August; further rise in security prices, spring; stock exchange panic after election.
Agriculture depressed; poor wheat and corn, excellent oats and cotton crops; severe fall in prices of agricultural commodities.

1845   *In spring 3,000 leave for Oregon.*
Prosperity; brief recession.
General prosperity, aided by marked improvement in South; slump ascribed to political difficulties, May; return to activity, October; slight rise in commodity prices; exports increase, smaller imports.
Money tight; stock market depressed, summer, but revives with active railroad speculation late in year.
Excellent wheat, fair cotton and oats, and poor corn crops; rising prices; active wheat speculation, last quarter.
Annexation of Texas, March; Oregon trouble with England, April.

1846   *In spring about 2,000 leave for Oregon. Mormons driven from Nauvoo.*
Recession; mild depression.
Slackening of activity to dullness; some advance of commodity prices; prosperity continues in South; smaller exports, larger imports.
Severe pressure in money market, May, and late in year; sub-treasuries established; security prices fall.
Large wheat, short cotton crop; agricultural prices rise late in year.
War with Mexico declared, May, followed by rapid successes; Oregon controversy settled, June; more liberal tariff becomes effective, December.

1847   *Mormons go to Salt Lake City; many settlers go to Oregon Territory and California.*
Revival; prosperity; panic; recession.
Rapid improvement begins, January; great activity; full employment; high commodity prices; activity slackens with collapse of English exchange and cotton prices, November; large foreign trade.
Money eases with large importation of specie; panic, November; tight money and break in security prices.

1848   Mild depression; revival.
Dullness in industry and trade; gradual improvement late in year with California boom; commodity prices decline; failures; foreign trade slackens, though exports of foodstuffs continue large.
Very tight money eases slightly; bonds advance late in year, stock prices decline; Mexico makes indemnity payments.
Record crops, very low prices.

Gold discoveries in California, January; treaty with Mexico, February; Taylor, Whig, elected.

1849   *Gold rush by land and sea; 20,000 left Missouri in April and many thousands more in May.*
Prosperity.
Widespread activity in industry; California expansion and speculation; commodity prices reach minimum; very active railroad construction; foreign trade recovers.
Money eases, summer; rising security prices, first half-year.
Excellent crops except cotton; higher prices.
Cholera scare, summer.

1850   *Gold rush by land and sea.*
Prosperity.
Unusual activity and expansion; commodity prices advance; very active railroad construction; foreign trade booms, especially import trade.
Money easy; revival of stock market, especially railroad securities, late in year; influx of gold from California commences.
Fair wheat, poor cotton crops, good wheat price, very high cotton.

1851   *Western migration continues.*
Prosperity.
Continued activity despite failures, summer, due to collapse of speculation in California shipments; further advance in commodity prices; enormous expansion in foreign trade, especially exports.
Money tightens, July; railroad stock prices reach peak, May, decline sharply to September, and then partially recover.
Fair wheat, very large cotton crop; high wheat price, rapid decline in price of cotton.

1852   *By this year, probably 100,000 had gone overland.*
Prosperity.
Widespread activity and expansion; lower commodity prices; active speculation; real estate boom; large foreign trade.
Money easier; security prices rise; railroad stocks reach peak, end of year.
Good wheat and record cotton crops; much lower prices.
Pierce, Democrat, elected President.

1853   Prosperity; recession.
Continued activity and expansion, slackening last quarter; iron and steel industry severely depressed; commodity prices rise rapidly; very active railroad construction; extensive speculation; great activity in foreign trade.
Money tightens severely; panics and distress in interior cities; decline in railroad stock prices.
Record wheat, poor cotton crops; wheat price low.

1854   Recession; depression.
Declining industrial activity; unemployment appears, autumn; continued rise of commodity prices and feverish speculation to autumn; railroad construction halted; many failures; continued activity in foreign trade.
Schuyler frauds bared, July, precipitating stock exchange panic; money very tight; financial panic, September; many private bank failures; financial distress especially severe, San Francisco; railroad stock prices steady to June, and then collapse.
Very small wheat and cotton crops; wheat price rises strongly.
Japan opened to the United States.

1855   Depression; revival.
        Dullness continues to autumn, when revival sets in; slack foreign trade,
        especially imports.
        Money eases, but tightens, autumn; railroad securities reach low point
        and recover somewhat.
        Excellent wheat, oats, corn and cotton crops; high prices.

1856   Prosperity.
        General activity and expansion; revival in railroad construction; in-
        creased number of failures late in year; very active commodity speculation;
        foreign trade recovers with favorable balance.
        Money very easy to autumn; severe stringency, November; excited and
        declining stock market with prices fairly steady and higher, summer.
        Excellent wheat, small cotton crop; wheat price falls.

1857   Prosperity; panic; recession; depression.
        Activity gives way to dullness, spring, and stagnation, autumn; com-
        modity prices decline late in year; many failures; enormous foreign trade
        checked.
        Money very tight; panic, August; runs on banks and bank failures,
        October; specie payment suspended, October to December; stock prices
        collapse with low point, October; bonds collapse temporarily, autumn.
        Good wheat and cotton crops, lower prices.

1858   Depression.
        Dullness continues; many failures; commodity prices decline; further
        reduction in construction; foreign trade restricted.
        Money eases; security markets depressed after temporary recovery, first
        quarter.
        Excellent crops, low prices.

1859   *Gold stampede to Colorado.*
        Revival.
        Gradual improvement; commodity prices steady; foreign trade very active.
        Money easy; further decline in railroad stock prices to low point, August;
        lower bond prices.
        Good wheat, enormous cotton crops; price for wheat low, high for cotton.

1860   Prosperity; recession.
        Continued activity, slackening late in year; foreign trade booms.
        Money tight after easing, summer; financial panic, November, neces-
        sitates issuing of clearing house certificates; slight recovery in railroad
        stock prices to peak, September; bond prices advance to summer and then
        decline.
        Good wheat and cotton crops, lower prices.

(Reprinted, with exception of statements on migrations, from *Business
Annals* (1926), courtesy of the National Bureau of Economic Research.)

BIBLIOGRAPHY

Abbey, James. *A Trip Across the Plains*. New Albany, Ind., Kent & Norman, and J. R. Nunemacher, 1850.

Bryce, George. *The Remarkable History of the Hudson's Bay Company*. London, S. Low, Marston & Co., 1902.

Burton, Richard F. *The City of the Saints*. New York, Harper & Bros., 1862.

Chambers, J. S. *The Conquest of Cholera*. New York, Macmillan, 1938.

Chittenden, Hiram Martin. *The American Fur Trade of the Far West* (2 vols.). Introduction and notes by Stallo Vinton. New York, R. R. Wilson, Inc., 1936. Best volume available on early fur trade, though both text and notes are occasionally inaccurate.

Clayton, William. *Journal*. Salt Lake City, *Deseret News*, 1921. Diary of the Clerk of the Mormon Pioneers.

Driggs, Howard R., Proctor, Arthur W., and Meeker, Ezra. *Covered-Wagon Centennial and Ox-Team Days*. New York, World Book Co., 1931.

Driggs, Howard R. *The Pony Express Goes Through*. New York, Frederick A. Stokes Co., 1935.

Frémont, Capt. John C. *Report of the Exploring Expedition to the Rocky Mountains in the Year 1842, and to Oregon and North California in the Years 1843-4*. Washington, Gales & Seaton, 1845.

Fuller, George W. *A History of the Pacific Northwest*. New York, Alfred A. Knopf, 1931. Very valuable.

Ghent, W. J. *The Road to Oregon*. New York, Tudor Publishing Co., 1934. Most comprehensive book on Oregon Trail, but prejudiced on Indian material.

Greeley, Horace. *An Overland Journey from New York to San Francisco*. New York, C. M. Saxton, Barker & Co., 1860.

Gregg, Josiah. *Commerce of the Prairies* (2 vols.). New York, H. G. Langley, 1844.

Historical Records Survey, Works Progress Administration, Washington. Copies of many unpublished early Mormon and other travel diaries.

Hulbert, Archer B., ed. *Overland to the Pacific* (6 vols.). Denver, Public Library, 1932-36. Annotated early travel journals.

Humfreville, J. Lee. *Twenty Years Among our Hostile Indians*. New York, Hunter & Co., 1899.

Irving, Washington. *Astoria*. New York, Belford, Clarke & Co., 1836. Based largely on the American Fur Company records of his friend, John Jacob Astor.

Irving, Washington. *Adventures of Captain Bonneville*. New York, Belford, Clarke & Co., 1837. Romanticized revision of the Bonneville notes.

Langford, Nathaniel P. *Vigilante Days and Ways* (2 vols.). Boston, J. G. Cupples Co., 1890.

Lewis, Meriwether, and Clark, William. *Original Journals of the Lewis and Clark Expedition, 1804-6* (8 vols.). Edited by Reuben Gold Thwaites. New York, Dodd, Mead & Co., 1904-5. The most comprehensive and authoritative publication on the Lewis and Clark expedition, unfortunately printed in an expensive and small edition. The notes are as valuable as the *Journals*, which were copied from the official documents. These were placed in the custody of the American Philosophical Society by Thomas Jefferson who feared their loss in the absence of any safe repository for national documents.

Mackenzie, Sir Alexander. *Voyages from Montreal through the Continent of North America to the Frozen and Pacific Oceans in 1789 and 1793* (2 vols.). New York, Allerton Book Co., 1922.

Marcy, Capt. Randolph B. *The Prairie Traveler.* Edited by Richard F. Burton. London, Trubner & Co., 1863. Published in U.S. by authority of the War Dept.

Montgomery, Richard H. *The White-Headed Eagle.* New York, Macmillan, 1935. Best account of McLoughlin.

Old Oregon Trail, The. Washington, Government Printing Office, 1925. Hearings before the Committee on Roads, House of Representatives, show confusion as to where the Oregon Trail ran; idea of officially marking trail was subsequently abandoned.

Ordway, John, and Lewis, Meriwether. *Journals of Captain Meriwether Lewis and Sergeant John Ordway, 1803-6.* Edited by Milo M. Quaife. Madison, Wisconsin Historical Society, 1916.

Oregon Historical Quarterly. Portland, Oregon-Statesman Publishing Co.

Pacific Northwest Quarterly. Seattle, University of Washington.

Palmer, Joel. *Journal of Travels over the Rocky Mountains, 1845-6.* Cincinnati, J. A. & U. P. James, 1847.

Parker, Rev. Samuel. *Journal of an Exploring Tour beyond the Rocky Mountains, 1835.* Auburn, J. C. Derby & Co., 1846. (First edition, 1838.)

Parkman, Francis. *The California and Oregon Trail.* New York, G. P. Putnam, 1849.

Paullin, Charles O., and Wright, John K. *Atlas of the Historical Geography of the United States,* Washington, Carnegie Institution, and New York, American Geographical Society, 1932.

Paxson, Frederic L. *History of the American Frontier, 1763-1893.* Boston, Houghton Mifflin, 1924. Very valuable.

Sage, Rufus B. *Rocky Mountain Life.* Boston, F. Hewes & Co., 1857.

Sawyer, Lorenzo. *Way Sketches, St. Joseph to California in 1850.* Edited by Edward Eberstadt. New York, 1926. Volume valuable for its quotes from and notes on rare unpublished manuscripts.

Stuart, Robert. *The Discovery of the Oregon Trail.* Edited by Philip Ashton Rollins. New York, Charles Scribner's Sons, 1935.

Thwaites, Reuben Gold, ed. *Early Western Travels, 1748-1846* (32 vols). Cleveland, A. H. Clarke Co., 1904-7. Annotated reprints of some of the best and rarest contemporary travel volumes.

Wagner, Henry R. *The Plains and the Rockies.* Revised by Charles L. Camp. San Francisco, Grabhorn Press, 1937. Comprehensive bibliography of original travel narratives, 1800-1865.

Washington Historical Quarterly. Seattle, University of Washington.

Werner, M. R. *Brigham Young.* New York, Harcourt Brace, 1925.

INDEX

INDEX

233